Another Kind of Justice

Chris Madsen

Another Kind of Justice: Canadian Military Law from Confederation to Somalia

UBCPress / Vancouver

Printed in Canada on acid-free paper ∞

ISBN 0-7748-0718-0 (bound)
ISBN 0-7748-0719-9 (pbk.)

Canadian Cataloguing in Publication Data

Madsen, C.M.V. (Chris Mark Vedel), 1968-
Another kind of justice

Includes bibliographical references and index.
ISBN 0-7748-0718-0 (bound)
ISBN 0-7748-0719-9 (pbk.)

1. Military law – Canada – History. I. Title.
KE6800.M32 1999 343.71'01 C99-910338-5
KF7209.M32 1999

This book has been published with a grant from the Humanities and Social Sciences Federation of Canada, using funds provided by the Social Sciences and Humanities Research Council of Canada.

UBC Press gratefully acknowledges the ongoing support to its publishing program from the Canada Council for the Arts and the British Columbia Arts Council.

We also wish to acknowledge the financial support of the Government of Canada through the Book Publishing Industry Development Program (BPIDP) for our publishing activities.
Canadä

UBC Press
University of British Columbia
6344 Memorial Road
Vancouver, BC V6T 1Z2
(604) 822-5959
Fax: 1-800-668-0821
E-mail: info@ubcpress.ubc.ca
www.ubcpress.ubc.ca

Contents

Acknowledgments

The R.B. Byers Postdoctoral Fellowship from the Department of National Defence during 1996-7 funded travel, research, and writing for this book. The Strategic Studies Program at the University of Calgary provided an office and secretarial support. I extend my thanks to Dr. David Bercuson, Dr. Holger Herwig, Dr. Terry Copp, Dr. David Zimmerman, Dr. Perry Biddiscombe, Dr. Doug Bland, Marc Whittingham, Mike Lonergan, and Dr. Louis Knafla. Parts of Chapter 1 were presented in a paper entitled "Military Law under Fire: The Canadian Militia and the Northwest Rebellion of 1885" at the Law for Buffalo, Law for Musk Ox Legal History Conference at the University of Calgary on 5 April 1997 and subsequently published by The Osgoode Society for Canadian Legal History in a collected work of proceedings. Dr. Bill McAndrew, Dr. Roger Sarty, and Dr. Steve Harris at the Directorate of History and Lieutenant Colonel Joe Holland and Commander Paul Corbett at the Judge Advocate General's Office at the Department of National Defence Headquarters gave the benefit of their expert knowledge and allowed access to historical materials. Bill Fenrick, a former member of the Judge Advocate General's Office who is now associated with the prosecution team for the International War Crimes Tribunal for the former Yugoslavia, read over earlier writings incorporated into this present study. Paul Marsden at the National Archives of Canada furnished valuable advice on archival materials, particularly for the period before 1920 and later accessions. The Royal Westminster Regiment, the 15th Field Artillery Regiment, the Princess Patricia's Canadian Light Infantry Regiment, and the Calgary Highlanders Regiment graciously made available their private regimental archives. Brian King and Don Munro, in particular, gave a great deal of their time to my research efforts. The CFB Esquimalt Naval and Military Museum and the library at the Museum of the Regiments proved indispensable repositories on naval law and military law respectively. Sylvain Roy at the JAG library answered last-minute queries. Material is used with permission from Great Britain's Parliamentary Counsel and the trustees of the Liddell Hart Centre for Military Archives at King's College, University of London. Laura MacLeod, Jean Wilson, and Camilla Jenkins at UBC Press guided the work from a manuscript into a finished book. Finally, I must thank my wife, Siân, for her patience, hard work, and support through another book.

Abbreviations

ADJA	assistant deputy judge advocate
ADM	Admiralty (London)
AG	adjutant general
AJAG	assistant judge advocate general
BCA	British Columbia Archives
CEF	Canadian Expeditionary Force
CF	Canadian Forces
CFAO	Canadian Forces administrative order
CFB	Canadian Forces base
CFP	Canadian Forces publication
CMHQ	Canadian Military Headquarters (Great Britain)
CO	commanding officer
COSC	Chiefs of Staff Committee
COTC	Canadian Officers Training Corps
CVA	City of Vancouver Archives, Vancouver
DHist	Directorate of History, Department of National Defence Headquarters, Ottawa
DJA	deputy judge advocate
DJAG	deputy judge advocate general
DM	deputy minister
DMD	Department of Militia and Defence
DND	Department of National Defence
ENMM	Esquimalt Naval and Military Museum, Esquimalt
GMA	Glenbow Museum and Archives, Calgary
HCL	Hove Central Library, Sussex
HMCS	His/Her Majesty's Canadian Ship
IWM	Imperial War Museum, Lambeth North
JA	judge advocate
JAG	judge advocate general
KC	King's Counsel

KR&O	King's Regulations and Orders
LHC	Liddell Hart Centre for Military Archives, King's College, University of London, London
MD	military district
MITCP	militia individual training and career profile
NAC	National Archives of Canada, Ottawa
NAM	National Army Museum, Chelsea
NATO	North Atlantic Treaty Organization
NCO	non-commissioned officer
NDA	National Defence Act
NDHQ	National Defence Headquarters
OPDP	Officer Professional Development Program
PAM	Provincial Archives of Manitoba, Winnipeg
PCO	Parliamentary Counsel's Office, Whitehall
PMC	Personnel Members Committee
PRO	Public Record Office, Kew
QC	Queen's Counsel
QR&O	Queen's Regulations and Orders
RA	Royal Artillery
RAF	Royal Air Force
RCAF	Royal Canadian Air Force
RCN	Royal Canadian Navy
RCNR	Royal Canadian Naval Reserve
RCNVR	Royal Canadian Naval Volunteer Reserve
RE	Royal Engineers
RMC	Royal Military College of Canada
RN	Royal Navy
ROTP	Regular Officer Training Plan
UN	United Nations
US	United States
VJAG	vice judge advocate general
WO	War Office

Another Kind of Justice

Introduction: Military Law in Canada

"Military justice," French Prime Minister Georges Clemenceau once pronounced, "is to justice, what military music is to music." The form is similar, but the character is very different. With little pretence to lofty ideals, military law serves strictly utilitarian and practical purposes in the maintenance of discipline within armed forces. Its endearing qualities are few. The application of military law is sometimes arbitrary and is heavily influenced by situation; it places the interests of service and group before the individual, and tends toward severe punishments.

Yet a general recognition exists that military law is absolutely essential for the good government and effectiveness of armed forces, particularly during times of war or crisis when conventional sanctions no longer suffice. Lack of discipline portends potential defeat and disaster, conditions that can threaten the very fate and livelihood of a nation. Fortunately, Canada has never faced such a situation. Perhaps more than any other institution in society, armed forces demand expected and predictable behaviour from its representatives. Military law simply sets out the prescribed rules. Soldiers who ignore, eschew, or overstep the laws, regulations, and orders governing the armed forces face the full wrath of a military justice system, which is designed for the main purpose of enforcing discipline and ensuring expected behaviour in battle.

If military law is a necessary tool, then efforts to temper, and prevent abuse of, the military's sweeping powers are equally legitimate. Democratic societies such as Canadian society share the added burden of reconciling the tension between military needs and the recognized rights of the individual. Although subject to military law, a Canadian soldier remains a citizen with all the protections and responsibilities that such status entails under civil law.[1] At times, the relationship has been problematical and unclear. But without proper control and supervision, armed forces have the potential to become dangerous and aggressive. In keeping with a long political tradition, Canada's military is firmly subordinate to civil authority.

Concerns over the proper place of the military in a democratic society underscored the historical development of military law in Great Britain and North America.

That military law, from which Canadian military law drew its inspiration, sprang from traditions and practice as old as common law. The earliest recorded British courts dealing with military matters date from the Crusades and subsequent courts of chivalry. Although special ordinances issued by the Crown governed naval and military forces that were raised during times of war, a semi-permanent court was established under the high constable – the English king's military commander-in-chief – and the earl marshal – the high constable's chief of staff. Henry VIII, fearful of a usurpation of his royal prerogative, had the high constable, Edward Duke of Buckingham, executed in 1521, thereby placing all responsibility for military discipline under the earl marshal.[2] The court martial eventually derived its name and form from the court of the marshal. During the English Civil War, both the Crown and Parliament issued separate Articles of War to their respective military forces.[3] A standing army on British soil stayed in existence after 1660, but the civil courts reasserted their authority over soldiers when the regulations lapsed at the end of the hostilities. A formal military code for peacetime came into existence after Parliament passed the Mutiny Act in 1689, in response to a revolt among British units embarking at Ipswich for service on the continent of Europe.[4] The Mutiny Act, renewed almost annually thereafter, and various Articles of War that governed British military forces who were sent abroad in time of war regulated military law until the separate laws were consolidated into a single statute, the Army Discipline and Regulation Act, in 1879, and subsequently the Army Act in 1881. The Royal Navy, on the other hand, underwent a separate, parallel development. Articles of War, incorporated into single legislative Acts in 1749 and 1866, governed naval discipline and naval courts martial. British law and practice provided a basis for the evolution of military law across the Atlantic in North America.

While the Articles of War were almost continually in force during the incessant European and colonial warfare of the eighteenth century, the Mutiny Act had no force outside Great Britain. During the American War of Independence, the rebellious thirteen colonies created Articles of War based closely upon the British model. The US and British armies not only fought along largely European lines, but also maintained similar disciplinary codes. The US Constitution, framed in 1787, became the source for all regulations governing military and naval forces in the new American republic. Separated from its British roots, US military law henceforth developed along an independent path.

Unlike the Americans, British subjects in the territories of Upper and Lower Canada, Nova Scotia, New Brunswick, and Prince Edward Island continued to follow British military law. In anticipation of the Treaty of Amiens with Napoleon in 1802, the British Parliament extended the Mutiny Act to all military forces outside Great Britain, including those in the colonies.[5] The Mutiny Act and the Articles of War applied to British troops stationed on garrison duty in North America as well as to various provincial militia called out from time to time on training and active service. To supplement applicable British regulations and orders, the militia published their own rules and regulations for mobilization purposes.[6] Although the provincial militia played a significant role during the War of 1812, the presence of regular troops guaranteed British interests in North America and protected the colonial territories against possible invasion from the United States. During peacetime, the local inhabitants normally showed a marked indifference to military matters. The poorly equipped and inadequately trained militia became little more than auxiliary forces, to be placed under British command and supervision in an emergency until reinforcements arrived from overseas.

This relationship remained unchanged until the incremental withdrawal of British troops from North America during and after the Crimean War. The British government attempted to shift an ever-increasing burden onto the Canadians for their own self-defence. It proved a difficult task. American posturing during the Trent Affair sparked some brief interest in the volunteer militia, but the colonial legislature's defeat of a Militia Bill in 1862 ousted the governing Conservative Party from power. John A. Macdonald, the minister of militia whose effectiveness usually depended on which end of a drinking binge he was on, shared part of the blame. The result reflected more than just a protest vote against an unpopular political party.[7] Segments of the Canadian population distrusted what they perceived as growing militarism, saw little need for expansion of the existing militia, and believed even more firmly that they did not want to pay the associated costs. As part of Confederation in 1867, the British North America Act gave the new Dominion of Canada responsibility for defence and maintenance of its own military forces during peacetime. Whether desirable or not, the provision of adequate armed forces became the price of nationhood. The Militia Act came into effect after its passage by the Dominion Parliament in 1868.

Although drawing upon a longer tradition and history for its legitimacy, Canadian military law has pursued a peculiar course of development since Confederation. It is a story largely unknown to soldiers, lawyers, scholars, and the public at large. What statutes and regulations governed Canada's Armed Forces? Who was responsible for the administration and supervision of military law? How was knowledge about military law disseminated within the Armed Forces? These questions, made even more pertinent by recent public concerns about the behaviour of Canadian soldiers in

Somalia and allegations of endemic sexual harassment within the Canadian Armed Forces, are fundamental to understanding the operation of Canadian military law today and in the past.

Contrary to some common assumptions, Canadian military law and the legal office within the Armed Forces that interprets and administers it did not evolve from some quest for national autonomy or supposed drive toward Canadianization. Military law in Canada instead responded to practical needs and matters of expedience. The result was a reactive, haphazard, and at times confused development with little apparent sense of direction or strategic vision. Although certainly not the first time the Canadian Armed Forces have been involved in questionable conduct, the misbehaviour in Somalia and subsequent revelations by an appointed commission of inquiry and the media focused public attention as never before on the military justice system in Canada. Many people attributed shortcomings to particular individuals and societal influences rather than examining the long-term, systemic reasons within the Canadian Armed Forces for what went wrong. Indeed, the Canadian military has proved reluctant to concede that it can blame no one but itself for the misdeeds in Somalia. Through ignorance and neglect, military authorities allowed serious deficiencies to persist over a long period of time. The content of Canadian military law and its relation to Canadian civil law were misunderstood, legal activities within the Armed Forces were inefficiently organized, and service personnel received a decreasing amount of instruction and practice in military law. The failure in Somalia was an inevitable consequence of these factors. Canadian soldiers broke the law because they were ignorant of what was expected of them and inadequately prepared for the situation in which they found themselves. The Canadian Forces bear full responsibility for the shocking unfamiliarity among its members with the legislation governing defence in this country.

The legislative basis for Canadian military law evolved over time. British influence was particularly persuasive during the nineteenth and early twentieth centuries. Canada's military and naval forces predominantly used British military law, modified by Canadian legislation and regulations to meet particular circumstances in Canada. Unlike other self-governing colonies such as Australia, which exerted some degree of independence, Canada willingly placed its Armed Forces overseas under British control and military law in support of imperial interests. Visiting forces agreements, concluded after the constitutional changes resulting from the Statute of Westminster, governed the application and administration of military law through the Second World War. The Canadian services obtained a truly national Code of Service Discipline with introduction of the National Defence Act in 1950. In subsequent decades, the National Defence Act and its accompanying *Queen's Regulations and Orders* (QR&O)

were amended to satisfy the requirements of unification, new operational commitments, and constitutional changes in Canadian law. The Canadian Bill of Rights and the Charter of Rights and Freedoms demanded a higher standard of fairness within the military justice system. Military authorities adjusted to the improved legal regime with some difficulty and untoward complaining.

The organization of the institutions responsible for administration and supervision of military justice in Canada impeded proper integration of civil and military law. Throughout the nineteenth century, the adjutant general handled disciplinary and other legal matters affecting the militia and conferred regularly with British officers in Canada, the War Office, and the judge advocate general in London. The appointment of a military officer as Canada's first judge advocate general (JAG) owed as much to patronage as to the requirements of the post itself. The JAG branch grew during the First World War to meet increased demands, but returned to a small staff in the interwar period. Regimental, squadron, and ship officers handled most court martial work and summary punishments under the JAG's overall guidance.

Expansion and ever greater specialization characterized the JAG office during and after the Second World War. Although proposals for partial civilianization were suggested in the immediate postwar period, the JAG and his staff remained military officers. Canadian legal officers increasingly focused on legal activities within the JAG office. Military lawyers distanced themselves from close interaction with Canadian society, the larger legal profession, and the rest of the Armed Forces. The negative impact of this trend was most apparent in the general level of knowledge and instruction in military law within the Canadian Armed Forces. The effectiveness of military justice relied upon officers having a sound working ability in the intricacies of military law and basic legal principles. During the nineteenth and early twentieth centuries, the Canadian services benefited from formal courses of legal instruction by British and Canadian officers at military schools, as well as from the availability of official and privately published manuals, handbooks, and pamphlets. Promotion and professional qualification required an appropriate knowledge of military law at every increase in rank. Until the mid-1970s, military lawyers played an active part in teaching military law through lectures, courses, and preparation for promotion examinations.

When the Canadian Armed Forces replaced competitive promotion examinations with a modulized self-study and formal course system, the JAG office began to train its own military lawyers rather than the whole Armed Forces. No published manual or up-to-date training pamphlets on Canadian military law existed to fill the void. Consequently, several generations of Canadian officers prior to the incidents in Somalia obtained little formal instruction or sustained practice in military law beyond an outdated self-study module, an occasional lecture on the Geneva Conventions, or what they picked up piecemeal along the way in their careers. The Canadian Armed Forces stopped teaching military law on a consistent basis. Canadian service personnel were sent into dangerous operational situations with a poor understanding of their rights, obligations, and responsibilities under military and civil law.

It was a recipe for disaster. In Somalia, rules of engagement were misinterpreted, regulations and orders were ignored, and international law was flouted. The Canadian Armed Forces paid dearly for their neglect of military law. The good name of Canadian peacekeepers became associated with the stigma of torture and murder. Without serious efforts now being made to improve deficiencies in training, overall knowledge of military law, and organization of legal activities within the Canadian Forces, there is greater likelihood of another event like the Somalia disaster happening again sometime in the future.

1
Modest Beginnings

Military law secured a solid foundation in Canada between Confederation and the end of the nineteenth century. Since changes to British military law indirectly influenced Canadian military law, the Militia Act and regulations issued under its authority supplemented and incorporated British statutory authorities. Although fiscal restraints imposed by Parliament placed practical limits on training and delayed creation of a proper instructional cadre within the Canadian militia during the last decades of the nineteenth century, military law became a serious subject for study at provisional and permanent military schools. Canadian officers and other ranks learned about military law through lectures and courses by seconded British officers, through reading in various official and private publications, as well as through actual practice in battalions or companies. Restricted legislatively from employment beyond the territories of Canada, the militia suppressed armed uprisings against the authority of the central Dominion government, aided the civil power, and deterred possible invasion. In spite of remarkably few resources and acknowledged organizational weaknesses, the Canadian militia attained at least a working knowledge of military law and regulations.

The early evolution of Canadian military law remained closely connected with major developments in British military law during the nineteenth century. Demands for reform in Great Britain primarily came from opposition to the infliction of corporal punishment within the armed forces, in particular flogging and branding. In an emotional campaign advocating total abolition, the popular press and influential persons within the British Parliament depicted the practices as demeaning and inhuman.[1] Public pressure became so strong that the British government under Sir Robert Peel appointed a royal commission in 1835 to examine the whole system of military punishments. The commissioners heard testimony and took evidence from the Duke of Wellington, experienced military officers, and the principal opponents of flogging.[2] The royal commission's conclusions recommended some restrictions on quantity and severity, but rejected the suggested complete elimination of flogging. Service authorities remained firmly convinced that corporal punishment was essential for the proper maintenance of military discipline.

Although the issue remained unresolved for several decades afterward, vocal outcries against flogging following the Crimean War eventually forced the appointment of another royal commission. In late 1867, the JAG warned that a motion in the British House of Commons was imminent, and he wished "to prevent any vote which the Authorities at the Horse Guards consider would be very prejudicial to the service by the appointment of a Commission."[3] Growing public outrage against flogging and other objectionable punishments could not be ignored any longer. Over protests from military authorities, the British government imposed restrictions on corporal punishment. From 1868 onward, flogging required proper sentence from a court martial, and then only for offences on active service involving mutiny or insubordination accompanied by personal violence.[4] While curbing the worst abuses associated with military law, the political decision left the British armed forces without their familiar means of enforcing discipline.

The royal commission, chaired by Colonel John Wilson Patten, explored alternative forms of punishment such as fines, imprisonment, and discharge of convicted soldiers. Between March 1868 and April 1869, the commissioners heard testimony from distinguished members of the legal profession and senior military officers, including His Royal Highness the Duke of Cambridge, the commander-in-chief of the British Army. A final report concluded that the existing court martial system worked sufficiently well under the new conditions, but found the sources of military law too complicated, guidance and instruction for officers insufficient, and certain procedures unfair.[5] The Duke of Cambridge, who took a sincere interest in the reform of military law, questioned whether the restrictions on flogging were having a negative effect on discipline within the army. Court martial returns showed that cases resulting in sentences of imprisonment were reaching alarmingly high numbers at home and abroad.[6] The trend may have only reflected the greater visibility of proceedings that had been previously handled informally at the discretion of individual commanding officers. But the actual amount of punished crime within the armed forces somewhat startled military authorities. The royal commission's main recommendations seemed to offer practical improvements in the existing military justice system to the satisfaction of the War Office and the Duke of Cambridge.

Officials began taking steps toward consolidating the numerous legislative sources behind British military law into a single service code. Charles Clode, a civilian lawyer employed in the War Office who devoted much attention to general questions of administration and military discipline, acknowledged that the Mutiny Act required revisions in light of the royal commission's findings.[7] In fact, the proposed alterations were so extensive that a more comprehensive statute, which incorporated both the Mutiny Act and the Articles of War, appeared preferable. Accordingly, the secretary of state for war asked Sir Henry Thring, the parliamentary counsel, to draft a suitable bill for submission to the British Parliament. Between 17 May and 26 July 1878, a select committee, chaired by Sir William Harcourt, examined the bill and heard oral testimony from a number of witnesses, including Thring, Clode, the Duke of Cambridge, and George Osborne Morgan, Great Britain's JAG.[8] Despite working under unreasonably wide terms of reference, Harcourt's committee agreed that the draft bill was a great improvement over existing legislation. In 1879, the Army Discipline and Regulation Act came into force, replaced two years later by the Army Act.[9] Like the previous Mutiny Act, the Army Act received annual approval from the British Parliament after 1881.

Although the Army Act silenced the harshest critics of the military justice system for the time being, military authorities disparaged what they perceived as encroaching civilian influence over military law. The British JAG was a political appointee who advised service authorities, the government, and the sovereign on points of law concerning military matters and courts martial.[10] During the nineteenth century, he sat in the British House of Commons, was a member of the Privy Council, and usually came and went with the political party in power. Proposals were occasionally put forward to extend the JAG's duties and responsibilities beyond simply the advisory role.[11] These proposals proved more popular among members of Parliament than military authorities. Under the existing system, the adjutant general, Major General Sir Garnet Wolseley, was responsible for the administration of military discipline within the army, and he personally opposed a suggested formal right of appeal to the JAG or some other civil legal authority: "Those who know how difficult it is to maintain discipline in an army – especially in an army constituted as ours is upon almost purely civilian principles with a Parliament always on the watch to check and find fault with the conduct of those in military authority – know also how essential it is the soldier should learn to look to his officer alone for justice."[12]

Unfortunately, some officers and soldiers coming before courts martial did not share Wolseley's faith in the impartiality of the military hierarchy. The Duke of Cambridge noted that defendants were increasingly hiring solicitors or barristers to represent them at trial.[13] The intervention of legally trained civilians at various levels of the military justice system demanded a higher standard of knowledge and proficiency in law among military officers.

The royal commission recommended the preparation of an official textbook on military law, issued by authority, for the general reference of the armed forces. Standard works on military law and courts martial by such authors as Captain Thomas Simmons, Major General Charles Napier, and Major General George D'Aguilar were still in use, but they were hopelessly outdated.[14] To be of any practical value, handbooks and manuals needed to stay current with constant changes in the statutes and regulations. Many irregularities in the application and administration of military law were undoubtedly due to some overreliance on old books. Charles Clode, who argued that military law could only be understood in its historical context, produced his own book through a private publisher, pending issue of an official manual.[15] The legitimacy of military law, he asserted, rested upon a separate and parallel development to the common law. A committee, which assembled at the Horse Guards on 2 May 1877 under instructions from the secretary of state for war, endorsed preparation of an official textbook, designed to enable all ranks to understand more clearly the connection between civil and military law and to promote more uniformity in courts martial.[16] The parliamentary counsel's efforts, however, overtook the endeavour. Colonel Robert Carey, a deputy judge advocate, wrote a book explaining the principles behind the Mutiny Act and Articles of War, but it was never published outside the War Office because the new statute superseded these authorities.[17] Instead, military authorities used the opportunity to suggest a more ambitious and comprehensive manual that drew upon extensive civil legal experience.

The first official British *Manual of Military Law* was prepared and arranged under the direction of the parliamentary counsel. The process began in July 1879 when the secretary of state for war asked Thring to produce rules of procedure for the new statute and to incorporate them into a textbook that would include the Act and explanatory notes on military law.[18] The original intention was to publish two versions of the manual, one for use in orderly rooms and another abridged and portable form to be taken into the field. Gerald Fitzgerald, a member of the parliamentary bar, acted as general editor, and several authors wrote individual chapters. Contributors included Thring; Fitzgerald; Henry Jenkyns, the assistant parliamentary counsel; Courtney Ilbert, legal member of the Council of the Viceroy of India; Lieutenant Colonel Blake; Albert Meysey-Thompson of the Inner Temple; and William Selfe of Lincoln's Inn. They referred extensively to the books by Simmons and Carey in writing the manual's chapters. At Thring's suggestion, the JAG added notes to and thoroughly revised the draft manuscript on the basis of the recently enacted Army Act.[19] The finished product then received approval from the Duke of Cambridge.

The War Office officially published the *Manual of Military Law* in 1884. Its fourteen chapters and appendices dealt authoritatively with the history of military law, military crimes and punishments, powers of arrest, courts martial, the law of evidence, English criminal law applicable to soldiers, the relation of civil courts to courts martial, billeting, constitution of the Crown's military forces, enlistment, the soldier's relation to civil life, the law of riot and insurrection, as well as the laws and customs of war.[20] The *Manual of Military Law* was available for purchase through Her Majesty's Stationery Office and received a wide public circulation. Republished in several editions in subsequent years, the book became an invaluable source on military law for officers, soldiers, and civilian lawyers involved with military justice in Great Britain and self-governing colonies like Canada.

In contrast to the interest in military law in Great Britain, the Canadian variant attracted less attention. The scale of Canadian public inquiry never matched that of the British royal commissions. Beyond matters of fiscal responsibility and blatant political patronage, the Dominion Parliament seldom showed any sustained interest in military matters. Flogging, which was less common in Canada, hardly caused the level of emotional debate exhibited in Great Britain. British commanders of troops in North America faced a major problem with desertion, particularly when labour markets in the United States offered the attractions of high wages and steady employment.[21] Flogging proved a poor deterrent because severe punishments merely gave dissatisfied soldiers another reason to run away. Military authorities recognized the dilemma. A memorandum, issued for the guidance of officers in understanding the Army Discipline and Regulation Act, stated that maximum punishments were to be the exception rather than the rule and were only to be imposed "when the offence committed [was] the worst of its class, and [was] committed by an habitual offender, or [was] committed under circumstances which require[d] an example to be made by reason of the unusual prevalence of that offence in the force to which the offender belong[ed]."[22] The voluntary nature of enlistment in the Canadian militia further militated against stern punishments. Aggrieved or disgruntled men simply chose not to re-enlist at the end of their three-year engagements.

Officers and non-commissioned officers in the small Canadian militia relied upon other means of persuasion and control. The British criticized Canadians for frequently forgetting "the line of demarcation which should exist between the officer and soldier, and without which no discipline can be properly carried out."[23] They overlooked the issue of whether the separation was even viable among part-time soldiers who were comparatively well educated by the standards of the day, integrated into their general civic and social communities, and more often related to each other through family, business, and political connections. The Canadian public, of which many officers and soldiers formed an influential part, disdained the abuses and outdated practices associated with traditional militaries. In this regard, the Canadian militia considered itself superior to the British and other European standing armies.

Although still subject to the Army Act and relevant QR&O in force within the British Army when called out on training and active service, the militia ordered its affairs to suit particular Canadian circumstances. The Militia Act of 1868 authorized four classes of men liable for military service, different types of volunteer and reserve militia, separate military districts, and an annual paid drill of no more than sixteen days, subject to parliamentary vote.[24] In practice, arrangements and organization fell far short of the legislation. While acknowledging the regional and cultural differences within the new Dominion, Colonel Walker Powell, a Canadian officer who eventually became adjutant general, felt confident that "a system will be reached, calculated to meet the necessities of the country, and be within the resources of the people."[25] The militia mobilized with some success during the Fenian scares and the Red River Rebellion. In 1870, the Department of Militia and Defence published *Regulations and Orders* for the active militia, based on practical experience in the field.[26] These superseded previous regulations issued on an interim basis by the adjutant general and promoted greater uniformity among Canadian military forces. In terms of discipline and organization, the Canadians compared themselves favourably to the Territorial Army in Great Britain.[27] The Militia Act and its accompanying regulations sought to bring the militia as close as possible to the standard of volunteer British troops to meet the Dominion's minimal defence needs.

The militia still relied heavily upon British command and legal expertise. The general officer commanding the Canadian militia was a British officer with the rank of major general, appointed by Queen Victoria in consultation with the Duke of Cambridge, the War Office, the Colonial Office, and the Canadian government.[28] The effectiveness of individuals in this position usually corresponded with their professional competence and astuteness in working within the volatile Canadian political culture. The general officer commanding the militia held a warrant from the Crown to convene and confirm courts martial within Canada, but he usually consulted the governor general and the civilian minister of militia and defence, who in turn made known the concerns of the Canadian cabinet and the Department of Justice. Colonel Powell, who served as adjutant general under successive British generals until his retirement in 1896, was responsible for overall supervision and administration of military law within the militia. Since no permanent military staff existed, civilian clerks, such as Benjamin Sulte, handled the administrative routine within the department on behalf of the adjutant general and the minister of militia and defence. Each military district had a deputy adjutant general and a brigade major. Although most matters dealing with courts martial and discipline were handled within Canada, difficult cases or legal questions were referred to the War Office and the JAG in London for advice. The system combined tangible Canadian involvement with the benefits of British professional expertise.

British assistance was indispensable in the progressive development of the Canadian militia as a professional military force. The late nineteenth century saw the transition from older traditions of amateurism to a growing sense of professionalism among British and Canadian officers.[29] Education, ability, and experience gradually took precedence over financial means, social background, and personal connections. The War Office formally abolished the purchase of commissions in 1869. Thereafter, prospective officers were required to achieve their qualifications through merit and demonstrated knowledge in the art of war and regimental duties. The introduction of formal instruction in military law resulted from a general effort to instill a higher degree of professionalism among officers. In a lecture to cadets at the Royal Military College at Sandhurst, General Sir Henry Murray emphasized the importance of the subject:

> Formally a notion used to prevail that Courts Martial in their proceedings and decisions were to be governed rather by honour than law – now this altogether is a mistake; honour, it is true is a noble influence, but it is rather of a capricious nature – each Gentleman seems to exhume the right of having his own code of it. Whereas law goes doggedly to its point – one counsel may represent it in a particular light and another counsel may show it in a different one, but still there remains the law founded on experience and reflection as a safe path to the administration of justice. For this reason I think that the study of military law is an important branch of education in any candidate for a Commission in the Army.[30]

Professional qualification required an appropriate knowledge of military law. With every increase in rank, an officer was expected to have a better level of understanding.[31] Self-study and formal courses of instruction, tested by written examinations, guaranteed a minimum knowledge. Not all officers in the Canadian militia eagerly embraced the concept of professionalism that the study of military law entailed, but those who took advantage of the available opportunities became more proficient soldiers.

As long as British regular troops remained in Canada, the militia enjoyed substantial facilities for training and education. In 1864, fearing an attack on Canada after tense relations with the Americans over seizure of the British steamer *Trent* during the American Civil War, the British attached military schools of instruction to British regiments on garrison duty in Ontario and Quebec.[32] Although originally provisional, the schools soon expanded in number and location, becoming more or less permanent institutions. British instructors provided officers and non-commissioned officers from the Canadian militia with a structured course of study, which imparted a basic knowledge of military law and relevant regulations.[33] Successful graduates from the military schools obtained certificates of qualification allowing them to act as company or battalion commanders.

Some militia officers took full advantage of British instruction. Two chapters in a handbook compiled by Major Thomas Scoble for the guidance of Canadian volunteers on active service dealt with the Militia Act, the QR&O, and the Articles of War.[34] Although little original thought was evident in the small work, Scoble sought to share with a wider audience the teaching he had received at the military school in Toronto. Such books were important because many militia officers were too busy with their own civil and business affairs to take the necessary time to attend British military schools. Geographical distance and other constraints always worked against greater participation in formal instructional courses with the British regiments, and other ways of learning more about military law were required.

Regardless of proximity to a major urban area or a British garrison, many militia officers independently read and studied books and regulations available locally to increase their professional knowledge of military law. Libraries and the private holdings of individuals who took an interest in military matters were the main sources. Officers bought books by mail order directly from publishers or borrowed from friends and neighbours. British and American veterans who settled in Canada with their families after retirement or discharge often possessed first-hand knowledge, if somewhat dated, about military law and discipline. Militia officers who read newspapers probably also had some awareness of leading foreign legal authorities, such as Dr. Francis Lieber's code for the Union army during the American Civil War, the 1864 Geneva Convention, or even Prussian regulations and orders with regard to military occupation during the Franco-Prussian War.

Individual study in military law often lagged behind other military subjects that seemed more interesting and soldierly, and less complex. Militia officers, if they studied at all in their spare time, usually gravitated toward reading about tactics or strategy. It was easy to ignore military law in an unregimented and unsystematic environment that left much to individual choice and preference. Officers who had an interest in military law and the regulations studied the subject, whereas those who did not never bothered. When some expertise in military law was actually demanded, many militia officers crammed from relevant regulations and books.

The presence of British troops in Canada generally meant that British books were most readily available. Captain Alexander Tulloch, a garrison instructor with the 69th Regiment in Halifax, published a set of lectures on military law to "facilitate the study of a subject which some officers consider rather a dry one."[35] Tulloch remarked that up-to-date books on military law were scarce in Canada; in the preparation of his book, he consulted staff college lecture notes and published works by Thomas Simmons, Charles Clode, and Major Charles Gorham.[36] British officers like Tulloch often brought books with them for their own use and then left some of these behind with friends and acquaintances when transferred again overseas. After concluding the Treaty of Washington with the Americans, the British government decided to withdraw its remaining regular troops from Canada, except for small garrisons at the naval fortresses of Esquimalt and Halifax.[37] The Canadian militia assumed sole responsibility for its own military training and education.

Although British military schools closed following the withdrawal of imperial troops, the Dominion government was eager to open comparable Canadian military schools of instruction as soon as possible. Plans called for various schools in all arms of the forces but organizational problems, limited funds from Parliament, and a country-wide economic depression meant that only two schools of gunnery, attached to artillery batteries at Kingston and Quebec, were initially established. The British government made available to the Canadian militia two Royal Artillery officers, Lieutenant Colonel George French and Lieutenant Colonel Thomas Strange, to organize and command the batteries. Both men had extensive operational and administrative experience. Strange was previously an artillery instructor and superintendent at the Royal Military Academy at Woolwich, the British Army's main educational institution for the Royal Artillery, over a five-year period.[38] The academic program at Woolwich was particularly intensive because the intellectual demands of the artillery were higher than in other military branches. Officers were required to demonstrate a good knowledge of mathematics, geometry, and other scientific subjects beyond the typical military topics.[39] As a result, the Royal Artillery was generally more selective in its choice of recruits. More than any other branch, the artillery represented the intellectual side of the army, and Canada drew immediate benefits for its own military training and organization.

Under the supervision of French and Strange, the curriculum at the Canadian gunnery schools resembled the curriculum at the Royal Military Academy. The gunnery schools offered long and short courses of instruction, lasting twelve and three months respectively. Enrolments were small, and the quality of instruction was kept very high.[40] The courses provided officers and other ranks from the militia with a thorough grounding in technical, military, and administrative duties. In regard to military law, non-commissioned officers and drivers mostly concentrated on the practical development of discipline through drill and attention to interior economy, whereas officers learned about the *Militia Regulations,* the QR&O, and the Articles of War, as applied under Canada's Militia Act. Questions for officers in the short and long course examinations at Quebec in November 1874 expected a detailed knowledge of courts martial, grievance procedures, punishments, framing of charges, types of evidence, and the rules governing arrest.[41] If successful in the written examinations and practical exercises, officers obtained first or second class certificates, depending on their final aggregate marks.

Although a select few secured engagements with the permanent batteries, the majority of graduates were expected to return to their battalions or companies to act as instructors during training and drill in camp. Printing presses at the gunnery schools distributed to the militia 1,800 copies of examination questions and 1,000 copies of an artillery manual with a section on discipline.[42] The gunnery schools represented the only truly efficient military schools in the country at the time. Like the Royal Military Academy that taught both engineering and artillery officers, the gunnery schools accepted officers from other branches. An infantry short course, offered at the Quebec school, required officers to pass written examinations on the Militia Act, the QR&O, and interior economy.[43] The gunnery schools, which received the prefix "Royal" in 1880, offered good quality instruction in military law for a select number of motivated militia officers.

The opening of the Royal Military College of Canada at Kingston in June 1876 furnished additional opportunities for formal military legal instruction. Despite misgivings within his own political party, Liberal Prime Minister Alexander Mackenzie accepted the need for an institution in Canada to educate young men for military service.[44] Whether Mackenzie saw the college as a preferable alternative to the militia schools or as a foundation for a future Canadian army was not clear. And given the limited employment available in the militia as it was then organized, the Royal Military College struggled for legitimacy in the early years. From the beginning, the Royal Military College of Canada emulated the United States Military Academy at West Point rather than Sandhurst or Woolwich.[45] The curriculum comprised a mixture of civil and military subjects with a strong emphasis on engineering. Even so, the War Office offered a small number of commissions in the British Army on a competitive basis to cadets with the highest standing in each year.

With few prospects of professional military careers, remaining cadets entered civil vocations or government service. Graduates of the Royal Military College of Canada were under no obligation to serve in the active militia, and some chose not to. On the one hand, the Royal Military College provided little more than a publicly subsidized education for the sons of better families within the Dominion; on the other hand, it produced a well-disciplined and educated body of men with an intimate appreciation of military concerns. Cadets received instruction in military administration and law in the third and fourth years of the Royal Military College's four-year academic program.

Instruction in military law at the Royal Military College of Canada initially started slowly. The predominantly British instructional staff was small. Lieutenant Colonel Edward Hewett, RE, the college's first commandant, regretted that some instruction in military administration and law, which cadets should have received in 1878 under the military college's regulations, was postponed until the next term because the instructor, Major Edgar Kensington, RA, was required to teach mathematics and artillery.[46] Notwithstanding, examiners remarked that results from final examinations indicated that cadets gained as much information on military law as the short instructional time allowed.

Military law received better coverage with minor staff changes in the following year. Cadets in the fourth and fifth classes learned about laws relating to soldiers, the history of British military law, military crimes and punishments, courts martial, and rules of evidence.[47] The focus was still primarily British rather than Canadian. Wolseley's popular *Soldier's Pocket-Book for Field Service,* privately published in Great Britain and the United States, and widely available in Canada, was used as a textbook.[48] The book was a forerunner to the British Army's later published *Field Service Regulations.* The appointment of a dedicated professor in military history, military administration, and law greatly improved the standing and teaching of the subject, although the Canadians chose not to create a separate Department of Law as existed at West Point.

A Royal Artillery officer, seconded from his regiment by the War Office, filled the professorship. Major Douglas Jones, RA, arrived at Kingston in the summer of 1879. Besides considerable experience in teaching military administration and law as a former instructor at Woolwich, he was knowledgeable about recent changes in British legislation and regulations. Major Jones broadened legal instruction at the Royal Military College of Canada to include comparisons between military and civil law, preliminary steps before trial, court martial procedure, the Militia Act and regulations applicable to the Canadian militia, courts of inquiry, and martial law.[49] The increased scope and sophistication of the course were now more in line with similar instruction in Great Britain. Examination questions at the Royal Military College at Sandhurst and for entry of militia officers into the British Army required candidates to have a wide range of knowledge on the content and administration of military law.[50] The course at the Royal Military College of Canada included British military law with a strong Canadian emphasis.

At Hewett's suggestion, Major Jones prepared notes on military law for the cadets to use. This publication received a wider circulation outside the

Royal Military College of Canada and became recommended reading for serious militia officers.[51] But changes necessitated by introduction of the new Army Act soon diminished its value as a reliable reference source. Consequently, Jones revised and expanded his notes into a full textbook on military law in 1882.[52] His classes consisted of lectures, followed by reading from the textbook and questions put to the students by him. The textbook provided greater detail on particular topics. This method of teaching, said Jones, "gain[s] the full attention of the Cadets to my lectures, which I should fail in doing had they to be busily engaged in taking copious notes, and enables me to proceed more rapidly."[53] Although a conscientious teacher, Major Jones held strong opinions on certain controversial military issues, and he resigned from the Royal Military College of Canada in 1884.

Major Edward Nash, another British artillery officer, became professor of military history, military administration, and law on 14 August 1884. Major Nash may not have possessed the same work ethic as Jones, but he was just as capable as his predecessor. His classes were taught in a thorough and comprehensive manner. Nash reported steady improvement from the cadets in their comprehension of military administration and law.[54] Among the chief reasons for establishing the Royal Military College in the first place was to produce a class of officers familiar with staff duties, a field generally recognized as lacking within the Canadian militia. Good regimental staff officers required a sound knowledge of military law and regulations. Besides the cadets, a select number of officers from the militia attended a special long course of instruction at the Royal Military College of Canada. Nash lectured on various aspects of military administration and law to both groups until his voluntary retirement. The professorship then remained vacant until Major Eustace Edwards, RA, became professor of artillery, military administration, and law in early 1891.[55] Courses at the Royal Military College of Canada provided good quality instruction in military law for militia officers and cadets, some of whom subsequently entered British and Canadian service.

The British officers who headed the Canadian militia exerted pressure for the creation of infantry and cavalry schools of military instruction, in addition to the Royal gunnery schools and the Royal Military College of Canada. Parliament's drastic reductions in funds allocated to the militia after 1876 delayed the opening of military schools in other arms and restricted paid training to twelve days every two years instead of annually. Lieutenant General Edward Selby-Smyth, the general officer commanding the militia, questioned the prevailing attitude toward defence in Canada:

> It is sometimes asked by a class of persons of peculiar habits of thought – "Why spend money on military establishments?" "Who are you going to

> fight?" It is hardly necessary to answer; happily we may have no one to fight, but military expenditure is a description of insurance that every country has to pay against loss by war, the amount of insurance in a great measure depending upon the value of the property, the risk, and the means of the insurer.
>
> It is a mistake, frequently made that an army is maintained solely for the purpose of fighting with somebody. No doubt it should be in a fit state to do so if required, but it is much more a guarantee for peace instead of war, for the nation that is able to back its opinions is pretty certain to prevail over the weak country that has no power beyond simple argument, be that ever so sound and sensible, but wanting the unanswerable logic of force to support it.[56]

Severe fiscal restraint restricted the militia to such an extent that its potential effectiveness was in doubt. A military force without discipline and training, Selby-Smyth asserted, was little more than an armed mob. He and his successor, Major General Richard Luard, repeatedly stressed the importance of military education in the professional development of officers and non-commissioned officers. Although proposals for reductions in size of the active militia and application of consequent savings to a smaller permanent force remained politically unpalatable, the Dominion government redistributed limited funds for more military instruction.

Military law constituted an important subject at the military schools. Examining boards and provisional schools were held in various parts of the country close to fairly large population centres. Examinations for second class militia certificates in May 1878 asked questions on the constitution of different types of courts martial, disciplinary powers of commanding officers, procedures and responsibilities in using troops to aid the civil power, and the nature of courts of inquiry.[57] Candidates answered in either English or French and required at least a score of fifty percent to pass. Questions for first class certificates in Montreal the next year demanded a detailed knowledge of the Militia Act, punishments for certain offences, enrolment and terms of service, as well as duties in relation to aiding the civil power.[58] As candidates were not allowed to bring books into the examination, the answers reflected a remarkably good grasp of the subject-matter. In Quebec, officers were also compelled "to attend as supernumeraries on District Courts Martial, and to make special reports as to how the proceedings were carried out."[59] Wherever possible, this type of practical observation reinforced theoretical instruction.

The long-awaited permanent schools of military instruction adopted long and short courses of instruction with a military law component. The deputy adjutant general suggested that before first and second class certificates were granted at the infantry schools, candidates should demonstrate a knowledge of the Militia Act and its accompanying regulations, the Army Act, the QR&O, powers of commanding officers, and courts martial.[60] In January 1884, permanent military schools – three infantry and one cavalry – opened at Toronto, Fredericton, St. John's, and Quebec City. Amendments to the militia regulations stipulated that officers required qualification, either through certificates obtained at a military school or before a board of officers, within a year of appointment to the active militia. In the absence of a British system of promotion examinations, the demand for qualification ensured at least a minimum standard of professional competence in military law within the Canadian militia.[61] As the permanent military schools of instruction swung into full operation, more and more qualified officers and non-commissioned officers returned to rural and city corps.

Under the tight fiscal regime imposed by the Dominion's Parliament, the militia was authorized to perform paid training of sixteen days for artillery and twelve days for all other arms every two years. The Militia Act required officers to read the conditions of service to soldiers upon mustering and to inform them that they were now subject to military law. Already restricted by the brief time available, training in camp involved instruction in a range of theoretical and practical subjects. A nucleus of trained officers who graduated from the Royal Military College of Canada and the permanent military schools of instruction set a disciplined example for the rest of the company or battalion.

For guidance, officers referred to the pocket-sized *Militia Orders and Regulations,* the latest published in 1883, and other official or semi-official books on hand. Current information on military law and courts martial was available in the British *Manual of Military Law*; a book in French by Major Joseph Taschereau; and sections on discipline, courts martial, offences, complaints, and defaulters in Lieutenant Colonel William Otter's popular guide for the administration of an infantry formation.[62] Although instruction was far from uniform, most soldiers gained some sort of familiarity with military law and certainly learned enough to recognize the difference between right and wrong within the military environment. The general availability of published manuals and regulations shifted the onus onto the individual to read and know what was expected of him. In general, city corps were in a much better state than their rural counterparts because literacy was more widespread, and money from interested patrons and businessmen enabled the purchase of additional books and supplies. The militia's conduct during the North-West Rebellion highlighted the progress and the problems with putting military law into practice during active operations.

In 1885, after Louis Riel and his supporters fought a number of engagements with the North-West Mounted Police and declared a provisional government at Batoche, the Dominion government raised and dispatched military forces under the command of the general officer commanding the militia, Major General Frederick Middleton. The North-West Field Force divided into three columns: Middleton proceeded against Riel and Gabriel Dumont, the rebel military leader, in the direction of Batoche; Lieutenant Colonel Otter relieved Battleford and engaged defiant natives under Chief Poundmaker north of the town; and Major General Strange, recalled from retirement near Calgary, moved to Edmonton and thence to besieged Fort Pitt along the North Saskatchewan River. Unlike the earlier Red River expedition, the military forces in 1885 were completely under Canadian control and administration. Major General Middleton received directions directly from the Dominion government in Ottawa, which gave him considerable latitude to conduct operations in the field as he saw fit.[63] The large-scale internal security operation represented Canada's first major national military experience since Confederation.

The number of punished offences during the North-West Rebellion was relatively low. The short campaign involved considerable movement and marches, troops were concentrated in camp when not deployed in combat, temptations of towns and settlements were far away, and liquor was prohibited in the North-West Territories. Lieutenant John Preston attributed an apparent lack of offences within the Midland battalion to the strictly enforced ban on alcohol: "Our Battalion had been recruited largely in the towns of the Lake Ontario waterfront, from hard-bitten sailors and dock workers, who, if liquor had been generally available, would sometimes have been in trouble; but without anything strong to drink they were the finest and best-behaved and most loyal troops possible; and the same was generally true of all our rank and file."[64]

Clear instructions and decisive action by officers and non-commissioned officers to prevent crime reinforced expected behaviour. Common infractions against service discipline such as insubordination, negligent performance of duties, falling asleep during guard duty, improper up-keep of equipment, misappropriation of supplies, and accidental shootings were handled in a summary fashion in accordance with the scale of punishments under the Army Act. In the field, summary punishments were usually preferred to more formal legal proceedings, even for obstinate or repeat offenders.[65] Facilities for imprisonment were limited, and every convicted soldier removed from active service placed an added burden on the other troops. Available documentary evidence suggests that no general courts martial were held during the North-West Rebellion.[66] A shortage of officers with sufficient experience to sit on courts martial undoubtedly played a part, but soldiers also committed few serious offences that required trial by court martial under the regulations. Major General Middleton observed "an almost total absence of such Military crimes as are usual with Regular Troops."[67] Canadian troops preserved a commendable degree of discipline, certainly far above what could have been expected from their limited training and organization in the years before the Rebellion.

The downside of using hastily recruited and, at best, partially trained amateur soldiers was, however, never far from the surface. Deployment during the North-West Rebellion underscored Selby-Smyth's earlier warning about the relationship between discipline and control. Incidents of looting and plundering by Canadian troops were more prevalent than the minister of militia and defence was willing to admit in Parliament.[68] Existing law and custom allowed armies to destroy private property in the course of military operations and to requisition necessary supplies from local inhabitants. The march of General William Sherman's Union army across the southern United States during the American Civil War provided the most immediate precedent. Orders from Major General Middleton, read out after drill practice, prohibited troops from entering houses or farms on the line of march, except those authorized to collect provisions for the quartermaster.[69] Despite the threat of severe punishment, soldiers still seized goods and livestock for personal gain without apparently distinguishing between property belonging to supporters of the rebels and that belonging to the settlers they were sent to protect. At Battleford, complaints about unofficial requisitions became so frequent that Lieutenant Colonel Otter acknowledged that "stringent means must be taken to remedy it."[70] Punishment under military law was a deterrent against unauthorized activities. Parliamentary inquiries into allegations of looting during the Rebellion, including the questionable seizure of furs by the major general himself, eventually led to Middleton's resignation in 1890 and his return to Great Britain.

Unlike Sherman, Middleton was not willing to pursue a deliberate campaign of terror and retribution without some sort of provocation from the rebels. The occasion never arose because Riel refused Dumont's request to adopt guerilla tactics against the field force.[71] The rebels fought in the accepted ways of the day, respected flags of truce, and with the exception of the Frog Lake massacre, treated most prisoners reasonably well. In return, Middleton and the North-West Field Force handled the rebels and defiant Natives with fairness and respect. Dumont later claimed that Canadian troops had killed helpless defenders during the storming of Batoche.[72] Whether true or not, these alleged acts were committed in the heat of battle and under very confused circumstances. Unless some particularly brutal or malicious conduct was involved, military law generally did not hold soldiers responsible for killings during operations. Refusing quarter to other combatants, while deplorable, was not technically a crime under the existing mid-nineteenth century explication of the laws and customs of war. Before marching away from Batoche, Canadian soldiers destroyed gunpowder and ammunition, but they left Métis women and their belongings untouched.[73] In general, the North-West Field Force respected the status of non-combatants and seldom killed prisoners after capture.

Upon conclusion of the 1885 North-West Rebellion, the Canadian militia returned again to a state of restricted funding and little interest in military law. Enthusiasm for the achievements of the North-West Field Force was short-lived. The Royal Military College of Canada and the military schools of instruction received modest increases in expenditures, but Parliament kept a tight leash on the militia's budget. In 1886, Major James Pennington Macpherson published, with Middleton's endorsement, a book on military law aimed at presenting "those portions of the law which every officer ought to know, and which he might find himself called upon to administer."[74] Macpherson remarked that recent British books on the subject were available. For example, Colonel John Boughey, the assistant adjutant general in Great Britain and a former professor of law and military administration at Sandhurst, revised numerous editions of a standard textbook on military law.[75] Yet none of the British books covered the Canadian Militia Act or the *Militia Regulations and Orders* issued under its authority. Macpherson's work was tailored to a Canadian audience and included questions and answers on several themes, a large section on evidence, related forms, and advertisements for the Royal Military College of Canada and the military schools of instruction.

Recruitment problems necessarily had an influence on the administration of military law in Canada. On the occasion of Queen Victoria's Jubilee in 1887, all soldiers convicted of desertion, fraudulent enlistment, and absence without leave were released from prison, and the balance of their sentences were remitted.[76] Soldiers serving sentences in Canada were pardoned. But without formation of a suitable permanent force, the militia remained unable to attract and retain suitably qualified officers and other ranks for any protracted length of time. While Macpherson's book and the *Militia Regulations and Orders* were useful references, insufficient numbers of suitably trained and experienced officers severely restricted commanding officers from holding regimental or district courts martial, courts of inquiry, and boards.[77] Consequently, many improprieties and offences went uninvestigated and unpunished, to the detriment of overall discipline within the militia.

Extreme measures were required when the situation finally reached crisis proportions. Major General Ivor Herbert, who became the general officer commanding the militia in late 1890, cited large personnel losses in the military schools of instruction owing "to the more serious forms of military crime, and the necessary action of military law."[78] Almost half the entire establishment had prematurely deserted, been discharged, or been tried before courts martial. The ineffectiveness of local arrangements more and more often forced the militia headquarters in Ottawa to intervene directly in the administration of military justice at the district level. Major General Herbert's tough stand on discipline was reflected in the total number of courts martial in the militia during these years: 128 in 1891, 161 in 1892, 176 in 1893, 130 in 1894, and 118 in 1895. Drunkenness, desertion, and breaking out of barracks were the most common charges.[79] Authorities resorted to military law to deal with major problems afflicting the militia and its permanent component, in the face of Parliament's continued frugality and the Dominion government's refusal to implement Major General Herbert's suggested reforms for the permanent force. In 1894, the deputy adjutant general in British Columbia downheartedly remarked: "We must just go along as we are doing – The Govt are so hard up it is terribly hard to get anything out of them."[80] The strict application of military law allowed the militia to preserve its essential core capabilities in the interim until more money was forthcoming.

Despite organizational and disciplinary problems, the militia was used on several occasions to provide aid to the civil power. These events included riots and labour strikes, as well as the protection of polling stations and officials during rancorous civic elections. Under existing Dominion legislation, maintenance of law and order was a provincial responsibility. Only a mayor, magistrate, or similar public official could call out the militia.[81] It was left to commanding officers to collect any resulting costs directly from municipalities. The duty was unpopular among the militia because some bills remained outstanding when municipalities refused to pay after the immediate emergency subsided; furthermore, relatives, friends, and neighbours were often on the opposing side, and prosecution in civil courts was a possibility facing officers and soldiers who used excessive force resulting in death or injury.[82] In cases of intentional or accidental shootings, civil courts appeared quite willing to assert common law jurisdiction over members of the militia.

To avoid such problems, officers required a precise knowledge of the applicable sections in the *Militia Regulations and Orders* and general criminal law. In a presentation outlining the militia's rights and responsibilities in aiding the civil power, Lieutenant Colonel Henry Smith, the officer commanding in Military District Number 1, counselled that a wise officer or soldier "will do as little as possible, and will do nothing without a positive order from a justice of the peace."[83] The sage words became especially important after the subject was dropped entirely from the revised *Militia Regulations and Orders* in 1898. Thereafter, officers and soldiers relied solely upon the Militia Act and their own knowledge of military law to avoid trouble during operations in support of civil authorities. Aid to the civil power, whether on the picket line or during times of insurrection, accentuated the defensive nature of the militia.

Since Canadian military forces at the time existed primarily to defend Canada against the unlikely possibility of invasion from the United States or another foreign power, the Militia Act made no provision for use of the militia overseas or in other parts of the British Empire. In 1885, Prime Minister Macdonald had turned down a request from the British government for inclusion of Canadian troops on a relief and punitive expedition from Egypt into the Sudan.[84] Imperial supporters denounced the decision, but political considerations within the Dominion precluded unconditional participation in Great Britain's small colonial wars. Canada's contribution to imperial defence, Macdonald argued, was better served by the maintenance of a creditable military force within the Dominion. In the event of war, the Canadian militia was available for the defence of Halifax, thus freeing up imperial troops for service elsewhere or bolstering the existing garrison until the arrival of British reinforcements.[85] The British reluctantly accepted that the Canadian cabinet now possessed the final say over where and when the militia was deployed. Canadians who wished to serve outside Canada were required to join the British armed forces. In 1889, Wolseley stated that the likelihood of British and Canadian forces ever serving together overseas was "so remote that the question of their relation together to each other seems hardly likely to arise."[86] As long as the Canadian government remained diffident about sending military forces abroad, intricate questions of military law were avoided.

Legislative changes in other colonies, however, highlighted the ambiguity of existing arrangements. On the parliamentary counsel's advice, the War Office adopted the view that colonial forces were subject to military law in the same way as regular troops because when volunteers and regulars acted together, they constituted a unified body.[87] In this respect, the Canadian militia and other colonial military forces were in an analogous position to volunteers in the British Territorial Army. Although section 177 of the Army Act appeared to cover the relationship in an adequate manner, the British JAG questioned the assumption that a colony would place its military contingents exclusively under British military law when they were sent abroad.[88] Colonial defence legislation differed in subtle ways from the Army Act, and certain colonies might not willingly put aside their own statutes. A volunteer law passed by the legislature of Natal, in South Africa, applied the Army Act to military forces acting in conjunction with imperial troops, "but only so far as the law of the Colony has not provided for the government and discipline of such a force."[89] In other words, the colonial statute took precedence over the Army Act, unless some particular deficiency required application of the imperial legislation. Since the change in emphasis would have far-reaching ramifications if Canada and the other self-governing colonies decided to follow Natal's lead, Wolseley suggested minor amendments to imperial and colonial defence legislation.

The War Office consulted the parliamentary counsel for his advice on this important point. Proposed amendments to the 1895 Army Act made regular troops serving with colonial forces liable to be tried for offences against colonial officers, soldiers, and institutions.[90] There was still some question whether colonial officers could lawfully exercise powers of command and discipline under the Army Act over regular troops by virtue of superior rank in the colonial forces. After careful consideration, Sir Courtney Ilbert, the parliamentary counsel, concluded that "the subject-matter is difficult and raises delicate questions, and it would not be desirable to initiate legislation upon it without proof of necessity."[91] The potential pitfalls were enormous; issues of military law trespassed into the political realm of imperial defence cooperation and the relationship of Great Britain with the self-governing colonies. With this in mind, Wolseley asked the JAG "to define ... the actual questions he wishes settled by regulations."[92] Meanwhile, British diplomats consulted representatives from the self-governing colonies directly. Canadian prime minister Wilfrid Laurier and other delegates agreed at a colonial conference in 1897 to institute uniformity in military law throughout the British Empire.[93] Although simple modifications to Canada's Militia Act appeared sufficient to meet the new arrangements, the decision offered to remove the main obstacle to Canadian military forces serving with imperial troops anywhere in the world.

Of course, Canadians already served with British regular troops within Canada. Under a warrant issued in January 1887, imperial officers no longer took precedence over colonial regimental officers in Canada.[94] The exemption, perhaps unique at the time among the self-governing colonies, solved the problem of finding suitably qualified officers to sit on courts martial. Utilizing officers from the Canadian militia avoided the apparently frowned-upon Australian practice of temporarily appointing civilian judges and magistrates.[95] The practical arrangement also made employment of mixed bodies of imperial and colonial troops easier. In 1897, Major General William Gascoigne, the general officer commanding the militia, exchanged a permanent force infantry company from Fredericton with a company of regular troops from the Royal Berkshire Regiment, then stationed in Halifax, with the consent of the Canadian and British governments.[96] It was intended that courts martial assembled in either formation would comprise both British and Canadian officers. But, as Gascoigne pointed out to the War Office, Canada's Militia Act still restricted imperial officers from sitting on courts martial convened to try members of the militia.[97] British officers could serve only on courts martial involving imperial officers or other ranks. Even though the British JAG was asked for an opinion on whether the limitation also applied to imperial and Canadian forces acting together, the question remained unresolved until the next year when a Canadian officer from the permanent force became president of a court martial to try a member of the Royal Artillery.[98] Through actual practice, imperial and Canadian officers were now clearly equal under military law.

Only the weaknesses of Canada's own military organization restricted further employment of the Canadian militia with British military forces. Although the Dominion had agreed in 1888 to the desirability of a defence scheme, no progress had been made in concrete terms. In 1896, the Colonial Defence Committee in London lamented that "Canada alone of the many parts which make up the British Empire, is absolutely without organization for utilizing its splendid personnel in war."[99] Canadian permanent force officers and non-commissioned officers had travelled to Great Britain since Major General Herbert's tenure as general officer commanding for instructional purposes with imperial regiments; but too few Canadian officers were trained properly in staff duties and military law within the militia. The twelve days of training allowed every year under Parliament's existing estimates were recognized as insufficient.

Major General Edward Hutton, a British officer with previous service with colonial forces in New South Wales, became general officer commanding the Canadian militia on 11 August 1898. Hutton observed that the standard of efficiency, discipline, and organization of the Canadian militia was "not equal to that which my experience with similar troops in other parts of the Empire had led me to expect."[100] In his view, reforms and training were urgently needed to turn the dilapidated militia into an effective fighting force for deployment with British and other colonial military forces. Wolseley, who became commander-in-chief after the Duke of Cambridge's resignation, was attempting a similar overhaul of the British Army, and he petitioned the queen to transfer responsibility for discipline from the adjutant general back to the commander-in-chief because the existing system "could not be carried out with an army in the field."[101] The probability of colonial and British troops soon fighting together added further weight to Wolseley's arguments. Both Wolseley and Hutton believed that military law required uniform and consistent application among all forces, whether imperial or colonial, to be truly effective. Hutton's efforts, however, upset colonial sensibilities in Canada. The British officer was abruptly forced to resign after tussles with Frederick Borden, the Liberal minister of militia and defence, which included an untimely letter written by Hutton to the press advocating dispatch of a Canadian contingent to South Africa before the Dominion government had made up its mind. In spite of Hutton's impudence, Canadian troops eventually went, under the jurisdiction and disciplinary provisions of the Army Act, to fight the Boers and preserve the British Empire.

2
In Defence of Empire

During the early twentieth century, Canada structured and organized its Armed Forces to assist Great Britain overseas and protect imperial interests. Canadian troops fought alongside British and other colonial formations in the Boer War and the First World War. Experiences during both conflicts raised complicated issues in terms of military law for all colonial governments involved. Methods of resolving such issues were distinctive. Australia, another self-governing colony, demanded greater control over the administration of military justice among its own forces. Canada, on the other hand, willingly placed troops under the Army Act and British supervision as long as Canadians remained in nationally distinct formations. The Department of Militia and Defence appointed a JAG to oversee the administration of military law and advise on legal matters affecting the Canadian Armed Forces. While legal staffs were largely Canadian, British example remained predominant. Various committees in London examined questions of discipline, punishments, and courts martial. Military legal instruction attracted considerable attention as Canadian officers attended militia staff courses and schools of higher military education in Great Britain.

The war in South Africa was Canada's first imperial adventure. In 1899, Paul Kruger and Dutch settlers in the Boer republics of the Transvaal and the Orange Free State, in an effort to stem encroaching British commercial interests and rival Dutch factions, broke off negotiations with Sir Alfred Milner and invaded British territory to the south. Although everyone in Great Britain believed that the ensuing war would be short, the British Army suffered a series of defeats and reversals at the hands of well-led and mobile Boer forces. The Boers were armed with modern weapons and enjoyed the tacit backing of Great Britain's European rivals, in particular imperial Germany under Kaiser Wilhelm II. Faced with stalemate or worse, possible defeat, in South Africa, the British colonial secretary appealed to the self-governing colonies to send troops and reinforcements to assist

British forces. Wilfrid Laurier bowed to imperial sentiment in English Canada and permitted the formation of a contingent of volunteers, recruited from across the Dominion and commanded by Colonel Otter.[1] Additional contingents of mounted infantry and artillery followed. Lord Strathcona, Canada's high commissioner in London, raised a unit of mounted rifles named the Strathcona's Horse at his own expense.[2] Even though members of the North-West Mounted Police formed a large part of the Strathcona's Horse, most of the volunteers were untrained and unfamiliar with military discipline. Canadian officers and other ranks signed attestation papers for one year of service in South Africa.[3] Under British direction, Canadian units participated in major battles and military operations against the elusive Boers.

Canadian troops became intimately involved in the nastier aspects of the South African war. Lord Roberts, the British commander-in-chief, and his chief of staff, Lord Kitchener, took the campaign into the heart of the Boer homeland by capturing Bloemfontein and Pretoria. Unwilling to admit defeat, Boer military forces separated into smaller commandos and adopted a strategy of guerilla raids and ambushes against the British. In this atmosphere of irregular warfare, the established laws and customs of war were sometimes disregarded. During fighting near Senekal in June 1900, Boer commandos set fire to the veldt, burning alive almost 150 wounded British soldiers.[4] The British responded with reprisals under their own interpretation of the existing legal rules. Canadian troops burned farmhouses for abuse of the white flag and concentrated Boer women and children into makeshift camps under official British orders.[5] As Roberts and Kitchener tried to deny the Boers their supply bases with a policy of systematic destruction, British and Canadian forces pursued the Boer leaders and remaining commandos. Colonial mounted troops proved particularly adept at this type of warfare. A British officer remarked that the discipline of the Canadians, "if not quite that of the regular army, was fairly good, their most marked fault being a tendency to struggle and live in a somewhat high-handed manner in the country."[6] Troops from the self-governing colonies still generally behaved better than those raised locally in South Africa. In what was tantamount to a civil war with imperial connotations, the Canadians adjusted, perhaps too easily, to unconventional and irregular means.

Despite frequent departures from the established rules, the law of war did exist in South Africa. Whether surprised or overwhelmed, significant numbers of officers and soldiers surrendered to the Boer commandos.[7] The Boers generally did not kill prisoners outright and treated them in a fair manner. Certain limitations, such as the nature of the warfare and food shortages, compelled the Boers to release British and colonial prisoners onto the veldt after stripping them of any useful equipment, accoutrements, and uniform.[8] The practice was a humane alternative in keeping with Boer religious beliefs, and it left the commandos mobile and unencumbered. Canadians directly benefited from Boer magnanimity. In a batch of 2,000 British prisoners released by the Boers in August 1900, nine soldiers belonged to the Strathcona's Horse.[9] Nonetheless, the Boers showed extreme ruthlessness toward soldiers who resisted longer than necessary or refused surrender upon reasonable demand. At Badfontein, a sergeant and three privates from the Strathcona's Horse, who had expended their rifle ammunition and shot down some of the advancing enemy with revolvers before their position was overwhelmed, "did not live long after getting in the Boer hands."[10] Foolhardy, if somewhat heroic, acts such as these made observance of the laws of war harder for both opposing sides. In spite of allegations of widespread use of expanding dumdum bullets and wearing of British uniforms for deceitful purposes, the Boer commandos were legal combatants, deserving of all the rights such a status entailed under international law. The Boers were a reasonable people and expected the same from the British and the Canadians.

The application of military law in South Africa aimed at maintaining a minimum standard of expected behaviour from imperial and colonial troops. Unfortunately, the nature of operations in the field fostered looting, horse-stealing, insubordination, and similar acts of ill-discipline among some formations. Officers, many of whom were inexperienced and ignorant of their duties and powers under military law, were initially reluctant to convene and confirm courts martial in the field and "passed without remark the irregularities and illegalities of their subordinates."[11] When soldiers were punished, the Army Act generally prescribed terms of imprisonment rather than more effective field punishments. For example, two privates from the Canadian Mounted Rifles, convicted of collecting arms from burghers and selling them back to the Boer commandos, each received sentences of ten years' penal servitude.[12] Courts martial made clear that such acts against military discipline were unacceptable, and sentences upon conviction were published in army orders and read out at parades for the benefit of all troops. In the earlier period of the conflict, military justice was sometimes swift in South Africa. A squadron sergeant major from Kitchener's Horse, who murdered another soldier on 29 November 1900, was tried, convicted, and shot the following day.[13] Stern punishments seemed necessary because the conduct of some troops in South Africa was especially bad.

Soldiers from the Strathcona's Horse participated in several questionable incidents involving the murder and mistreatment of captured Boer prisoners. On 15 August 1900, Boers flying a white flag from a farmhouse near Carolina shot down scouts from the South African Light Horse advancing to accept their surrender. A troop from the Strathcona's Horse then captured the place and proceeded to hang the Boers one by one after an impromptu trial.[14] After nine captives were dead, an officer intervened to stop the executions. Even though refusing quarter to enemy soldiers in combat represented an ambiguous area in existing law and custom until later codification under the Geneva Conventions, the Canadians had clearly exceeded the bounds of impropriety by killing Boer prisoners after the point of capture. A legal distinction existed between killing in the course of military operations and killing after the enemy's surrender. Prisoners of war were technically in protective custody and enjoyed certain legal safeguards in respect of their person and belongings. While the conduct of the Boers before capture was not above reproach, the deliberate and malicious killing of prisoners of war by the Canadians constituted murder. Consequently, the soldiers implicated in the unfortunate incident at the farmhouse were arrested and given severe reprimands for transgressing military law.[15] The Strathcona's Horse gained a reputation among colonial mounted troops as a hard-fighting, brash, and wild unit. In a diary entry for 12 October 1900, Trooper George Bowers described the arrest of several drunk non-commissioned officers, who were shouting, singing, and firing revolvers at Boer captives: "The prisoners were frightened they were going to be killed and no doubt will be glad when the Strathcona's Horse move camp."[16] Although the available evidence does not conclusively support a definite pattern, it is fair to conclude that some Canadian soldiers in the Strathcona's Horse committed illegalities outside normal military operations. They escaped severer punishment only because Lord Roberts was still in command.[17] Australians who committed remarkably similar crimes a year later did not receive the same leniency from Lord Kitchener.

The trial and execution of Australians in the Boer War, depicted in the Australian film *Breaker Morant,* took place under very different circumstances. In January 1902, a general court martial convened in Pietersburg to try Lieutenants Harry Morant, Peter Handcock, and George Witton for the alleged killing of Boer prisoners and a German missionary.[18] The three Australians were attached to a British mounted unit called the Bushveldt Carbineers, which, like the Strathcona's Horse, used unconventional tactics against the Boer commandos. From the outset, Australian public opinion opposed the trial, and representatives in Australia's legislature passed a resolution denouncing the charges as baseless and a stain on the honour of the people and soldiers of the British Empire.[19] In spite of political unease overseas, the British court martial found the three defendants guilty and sentenced Morant and Handcock to death by firing squad. Kitchener confirmed the sentences, and the two men were executed in Pretoria on 27 February 1902. Australian writers and historians contend that the British pushed through the trial and executions without consulting the Australian government because Kitchener was implicated in an alleged order to shoot

Boer prisoners, and he also needed to show good faith in upcoming peace negotiations.[20] Lesser sentences for British officers convicted of the same offences reinforced the view that Morant and Handcock were scapegoats. The probability that the Australians committed the acts for which they were convicted and deserved their punishment seemed less important than the high-handed manner in which the British, in particular Kitchener, handled the case.

In fact, the British commander-in-chief possessed exceptional powers over confirmation of courts martial in South Africa. In early November 1901, Kitchener had asked the War Office if he could extend his warrant to confirm cases involving cashiering or dismissal of imperial and colonial officers without referring to His Majesty the King.[21] Dispatch to and from London often entailed delays of several weeks. The War Office instead decided to issue a new warrant to Kitchener similar to one held by the commander-in-chief in India, which allowed confirmation of all courts martial on the spot. Sir Francis Jeune, the JAG, was concerned that the self-governing colonies would object to such sweeping authority, being "certain that sooner or later, probably sooner, some illegal sentence would be allowed to take effect, probably causing great scandal and possibly involving members of the Court Martial and even the Commander-in-Chief in serious consequences."[22] Jeune wanted convictions, especially those involving capital offences, referred to London for the purview of the British and colonial governments. The significance for Canada and the other self-governing colonies was obvious. Kitchener's new powers ran roughshod over national control and accountability.

Jeune's advice, however, was ignored because Kitchener had officers on his staff with considerable experience in military law, including Major General Sir Francis Kelly, the South African Field Force's adjutant general, and Colonel J. St. Clair, the deputy judge advocate general (DJAG). After promulgation of verdicts and sentences, all courts martial proceedings were forwarded to the latter for review before confirmation.[23] The DJAG department in Pretoria included two colonels named Sinclair and Pemberton; Chief Justice Richard Solomon, later made attorney general for Transvaal, also advised Kitchener on all legal matters. With the benefit of professional legal counsel, Kitchener felt reasonably competent in confirming courts martial under his all-encompassing warrant, applicable to both imperial and colonial forces.

Whatever the Australians may claim of the British commander-in-chief, Kitchener's correspondence with Sir John Broderick, the secretary of state for war, displayed a serious interest in the application and renovation of military law. Kitchener dealt with legal problems involving martial law, prisoners of war and paroles, trial and execution of Boer leaders, requisitions and foraging, and neutrals, as well as discipline within the imperial and colonial forces on an almost daily basis. As the Duke of Wellington had done a century before, Kitchener suggested changes in military law, based upon recent operational experience.[24] He carefully considered every verdict before confirmation. For Kitchener, military law was an essential tool for maintaining overall discipline within the South African Field Force:

> In my opinion strict-punishment is very necessary to impress on officers their very serious duties, but at the same time it does as good to act with fullest inquiry and strictly on legal lines. A hasty judgment creates a martyr, and unless military law is strictly followed a sense of injustice having been done is the result. Military law requires in my opinion considerable alteration to be effective, and to meet cases that have occurred during this war. The slight changes in the court of inquiry procedure are not in my opinion sufficient. It is always very difficult to elucidate by evidence an act by what has taken place is a fight. I have however tried my best, in every unpleasant case of mishap, to deal with the case on the above lines ... With regard to the remarks we so often see in the papers, the Army, I think quite rightly, feel that examples should be made, but when such an example has to be and is carried out, it should be published to the world as little as possible on the principle of washing our dirty linen at home. Examples are solely for the good of the Army, throughout which they are thoroughly known and appreciated and though the public may wish to "turn their thumbs down," it is felt that considering the honour of the Army at home and abroad, they should as far as possible be made to restrain their efforts for our good.[25]

In Kitchener's view, considerations of fairness and justice were solely the preserve of the informed commander. Officers and soldiers often made errors when difficult situations demanded quick and decisive action. Kitchener took severe measures against clear cases of wrongdoing, but he admitted that "dealing with Colonial troops and colonial feelings increases the difficulty considerably."[26] There is no evidence that Kitchener's immediate political superiors in London questioned his judgment. On the contrary, in the case of the Bushveldt Carbineers, Broderick wrote Kitchener: "It is a most deplorable performance and, if it gets out, as I fear it will, even the strong measures we are taking will not undo the disgrace it inflicts on our Colonial Forces. I should myself have been inclined to shoot all the three officers – but you are in the best position to judge."[27] In confirming court martial sentences on colonial troops, Kitchener acted on the merits of specific cases, the character of the accused, and the need to preserve confidence in military law. The test of a military institution's commitment to order and discipline was the timely punishment of atrocities, such as those committed by the Canadians and Australians. Kitchener was not the type of military commander to shirk from the responsibility of doing what he thought was right under military law and punishing inappropriate behaviour.

Kitchener's concerns and the British Army's dismal performance in South Africa ultimately led to calls for military reform following the Boer War. A British royal commission, which examined the dispatch, organization, and activities of the South African Field Force and heard testimony from key participants, exposed glaring defects in Great Britain's military structure.[28] The administration of military law, especially the inadequacy of imprisonment as a punishment on active service and the handing down of death sentences by British courts on British and colonial troops, attracted special scrutiny. In 1904, a committee under the chair of Major General Henry Douglas suggested the reintroduction of corporal punishment, although it recognized that the self-governing colonies were against inflicting such punishment on their troops, and "all the fighting units composing a field army ought to be subject to the same disciplinary regulations."[29] Given the recent experience in South Africa, senior British officers did not believe that self-governing colonies, some already uneasy about death sentences, would ever countenance flogging; it was incredible that the idea was even contemplated at the time.

The increasingly complex relationships within the British Empire complicated the implementation of sweeping changes to military law. When the War Office wanted to extend the Army Reserve Forces Act to men in India and the colonies, the Colonial Office insisted that self-governing colonies with responsible government – namely, the Dominion of Canada, the Commonwealth of Australia, New Zealand, Cape Colony, Natal, and Newfoundland – be exempted because they already possessed organized defence forces under their own legislation.[30] Any disciplinary or legal arrangements necessarily had to take into account different views from the self-governing colonies. Nevertheless, British officials were reluctant to disturb the existing system of military punishments. When the inspector general of forces suggested fines instead of confinement to barracks as a more appropriate minor punishment, he was told that "a tendency to violent change is to be deprecated."[31] The scale of punishments was the product of long experience and tradition. A committee under the chair of Major General Sir Francis Howard, which met between 31 March and 8 June 1906, recommended only minor administrative adjustments to improve the system of military punishments.[32] These were achieved through amendments to the annual Army Act and revisions to the *Manual of Military Law*. Whereas the British preferred gradual reform, the Canadians embarked on a major overhaul of the Dominion's defence legislation.

In the aftermath of the Boer War, the limitations of Canada's Militia Act, only slightly changed since 1868, were glaringly apparent. Although Canadian officers had gained staff and operational experience during the recent overseas deployment, a British officer, Major General Earl of Dundonald, still held the highest command in the militia.[33] The Dominion might have continued with the arrangement had Dundonald confined himself to his immediate professional military duties and stayed out of politics. Unfortunately, he did not. He took every opportunity to embarrass the Liberal government into spending more money on defence. In the House of Commons on 17 March 1904, Frederick Borden tabled a bill, which, among other things, offered command of the militia to suitably qualified Canadian officers, provided for equality in the status and rank of Canadian and imperial officers, removed delegated royal authority from the governor general, and increased the numbers and pay of personnel in the permanent force.[34] During a visit to London for a meeting of the Imperial Defence Committee, Borden learned of major reforms in the War Office, arising from the recommendations of Lord Esher's committee on military reorganization, whereby an army council comprising civil and military representatives replaced the commander-in-chief.

Borden returned to Canada determined to establish a comparable militia council under the Canadian legislation. After amendments at the committee stage and third reading, the new Militia Act received assent on 10 August 1904.[35] The statute stipulated that the British *King's Regulations and Orders* (KR&O) no longer formed part of Canadian law. Revised *Regulations and Orders for the Militia* were duly issued under the Militia Act's authority.[36] Unlike the British Army Council, Canada's legislatively created Militia Council served as an advisory body to the minister of militia and defence, thus ensuring complete Canadian control over the militia. Borden dismissed Dundonald and secured the services of a more popular and agreeable British officer, Major General Percy Lake.

At the same time that the Militia Act was being discussed, Canadian officers gained opportunities to study military law at the level of British standards. Beginning in November 1903, officers in the permanent force took the same promotion examinations as their counterparts in the British Army.[37] The examination papers, which included a section on military law, were obtained from the War Office and marked by the teaching staff at the Royal Military College of Canada. Large numbers of officers had attended long and staff courses in Kingston over the years. Captain Casimir Van Straubenzee and Major C.N. Buchanan-Dunlop, two former RMC graduates, taught military law and administration.[38] The Colonial Defence Committee also recommended that two permanent force officers be nominated to attend the British staff college in Camberley each year, subject to their successful qualification in the entrance examination.[39] It was hoped that this type of training would allow them to fill higher staff positions, with a view to creation of a general staff for the Canadian militia at some future date. Major D.I.V. Eaton was the first Canadian graduate from Camberley in 1903, but subsequent candidates repeatedly failed to qualify for entrance.[40] The Canadian officers' poor showing was blamed on the inadequacy of military instruction in Canada. At Borden's request, the War Office sent two general staff officers to the Royal Military College of Canada to teach a staff college preparatory course and staff courses for the active militia.[41] Helped by this additional assistance, more Canadians obtained entrance to the staff college.

The military law course that Canadian officers were required to pass at Camberley focused on the laws and customs of war and recent changes in British military law. In the previous decade, students had received detailed instruction on the Army Act from a civilian instructor.[42] After the Boer War experience and recent codification in the laws of war, instruction increasingly emphasized an international dimension. Professor Thomas Holland, an occasional lecturer at the staff college, produced a handbook "to set forth, in an orderly sequence, for the guidance of British troops, the rules of International Law applicable to the conduct of warfare on land."[43] The work was largely a reprint of the 1899 Hague Convention with explanatory notes. Colonel James Edmonds, who reviewed the staff college's 1907 military law examination paper, believed that the syllabus was too academic and that it ignored continental sources and important British precedents.[44] The range of legal topics taught was admittedly very large for most military officers. The 1909 course included declarations of war, recognition of belligerent status, sanctions against irregular troops, resistance by civilian populations, maritime blockade and contraband, stratagems, prisoners of war, martial law, field punishments, and amendments to the Army Act.[45]

Although useful for officers destined for senior positions, familiarity with the law was never intended to restrict freedom of decision in operations. Colonel Edmonds, who returned to Great Britain with a strong dose of military realism after a stint as military attaché in Berlin, told a military audience: "Remember, however, that when the fate of your command is in the balance and when by breaking any of the laws and usages of war you can extricate it from capture or annihilation, it is your duty to take that risk and obey only the law of necessity. *Salus populi suprema lex.* The safety of the country is paramount to all other considerations."[46]

This legal interpretation was excusable if his views were strictly personal. However, Colonel Edmonds co-authored an officially sanctioned replacement for Professor Holland's earlier treatise, and revised the relevant section in a new edition of the *Manual of Military Law.*[47] These books became the standard texts on the laws of war at the staff college and throughout the British and colonial forces. For better or for worse, Canadian officers were exposed to the latest British instruction in military law and the laws of war.

The revision of the Militia Act in 1906 and raising the education of Canadian officers to British standards coincided with concerns about the legal status of colonial troops placed on active service with regular imperial forces. In Australia, in the aftermath of the Boer War, the attorney general had ruled that Australian troops could serve under an imperial commander-in-chief but were subject only to the Commonwealth's 1903 Defence Act. There were to be no more Morants or Handcocks. Henceforth, courts martial were convened only under the Australian statute, and sentences required confirmation from Australia's governor general. The Australian action, while considered quite extreme at the time, attracted interest in the other self-governing colonies, particularly Canada. When Canada's adjutant general inquired whether a special Dominion discipline Act should supersede the Army Act, the Militia Council responded that the Canadian militia should "be kept as far as possible in touch with the British Army and with the law and regulations governing it; that any Bill which might be brought down should be as short and as comprehensive as possible, dealing with doubtful points only, and making the Army Act to apply in all other respects."[48] The Canadians chose not to follow the Australian example.

Indeed, the Department of Militia and Defence very much wanted to continue using imperial legislation. In a meeting with the chief of the general staff in London on 30 April 1907, Borden merely pointed out "certain disabilities affecting the administration of military law in the Canadian forces, consequent upon the present wording of certain portions of the Army Act."[49] Doubts had been expressed in Ottawa whether the term "His Majesty's Forces" applied to the permanent force, especially in regard to certain offences such as desertion and fraudulent enlistment. To remove any ambiguity, Borden suggested a small amendment to the Army Act.[50] Unlike Australia's Defence Act, Canada's Militia Act automatically made the militia subject to the Army Act on active service, at drill, or in training. Although Major General Lake personally discussed the matter with Colonel Cecil Macready at the War Office on several occasions, the parliamentary counsel ruled that the term "His Majesty's Forces" included every colonial force, and he believed that enactment of specific colonial legislation was more appropriate.[51] In spite of Australia's self-declared autonomy, the War Office still asserted that all imperial, colonial, and auxiliary troops were amenable to the Army Act on active service.

The British initiated steps to define this position. In July 1908, the Colonial Defence Committee invited the self-governing colonies to make amendments to their defence and militia statutes to achieve greater uniformity in military law within the empire.[52] Except in Australia, no governor general in the self-governing colonies, including Canada, held a warrant to convene and confirm courts martial; it was now intended to legalize the issue of such a warrant through the amendments intended to cover the entire British Empire. But Borden still felt that imperial authorities were incognizant of the unique legal difficulties facing the self-governing colonies. He informed the governor general that "Canada desires to place her forces under the Army Act, and does so, but is well aware that there is some legal risk and some legal difficulty involved in so doing."[53] Borden strongly argued that a change to the Army Act was required, if not essential, to define the legal position of any Canadian military forces sent overseas.

Canadian authorities sought clarification of the Canadian militia's exact status under military law. Frederick Borden's legal advisor Lieutenant Colonel Henry Smith cautioned that without an amendment to section 177, the wording in the Army Act was insufficient "to clothe a colony with such sovereign authority to enable it to maintain an army abroad."[54] The British North America Act constitutionally limited Canada in this sphere. During a conference at the War Office on 11 December 1908, Borden tabled a memorandum by Major General Lake that examined the entire issue from the Canadian perspective and questioned whether under the proposed legislation, the Canadian militia would "in so far as command and discipline are concerned, pass from the control of the Dominion authorities."[55] Although the British believed that the Canadians had accepted this condition earlier, the Dominion government now made clear that any forces sent abroad would remain under its control and direction, even though the Army Act still applied. In September 1909, the Army Council approved a warrant allowing the governor general to convene and confirm general courts martial within Canada's territorial limits.[56] In respect of Canadian military forces sent abroad, the War Office postponed amendment of section 177 along the lines proposed by Borden until unification of the self-governing colonies in South Africa. After careful consideration, the parliamentary counsel perceived no legal difficulties in applying the Army Act to the Canadian militia.[57] Major General Lake's departure to India in late 1910 and Frederick Borden's political defeat at the election polls eventually meant that the matter was pursued no further.

The complicated legal questions confronting the militia had already convinced the minister of militia and defence that the appointment of a judge advocate general was needed in Canada. In January 1905, Borden remarked that the department was taking serious risks without an officer to review courts martial, stating that he knew "a good man, a Lieut-Col, whose age is probably 50."[58] As the minister pointed out, several US states, including small Massachusetts with only a 5,000-strong militia, had dedicated legal officers. Since the advanced age and standing of Borden's nominee involved pension questions, the matter was referred to the military members of the Militia Council. After some consideration, they reported that the amount of work, projected at about 106 courts martial per year, hardly justified continuous employment of a military officer and instead asked "whether the object in view might not, perhaps, be more satisfactorily obtained by the appointment of a special military law officer as Judge Advocate-General to the Department of Justice who would work under the orders and instructions of the Minister of Justice, though paid by the Militia Department."[59] A qualified civilian lawyer as Canada's new JAG appeared preferable since the Department of Militia and Defence could then avoid any perceived conflict of interest. Sir Thomas Milvain's appointment as Great Britain's JAG in 1906, corollary to the Esher Committee's recommendations, provided a precedent as well as the logical model to emulate.[60] Although no longer independent of the War Office, the JAG in London remained an experienced civilian lawyer. On the other hand, the JAG in India, drawing upon older traditions in the presidencies of Bengal, Madras, and Bombay, had been a military officer since reorganization of all military legal matters in India into one department in 1888.[61] As in India, the JAG for the United States Army was also a military officer. As strong precedents existed for either a civilian or a military JAG, the choice was ultimately left to the minister of militia and defence.

For purely personal reasons, Borden championed the appointment of Lieutenant Colonel Henry Smith to the post of JAG. Borden and Smith were long-time friends and associates. In 1898, Major General Gascoigne's restructuring of the militia had forced Smith to retire prematurely from command of Military District 1 in London, Ontario. Feeling that some injustice had been done Smith, Borden eventually gained further work for him at militia headquarters in Ottawa. Smith, who possessed some legal knowledge, was specially employed in the adjutant general's branch on various legal matters and became chairman of the Pension Claims Board.[62] The work apparently suited him. Besides giving advice to Borden and militia officials, Smith discussed proposed amendments to the Militia Act with the Department of Justice, worked on a new edition of the militia's *Regulations and Orders,* and inaugurated a course of lectures on military history, tactics, military law, and administration at McGill University in 1907. In reviewing courts martial, he actually fulfilled the duties of a de facto JAG.[63] Only a shortage of money prevented the militia from putting the arrangement on a more permanent basis. Borden had originally hoped to make an official appointment by 1 April 1910.[64] But financial considerations and awkward questions about Smith's selection for the post delayed a final decision. Although no provision was made in the militia's 1911-2 fiscal estimates, Henry Smith, recently promoted to colonel, became Canada's first JAG on 1 October 1911.[65] Smith's appointment reflected the persuasiveness of patronage within the Ottawa political structure and the Canadian militia at the time. Ironically, the old militia officer outlasted his stalwart patron; Frederick Borden left Ottawa after the Liberal Party's defeat in the 1911 general election.

At the time of Smith's appointment, the military structure in Canada was in a state of change. In 1910, General Sir John French, the inspector general of Imperial Forces, had examined its shortcomings, noting that "only when the regulations which govern the constitution and maintenance of the Canadian Militia are strictly enforced will it be possible to say whether the present system meets the defensive requirements of the country or not."[66] While acknowledging the considerable progress made under Frederick Borden, General French expressed serious doubts about the militia's organization, staff training, level of competence among officers and non-commissioned officers, and commitment of the rank and file.

The British believed that Canada was not prepared to defend itself in North America, never mind send troops abroad. After a tour of inspection in 1913, General Sir Ian Hamilton hesitantly commented on the deficiencies of Canadian law in regard to defence: "An Imperial officer must approach with the utmost diffidence a subject so purely domestic as the legislation which determines where in the world a Canadian soldier may, or may not serve. Even among those most interested, namely the soldiers themselves, few seem to realize that not only can no Canadian militiaman in his capacity as such, volunteer for overseas service, but that it is extremely doubtful whether there exists in Canada any constitutional means of organizing any armed force whatsoever for extra territorial service."[67]

Like French, General Hamilton was critical of overall training and education within the militia and permanent force. There was much scope for improvement. The Department of Militia and Defence, Hamilton asserted, was not solely to blame since defence estimates in Canada always had to "run the gauntlet of a remorseless Finance Department, whose business it is to skin them as bare as it can."[68] The efforts of the new Conservative minister of militia and defence, the egotistical and vain Sam Hughes, somewhat relieved the situation. In a time of acute economic depression, Hughes wrung money from a tight-fisted government to fund additional training camps, build armouries, and replace worn-out equipment. Hamilton wrote to French: "The present Defence Minister will not last forever and, with good guidance, may do valuable work during his tenure if influenced by men he trusts, but an attempt to thwart him can only end in a smash of some kind which might be, militarily speaking, unremediable."[69] Despite his endless political machinations and desire for aggrandizement, Hughes made tangible improvements to the militia in Canada during the years leading up to the First World War.

As an indirect result of Hughes' labours, officers and non-commissioned officers learned more military law. The provisional schools and Royal schools of military instruction offered courses on a somewhat continual basis. The theoretical portion of a sergeant's course in Vancouver included written exams on interior economy, duties, and discipline.[70] Libraries and classrooms in the new armouries constructed by Hughes allowed officers and soldiers to study and discuss, throughout the year at their leisure, the 1907 edition of the *Manual of Military Law,* the *Field Service Pocket Book,* Part II of the *Field Service Regulations,* and the 1910 *King's Regulations and Orders* for the Canadian militia. Since formal instruction devoted to military law was limited, private study beforehand was essential.[71] A sound knowledge of military law was required to pass required promotion and qualification examinations. Specialized books from military publishers such as Gale and Polden kept pace with recent developments in the Army Act and provided sample examinations from previous years.[72] Lectures and courses were also offered through contingents of the new Canadian Officers Training Corps (COTC), established at selected Canadian universities. McGill University was the first to teach military law and other theoretical subjects on a continual basis in 1912.[73] The universities provided a good source of educated and partially trained men for the active militia. By early 1914, most regiments generally included a lecture on military law and discipline in theoretical instruction at militia armouries during the winter months.[74]

With the outbreak of the First World War, Canadian soldiers were sent to fight in the general European conflict. Canada's main contribution to the defence of the British Empire and ultimate victory in the First World War was the Canadian Expeditionary Force (CEF). The dispatch of so large a military force from Canada was unprecedented. To the dismay of Major General Willoughby Gwatkin, the militia's chief of the general staff, Hughes threw aside the prepared mobilization plan and proceeded to recruit, clothe, equip, and arm an entire army. In spite of the efforts at education and training in recent years, Canada was still ill-prepared for a large-scale conflict. The Duke of Connaught, Canada's governor general, wrote Lord Kitchener: "The material is very good, but the officers are still ignorant of their military duties which they have never been taught."[75] The legal position of the Canadian Expeditionary Force once it arrived in Great Britain and France was also unclear. When asked which regulations, Canadian or British, were to govern the contingent being sent overseas, the adjutant general replied: "The force will be imperial and have the status of British regular troops."[76] Unlike his predecessor Frederick Borden, Hughes rarely worried about legal technicalities. Canadians were needed on the Continent of Europe immediately to meet German advances, and he believed that command and disciplinary arrangements could be worked out later. Consequently, Canadian formations sent overseas came under the supervision of British commanders and the jurisdiction of the British Army Act rather than Canadian legislation. Disciplinary and legal matters affecting the Canadian Expeditionary Force were referred to the War Office and the JAG in London.[77] Even members of courts martial, convened to try Canadian officers and soldiers in France, were often British.

By 1916, the bloodletting on the Western Front and the growing unpopularity of Hughes led to a major reassessment of the situation. Prime Minister Sir Robert Borden became convinced that his conceited and erratic militia minister had to be reigned in somehow.[78] Hughes' activities and overlapping organization were disruptive and counter-productive. On the basis of a legal opinion from Edmond Newcombe, the deputy minister of justice, Borden created a separate Ministry of Overseas Military Forces of Canada in London, headed by Sir George Perley.[79] This new organization reasserted ministerial and administrative control over the Canadian Expeditionary Force. Perley and his successor, Sir Albert Edward Kemp, interceded with British military authorities on important issues of policy. The Canadian Expeditionary Force still remained subject to the British Army Act, but with considerably more Canadian participation in the administration of military law as time went on.[80] Reasserting national sovereignty and control over the administration of Canadian military forces arose from a determined effort to get rid of Sam Hughes.

Canadian officers with legal knowledge oversaw instruction, application, and supervision of military law within the Canadian Expeditionary Force. Every officer was expected to have a basic understanding of charges and courts martial, or least to know where to find relevant sections in the statutes, the 1914 edition of the *Manual of Military Law,* and the *King's Regulations and Orders*.[81] Considerable teaching in military law took place within the training division before the arrival of a dedicated legal officer at the Canadian Military Headquarters in London. In February 1916, Major Maurice Alexander, the assistant judge advocate general (AJAG), received a strongly worded rebuke from the Shorncliffe command for "very belated instructions containing as they do purely elementary points in the general procedure at Courts-Martial."[82] Over the previous eight months, an officer from headquarters had already given a considerable number of officers of all ranks thorough instruction in military law, and teaching in the subject was taking place on almost a continual basis. Books by Captain A.P. Birchall and Captain Francis Grierson as well as a number of pamphlets gave basic information on military law and discipline.[83] Under the regulations, officers were required to attend twenty-five courts martial as observers before being considered competent to sit on one themselves. The training commands were already far ahead of Alexander in instruction on military law.

Older officers who possessed professional legal credentials or practised law in civil life were designated permanent presidents or judge advocates at courts martial within the various commands. Besides the *Manual of*

Military Law, several reference sources were available to them, including notes distributed by the Canadian London headquarters, a War Office circular memorandum on courts martial, and recent books by Major E.W. Pope and Lieutenant Colonel Sisson Pratt.[84] The employment, on a regular basis, of presidents with legal training ensured continuity and relieved senior officers from time-consuming court martial work; however, the practice did not necessarily mean more justice or fairness for the accused. Major E.C. Hale, the president of a district court martial at Shorncliffe, chastised a defending officer for presuming the soldier on trial was innocent:

> Whatever the custom may be in Civil Courts it should be clearly understood by all who appear as Counsel that to endeavour to persuade a Court that a man is not guilty while the evidence decidedly shows that he is, or to try and fog the court by irrelevant cross-examination and the raising of technical points on which a man might get off in a Civil Court, is not in accordance with the spirit of the law as laid down in the Army Act; further to try to get a man off on a purely technical point is tantamount to encouraging Military Crime which it is the duty of every Officer to keep down and to prevent in every way possible.[85]

In spite of Hale's obvious bias, most presidents appeared to take their duties on courts martial seriously. On 19 July 1917, Lieutenant Colonel Robert Dennistoun became deputy judge advocate general (DJAG), taking over Alexander's job in London.[86] Dennistoun, a prominent lawyer from Winnipeg, had gone overseas with the Fort Garry Horse in 1914, returned to Canada to recruit and command the 53rd Battalion, served as chief compensation officer in the Shorncliffe and Brighton areas, and chaired the Regimental Funds Board. He was the author of two small works on military law and sat on roughly 100 courts martial and courts of inquiry before becoming the DJAG in London.[87] Dennistoun was an exceptional example of the level of legal expertise available within the Canadian Expeditionary Force.

The courts martial, on which permanent presidents and members sat, convened as circumstances demanded. Within the Canadian commands in Great Britain, soldiers came before general or district courts martial, whereas officers were tried by general courts martial only.[88] The type of trial depended upon the rank of the accused and the nature of the alleged offence. Desertion and absence without leave were the leading charges. British civil courts frequently claimed jurisdiction over cases involving civil offences, such as assault, murder, or rape.[89] In France, on the other hand, Canadian troops were tried primarily by field general courts martial. Convened only on active service, the field general court martial was less stringent in terms of membership and procedure.[90] Commanding officers used it as a convenient and speedy means to punish a variety of offences in line and reserve units. In the Princess Patricia's Canadian Light Infantry Regiment, charges included threatening or striking superior officers, insubordination, drunkenness, escaping confinement, desertion, absence without leave, assault, disobedience, theft, and self-inflicted wounds.[91]

To assist subordinate commands, officers with legal qualifications and knowledge of military law were assigned to each corps headquarters. These special court martial officers combined "the function of an ordinary member of the Court with those allotted to the judge advocate on a general court martial."[92] Their presence guaranteed that the rights of accused were respected and trials were conducted in a legal and proper manner. Eventually, Canadian military authorities in France assembled a central field general court martial on every Tuesday and Wednesday, comprising members and a president from the brigades and a court martial officer from the corps headquarters.[93] This policy considerably expedited the administration of military justice in the field. Although exact numbers are difficult to determine because the British JAG reviewed and took custody of all court martial records, upwards of 16,000 courts martial took place within the Canadian Expeditionary Force between 1914 and 1920.

By far the most controversial courts martial involved the imposition and implementation of death sentences. Although the number of death sentences passed by courts martial was far higher than the number actually carried out, British military authorities executed 346 officers and soldiers during the First World War.[94] The majority of cases involved desertion and cowardice in the face of the enemy. Twenty-five Canadians were among those executed.[95] Despite recent assertions by some historians, there is little evidence to suggest that these soldiers were "bad apples" or predisposed toward deviant behaviour. On the contrary, most were simply ordinary men placed in extraordinary situations.[96] The stress of combat and months of dismal living in the trenches inevitably caused psychological breakdown. The threshold was higher in some than in others, but once they were pushed over it, rational decision no longer became possible. The natural instinct was self-preservation; in other words, they ran away from the danger. During each offensive, the Canadian headquarters deployed military police "for duty in the Trenches to prevent a rearward movement."[97] The effects of battle exhaustion, commonly referred to as shell shock, were poorly understood at the time.

Military authorities treated such behaviour as a disciplinary problem rather than a medical condition. Most of those Canadians executed were simply in the wrong place at the wrong time. The likelihood of a death sentence being carried out or remitted depended more often on the operational situation and the perceived need of the higher command to set some examples than on the particular guilt of the individual. Field Marshal Sir

Douglas Haig vehemently insisted that Australia's legislative restrictions on imposing the death penalty among its troops was detrimental to discipline throughout the British and dominion forces.[98] Whether Haig was correct or not, no Australian was ever executed on the Western Front for a military crime, although French civil courts passed death sentences on Australian soldiers for capital offences against civilians. The Australians retained complete control over their own courts martial and disciplinary system. The Canadians were not confident enough to emulate the Australians and only disagreed on the way the War Office notified the next-of-kin of executed soldiers:

> A mother or father give up their son, probably the only son, so that he may proceed to France to fight the common enemy. Probably after several months in the trenches he develops "Nerves" and does something at the moment that he had no immediate control over; yet he is Court Martialled and shot.
>
> If his parents were informed in this cold-blooded way it would not only add to their grief but would more or less cast a shadow over the rest of their lives; not to mention the bad effect that it would have on the recruiting in our country if his parents were to get into their heads that an injustice had been done to their flesh and blood.[99]

The relatives of executed Canadian soldiers were not even told the truth. Even with some realization of the true nature of the problem and its potential consequences back at home, Canadian officials let military justice, as applied under the British Army Act, take its tragic course. Canadian soldiers paid with their lives for the policy decision.

Within Canada, the military districts handled the reinforcement demands of the Canadian Expeditionary Force. In March 1916, district commanding officers were empowered to convene and confirm district courts martial, appoint judge advocates, and mitigate or remit sentences.[100] Recruitment and training in the military districts sustained the overseas battalions. A small booklet, prepared to help officers qualify, defined military law as "the power given to the military authorities to enable them to deal with offences the civil power are not competent to deal with."[101] For officers with previous military experience or too old to go overseas, even the minimum requirement was sometimes waived. John Birney remembered that when he became a major in charge of an internment camp at Lethbridge "he had never actually qualified although he had written all the examinations except military law."[102] The main task was to impart a sense of military discipline and respect for the regulations among volunteers. At least once a month, sections four through forty-four of the Army Act were read at parade for the benefit of new recruits. Not all newcomers easily adjusted to the unconventional environment. Courts of inquiry kept a careful account of kit and equipment taken by soldiers who deserted or went absent without leave.[103] Keeping personnel in reinforcement formations long enough for training posed a significant problem. From 1916 onward, AJAGs were appointed to busier military districts to assist in the application of military law and convening of courts martial.

The legal establishment at militia headquarters in Ottawa also responded to the wartime emergency. Henry Smith, still JAG, became a major general on 23 June 1916.[104] Legal work within the Department of Militia and Defence had increased dramatically since the beginning of the war. Smith handled a variety of matters outside his normal day-to-day activities, including giving advice on the enlistment of minors, the estates of deceased soldiers, separation allowances, and pay questions.[105] Major H.M. Daly served as AJAG at militia headquarters. After winning re-election on a platform of conscription in late 1917, Prime Minister Robert Borden put through the Military Service Act.[106] Administration of the statute, in particular consideration and review of the enormous number of exemption applications, placed an added burden on the JAG.[107] By now very tired, Smith decided to step aside in favour of a younger man.

Although Smith stayed on in an advisory capacity, the JAG branch came under the direction of a competent civilian lawyer, merely placed in uniform for the war's duration. Major Oliver Mowat Biggar was appointed JAG on 30 January 1918 in the acting rank of lieutenant colonel.[108] Biggar was a well-known lawyer from Edmonton, who had joined the 101st Regiment as a lieutenant in 1916. His superiors quickly recognized his natural talents and legal abilities. Biggar served as AJAG in Military District 13 until 1917 and then as a member of the Military Service Council, a body established to advise and assist the government on administration of the Military Service Act. On 16 March 1918, a separate establishment for the branch of the JAG was created within the Canadian Expeditionary Force with Biggar as JAG.[109] Major Gregor Barclay was appointed AJAG, and Lieutenant Colonel W.B. Kingsmill subsequently became DJAG. As officially promulgated, Biggar's duties were to advise on questions of law and procedure, revise all orders, maintain a record of orders-in-council with regard to military forces, prepare draft amendments to regulations and orders, oversee and review courts martial, keep a record of all general and district courts martial, recommend and supervise AJAGs, direct distribution of the estates of deceased soldiers, and negotiate acquisition and disposal of property on behalf of the Department of Militia and Defence. During his short tenure, Bigger was perhaps one of Canada's most capable JAGs.

In contrast to the disciplinary arrangements for the Canadian Expeditionary Force and the militia, disciplinary procedures for Canadian naval forces remained unsettled during the war. The Dominion's Naval Service

Act had created the Royal Canadian Navy (RCN) in 1910.[110] Like the navies of most other self-governing colonies, the small Canadian naval force was closely integrated with the Royal Navy. For the purposes of discipline, Canadian officers and sailors came under the provisions of Great Britain's Naval Discipline Act of 1866 and its accompanying *King's Regulations and Admiralty Instructions*.[111] In the tiny Canadian naval service, few officers were qualified by experience and training to sit on or confirm courts martial. Therefore, power to convene courts martial was delegated to a British flag officer, and Royal Navy officers were usually called upon to sit as members on naval courts martial.[112] For legal review, proceedings were referred to the judge advocate of the Fleet, a civilian solicitor in London kept on retainer by the Admiralty.

The Admiralty tried to give the self-governing colonies more authority and control over discipline within their naval forces when they acted in conjunction with the Royal Navy and each other. In 1911, the Naval Discipline (Dominion Naval Forces) Act empowered dominion governments to apply the Naval Discipline Act without reference to London or a delegated British officer. Adoption of the imperial statute required enactment of legislation within the self-governing colonies. Australia and New Zealand applied the Naval Discipline (Dominion Naval Forces) Act to their navies in 1913 and 1914 respectively.[113] Canada, on the other hand, failed to do so before the outbreak of the First World War.

In matters of discipline and courts martial, the Royal Canadian Navy followed the Royal Navy's lead. In 1912, a committee on naval discipline, chaired by Rear Admiral Frederic Brock, RN, enquired into general disciplinary matters, devoting special attention to summary punishments: "There can be no doubt that discipline based on such sympathy and understanding is far more effective than any system which relies mainly on punishment."[114] Its recommendations included giving access to the *King's Regulations and Admiralty Instructions* to every rank on board ship, lectures on legal subjects to new entries, and small informational pamphlets explaining in a simple manner the rights and responsibilities of sailors. The Royal Navy, in particular, emphasized the effect of deprivation of good conduct badges for disciplinary infractions in terms of diminished pay and pension at later dates; it was a message even the lowest rating or stoker could understand. In a meeting at the Admiralty on 18 September 1914, the second sea lord "concluded that discipline could be well maintained in exceptional circumstances without resorting to extraordinary measures."[115] Under the Naval Discipline Act, captains possessed extensive powers of summary punishment over ships' companies. Earlier in the war, many inexperienced officers imposed unduly harsh punishments resulting in overcrowded detention barracks; but peacetime standards were generally maintained. As a temporary wartime measure, the second sea lord expressed a desire for a special court to try officers below command rank "without any of the serious consequences of delay that is occasioned by holding the Court Martial."[116] The resulting disciplinary court, which was also adopted in the RCN, proved a flexible and practical instrument for dealing with offences at sea and on shore.

As the Royal Navy and the dominion navies expanded, the existing scale of punishments, based mostly upon imprisonment and detention, proved less and less workable, especially in the case of habitual offenders. With no tradition of unpleasant field punishments or the death penalty as in the army, the Admiralty advocated return to the traditional practice of flogging because it would have "a very strong deterrent effect on the malingerers in question, and it might not be necessary actually to use it at all."[117] Fortunately, more sensible minds convinced the Admiralty that reintroduction of corporal punishment was not suited to modern conditions in the Royal Navy and the colonial naval forces. It was debatable whether Canada would have accepted flogging in its navy anyway because the RCN had never previously used this form of punishment to maintain discipline.

The RCN's lack of any clear sense of offensive mission during the war undoubtedly contributed to deferment of the legal question. In the absence of a clearly defined naval policy from the Dominion government or direction from the Admiralty, the Naval Service of Canada instituted defensive patrols of the Newfoundland and Canadian coasts.[118] The Naval Service Act applied as long as Canadian warships remained within Canadian territorial waters. In late 1917, officials in Ottawa wished to issue a commission, signed by the minister of the Canadian Naval Service, authorizing the British commander-in-chief on the North America and West Indies station to convene courts martial for the trial of Canadian offenders.[119] To the Canadians, it appeared a reasonable request since Canadian warships increasingly operated within his sphere of responsibility. The Admiralty, however, replied that the "course proposed would not be in accordance with the Naval Discipline Act, and could only be based on Canadian Law; it is also open to doubt how far Canadian legislation is operative outside the territorial waters of the Dominion."[120] Without the safeguard of legislation in Canada, the question remained whether British officers might be liable to legal action for false imprisonment in cases outside the Naval Service Act's jurisdiction. Left with little other choice, the Dominion Parliament passed legislation on 24 May 1918, bringing into force the Naval Discipline (Dominion Naval Forces) Act of 1911.[121] The RCN asked the Admiralty to amend the *King's Regulations and Admiralty Instructions* to allow interchangeability of Canadian and British naval officers as members on courts martial. King George V signed an order-in-council to this effect on 28 June 1920.[122] Although the imperial statute now legally applied, the arrangement still posed difficulties. Reviewing wartime courts martial and legal activities, the judge advocate of the Fleet remarked that the entire question of disciplinary relations between the Royal Navy and dominion navies required consideration and possibly even a revised Naval Discipline Act after a postwar imperial conference.[123] The First World War generally left the legal position of the RCN unresolved.

Across the Atlantic, important developments in the closing stages and immediate aftermath of the war finally created some awareness of the defects in the legal position of the Canadian Expeditionary Force. General Sir Arthur Currie, a Canadian officer, assumed command of the Canadian Corps in France. Under the supreme command of the French marshal Ferdinand Foch, the Canadians won a decisive victory at Amiens and then broke through the German lines in a series of bloody battles before the armistice on 11 November 1918. When Colonel Biggar, who accompanied Robert Borden to London and Paris to participate in the peace negotiations, asked a Canadian general whether Canada should fight another war under the same arrangements with the British, the latter "answered in the negative without hesitation."[124] The sense of pride in the achievements of the Canadian Corps over the last months of the war militated against Canada ever again placing its military forces unconditionally under British disciplinary authority. A.M. Munro, a Canadian soldier transferred to the British flying corps, deprecated "the way some of these Imperial officers attempt to get discipline. If Prussians are any worse, I do not know what it is like. At the present day, there is not a finer disciplined Corps in the world than the Canadian Corps, but they have a vastly different way of getting discipline than they do in this branch."[125] The Canadians knew enough about their rights under the law to recognize arbitrariness and injustice.

Disciplinary problems arose with the return and demobilization of the Canadian Corps. In March 1919, Canadian troops, impatient over delays in their repatriation from Great Britain and tired of squalid living quarters, rioted in Kinmel Park camp near Rhyl in Wales, causing extensive damage and several deaths.[126] Pressured by the British press, military authorities tried fifty-one alleged instigators before courts martial on charges of mutiny under the Army Act. Convicted soldiers received various terms of detention and imprisonment.[127] Many questions were subsequently raised about the conduct and the legality of the trials. In a letter to Robert Borden, Captain George Black, a defending officer for British Columbia soldiers involved in the disturbance, cited problems with members of the court, the shortness of the proceedings, and the abuse of legal procedures and evidence as reasons for the Dominion government to ask for release of remaining soldiers from incarceration.[128] The British appeared to show little understanding of the true circumstances behind the riots. For the bored Canadian soldiers who simply wanted to go home after a long war, the courts martial demonstrated the inflexibility of a heartless military justice system.

Despite Kinmel Park, the end of the war actually brought Canadian military lawyers into closer contact with British legal authorities. With some help from influential friends at home and with Borden's backing, Dennistoun was appointed a judge to the Court of Appeal in Manitoba.[129] For the time being, he remained in London to finish his duties as DJAG. Dennistoun's newly attained stature immediately provided an entry into the corridors of the British legal establishment through dinners, meetings, and similar engagements. By the time the Canadian JAG arrived in Great Britain with Borden's entourage, the connections were already well established. Biggar met with Felix Cassel, the British JAG, and members of his staff.[130] Taking full advantage of the opportunity, the two lawyers exchanged wartime experiences in their respective legal branches.

The Canadians obviously interested and impressed the British. Soon after, Biggar left for Paris as Borden's military legal advisor at the peace conference, where he sat on various committees and commissions as part of the Secretariat of the British Empire.[131] Surprisingly, in spite of the wartime death sentences passed on Canadian soldiers and British treatment in response to the Kinmel Park riots, the Canadian lawyers had few concerns about the way military law was applied by the British. During a dinner hosted by Cassel, Dennistoun "expressed complete satisfaction with the manner in which legal proceedings of a military character had been conducted during the war in so far as Canadians are concerned."[132] On the basis of these good relations, the British took the Manitoba lawyer into their confidence. Before returning to his new judgeship in Canada, Dennistoun met with Sir Charles Darling, a judge with long experience in criminal matters and recently chair of a committee on courts martial.[133] Through Dennistoun's association with Darling, the Canadians learned first-hand about the committee's main findings.

Darling's committee conducted the most comprehensive review of the military justice system since the royal commission in 1869. Besides Darling, members of the committee included the JAG, senior military officers, and selected members of Parliament, including Horatio Bottomley, an outspoken critic of court martial procedure in the British House of Commons.[134] The War Office intentionally appointed Bottomley to "educate" him in the finer points of military law. During twenty-two days of hearings, the committee heard testimony from a number of witnesses with legal qualifications, and received written submissions.

A majority report, delivered on 29 July 1919, concluded that the existing court martial system had worked sufficiently well during the war with regard to imperial and dominion forces, but recommended some improvements with special attention devoted to military legal education and the right of appeal. As the report noted, "no disciplinary code, however well drafted, can be expected to work satisfactorily unless officers chiefly concerned with its administration are not only thoroughly familiar with its provisions, but have also a fair knowledge of the principles of criminal law and of the rules of evidence, and are reasonably familiar with the practice and procedure in ordinary Criminal Courts."[135] To achieve this end, the committee recommended the simplification and abbreviation of the disciplinary code and the *Manual of Military Law,* employment of officers with legal qualifications within area commands for court martial work and legal instruction, as well as a higher standard of legal training for presidents of courts martial. If senior officers knew and applied military law properly, the committee believed that appeal to a higher civilian court was unnecessary and, in some respects, inappropriate. A minority report, submitted by Bottomley and other parliamentary members on the committee, suggested a court of appeal in cases involving the death sentence. The underlying conclusion of Darling's committee was that better military legal education was essential to ensure that the military justice system worked effectively.

The War Office carefully considered the Darling Committee's recommendations. The deputy adjutant general distributed the report to all commands for their comments and concerns. In the most detailed reply, Brigadier General Alfred James, the provost marshal, found few legitimate criticisms with its conclusions and suggestions, except he believed that military legal advisors should be chosen from officers already in units and should be provided with a formal legal education.[136] James stressed that there should be greater encouragement and opportunities for younger officers to attend lectures and criminal courts, arrangements for special courses on military law and evidence, as well as the consolidation of essential portions of the Army Act, rules of procedure, and regulations into a single, compact form. A circular memorandum on courts martial that was distributed in France in 1918 had shown the utility of such a publication in explaining the rudiments of military law in a simple manner.[137] The circular memorandum provided a basis for lectures to officers unfamiliar with the Army Act and the KR&O.

Field Marshal Haig agreed with James that military legal advisors and other officers acting on courts martial "should be soldiers with legal experience, and not barristers or solicitors with commissions."[138] Despite his earlier tough stance toward disciplinary offences at the front, the British commander-in-chief expressed concern about the stigma of wartime convictions on soldiers returning to civil vocations. After consulting his former adjutant general in France, Lieutenant General Sir George Fowke, and Charles Darling, Haig suggested convening a special review tribunal to consider all outstanding sentences from courts martial.[139] The bogey of appeal to a civil court was avoided since Haig carefully distinguished between a review of selected cases and a formal right of appeal against all sentences of courts martial. The review board was simply a one-shot affair to correct obvious injustices from the wartime situation. Now that the immediate emergency had given way to more rational conditions in peacetime, the War Office showed more compassion toward the plight of convicted soldiers who were imprisoned and detained.

Since the army raised no immediate objections, the War Office established committees, chaired by Cassel, to examine the Darling Committee's recommendations and work out precise details on how to implement its suggestions in regard to special military legal advisors and improved military legal education. The impetus came from the top. Winston Churchill, the secretary of state for war, wanted the matter "proceeded without any further delay as he wishe[d] the Committees to be well under way before the Army Annual Bill [came] up in the House."[140] Through witness testimony and numerous written submissions, the JAG and representatives from the War Office and the Air Ministry learned that existing legal officers were fully preoccupied with courts martial and other legal responsibilities, and little time was actually devoted to instruction in military law, even though it was recognized as an important part of their work. Once aware of the true situation, Cassel felt "considerable and constant anxiety as to whether some blunder may not at any moment be made, which would give rise to great trouble in the House of Commons, although hitherto we have been providentially spared from this."[141] Beyond the military colleges and the staff college, only the promotion examinations set and marked by the War Office with the assistance of the JAG required any demonstrated knowledge of military law.

Instruction in military law at the unit level remained the responsibility of commanding officers and often competed with other professional subjects. Although young officers were required to attend courts martial as observers, no formal system of lectures or courses existed. Cassel's committee recommended the creation of a specialized legal corps with officers qualified to provide instruction and administer military justice effectively within the commands, adding that it was important to take advantage of wartime lawyers in uniform before they demobilized.[142] Lawyers were considered preferable because soldiers were more aware of their legal rights than before the war, and courts martial needed to be conducted in such a manner as to inspire public confidence. But after the Treasury vetoed the scheme as too expensive, the War Office proposed a permanent military department within the JAG office, similar to the temporary one that had existed during the war. It was hoped that the JAG's greater involvement in the instruction of officers might "raise the standard of knowledge of military law throughout the army."[143] The distribution of a corps of military lawyers among the commands, the War Office's preferred arrangement, was postponed indefinitely because of a shortage of money in the public coffers.

While kept abreast of the debate and proposals in Great Britain affecting military law, Canada's JAG branch gradually wound down its wartime activities. Lieutenant Colonel George McFarland replaced Lieutenant Colonel Kingsmill as DJAG, and Major Reginald Orde, employed in the branch since 17 December 1918, became AJAG.[144] Questions over demobilization, settlement of claims and estates, and review of outstanding courts martial sentences continued for some time after the end of hostilities. In a letter from Paris addressed to Orde, Biggar wrote: "The work has no doubt become less, but I daresay there is still a good deal to do."[145] The JAG staff made every attempt to decrease the workload. Commanding officers in the military districts were encouraged to remit or mitigate sentences from courts martial whenever possible.[146] The effort inevitably produced inequality and lack of uniformity. Under instructions from the JAG branch in Ottawa, district officers commanding henceforth tried all cases of desertion by district court martial instead of general court martial; since a district court martial could hand down a maximum sentence of only two years imprisonment, soldiers who had been convicted and sentenced earlier in the war were serving substantially longer terms of imprisonment for essentially the same offences.[147] After discussions with Edmond Newcombe at the Department of Justice, Orde favoured an amnesty rather than a simple remission of outstanding sentences to two years. As a result, the Dominion government proclaimed a general amnesty on 20 December 1919 and released the remaining seventy-six soldiers in prison or detention from convictions at court martial.[148] The Canadian militia started afresh in the immediate postwar period.

The JAG branch returned to its former small size. The post of JAG was included in a proposed reorganization of the permanent force's headquarters and district staffs.[149] Perhaps with the earlier services of Henry Smith in mind, the Department of Militia and Defence decided to retain within the branch a military officer who had legal training. On 1 February 1920, Reginald Orde, promoted to lieutenant colonel, replaced Biggar as JAG.[150] With the change, the JAG again came under the purview of the adjutant general's branch. Biggar served as vice-chairman of the new Air Board until August 1921 and then resumed private practice in Ottawa, eventually becoming a leading authority on patent law and serving on various governmental commissions.[151] Orde started a three-decade tenure in the administration of military law within the Canadian Armed Forces, thereby becoming Canada's longest serving JAG through peace and war.

3
Coming of Age

Under Orde's stewardship, Canadian military law matured dramatically between 1920 and the late 1930s. The JAG assumed responsibility for legal activities and courts martial in all three services. Although severe financial restraint limited the size and training of the Canadian Armed Forces, instruction in military law, the cornerstone of an effective military justice system, received considerable attention from the JAG and military authorities. Senior officers recognized the relationship between the maintenance of good discipline and overall legal knowledge within the Armed Forces. Military legal instruction also justified additional staff in the JAG office. Constitutional changes consequent upon the 1931 Statute of Westminster and resulting visiting forces agreements established new command and disciplinary relationships between the Canadian services and forces from other British Commonwealth countries, including Great Britain.

In the early interwar period, Lieutenant Colonel Reginald Orde was the sole lawyer employed in the JAG office. The post of JAG was an auspicious opportunity for the young officer. At the time of his appointment, Orde was only twenty-seven years old. A graduate of the University of Toronto and Osgoode Hall Law School, Orde went to France with the first Canadian contingent as a gunner in 1914, received a commission in the Royal Field Artillery in January 1915, and then served with the Indian Army in France and Mesopotamia.[1] Owing to illness, Orde returned to Canada, whereupon he transferred into the Canadian Field Artillery in June 1917 and served as an artillery instructor at Petawawa in the rank of major. He soon became dissatisfied with the job and decided to finish his legal studies. Orde read law with the firm of Smith, Rae, and Greer in Toronto, passed the Ontario bar examination in early 1918, and then joined the wartime JAG branch. Biggar's favour and backing catapulted Orde into the JAG appointment less than two years after he had become a fully qualified lawyer. Major Henry Hanington, the last of the wartime lawyers, demobilized, leaving Orde as the only remaining legal officer. His support staff consisted of an assistant, two stenographers, and two orderlies.

Despite the limited size of the JAG branch, the work was varied and constant. In addition to the review of courts martial, Orde advised on questions concerning pensions and civil re-establishment, return of Canadian officers and soldiers imprisoned in British jails for civil offences, leases and agreements, legal cases referred by the Department of Justice, dishonoured cheques and mess accounts, and amendments to pay and allowance regulations.[2] Legal decisions were often complicated and difficult to make. For example, Orde ruled that no consideration could be given under the Regimental Debts Act to dependants of absentees from the Canadian Expeditionary Force who owed outstanding debts without extending the same treatment to other members whose misconduct had deprived them and their dependants of the war service gratuity.[3] Although arbitrary, the action was necessary because the government was in a particularly acute financial situation as boom times turned to bust in the early 1920s. Economy became the order of the day.

At the direction of the Militia Council, the JAG prepared lectures and short courses for instruction on military law and discipline in the military districts. To assist this endeavour, the adjutant general distributed extracts from the proceedings of recent district courts martial.[4] Opportunities to gain practical experience in military law were limited because the total number of courts martial in the permanent force and non-permanent active militia decreased from 168 in 1921 to 74 in 1922 and 49 in 1923. The numbers generally corresponded to reductions in Canada's Armed Forces at the time. The employment of specialized legal officers during the war meant that few officers in the permanent force had received any systematic or thorough training in military law under peacetime conditions.[5] With some dismay, Orde noted numerous mistakes and irregularities in proceedings submitted by presidents of courts martial and confirming authorities. At the time, his educational efforts represented a short-term measure to correct glaring deficiencies rather than a permanent feature in the administration of military law.

Since military lawyers were an expensive luxury in such a small military force, general officers applied and administered military law without the benefit of professional legal advice immediately on hand. They predominantly relied upon their own experience and knowledge of relevant regulations and books. As money became available, the Department of Militia and Defence reopened permanent schools of military instruction and resumed staff courses. Stencilled notes prepared by Colonel Thomas Anderson for the first militia staff course offered since the end of the First World War covered the Militia Act, the *Manual of Military Law,* the Army Act, military offences, courts martial, and courts of inquiry.[6] While the immediate crisis subsided as more officers again received formal instruction in military law and as discipline in the militia as a whole improved,

Orde became preoccupied with substantial administrative reorganization within the defence headquarters.

Orde's duties as JAG broadened with the establishment of the Department of National Defence. In 1922, Parliament passed the National Defence Act, effective from 1 January 1923, which provided for the reorganization and coordination of the work of the three existing services under a single minister and department.[7] Despite the change, each service preserved its identity and continued to use separate service codes for administration of discipline, pay, and matters of interior economy. The JAG passed from the charge of the adjutant general's branch to that of the deputy minister in the new department.[8] Orde became responsible for legal activities in all three services. Under the new arrangement, the JAG administered and supervised naval, militia, and air force law, received and recorded all court martial proceedings, advised the minister, revised naval, militia, and air force regulations, and gave legal advice on general matters pertaining to the Department of National Defence.[9] A desperate need for economy rather than any pressing requirement for rational consolidation inspired the 1922 National Defence Act. In spite of his increased duties, Orde received no additional staff or assistance. Like the rest of the Canadian Armed Forces, the JAG worked with the limited resources available.

The JAG contributed in a small way to the creation of an independent Canadian air force. In 1919, Parliament passed the Air Board Act to control all civil and military aviation within Canada.[10] The small air force comprised a collection of war-surplus planes, flown and maintained mostly by First World War veterans. Regulations for discipline and pay, prepared by the air staff, were approved on 31 August 1920.[11] The single volume of regulations drew heavily upon the British Air Force Act and corresponded in a general nature to the Canadian militia's KR&O. A proposal was made to amalgamate the air force into the active militia, but Orde deemed that the legislation and regulations governing the Canadian air force were sufficiently distinct to keep it separate from the other services.[12] For economic reasons, civil air operations had been the mainstay of the tiny force since its inception. However, after promulgation of the National Defence Act, the Canadian air force, prefixed with "Royal" after early 1923, increasingly emphasized a defence orientation.

The dual nature of the air force's activities left many officers unsure about the exercise of their authority under the Air Board Act and the 1920 regulations. Wing Commander William Barker, the acting director of the Royal Canadian Air Force (RCAF), noted "a feeling prevalent throughout the Force at the present time that Courts-Martial must be avoided at all cost, and this is to a certain extent prejudicial to good discipline."[13] To clear up any ambiguity, a committee was established to examine possible changes to RCAF regulations, and the task of drafting revised regulations was handed over to the JAG in early March 1923. Two officers spared from other duties, Major R. Nordheimer and Flight Lieutenant F.J. Mawdsley, produced an entirely new set of KR&O for the RCAF under Orde's general supervision.[14] Among other things, the draft regulations allowed militia officers commanding in the military districts to convene and confirm courts martial involving air force personnel. A precedent existed in Great Britain for this practice, and Barker believed "occasions may arise when there may be an insufficient number of Air Force officers available as members of a court martial, and there is no legal reason why the same procedure should not be followed in Canada."[15] Similarities between Great Britain's Army Act and Air Force Act, both made applicable to the respective Canadian services, allowed a certain degree of overlap.

Canadian authorities assumed at the time that the RCAF would serve with the Royal Air Force (RAF) under the provisions of the Air Force Act in the event of hostilities. The RCAF's *King's Regulations and Orders,* which Barker called "the Charter for the formation of the proposed re-organized Air Force," were approved and issued in 1924 to every officer at air stations across the country.[16] While these new regulations incorporated the Air Force Act and rules of procedure from the RAF KR&O insofar as they were consistent with conditions pertaining in the RCAF, the new regulations still closely paralleled the KR&O for the Canadian militia. All air officers were expected to interpret the 1924 regulations "reasonably and intelligently, with due regard to the interests of the Service, bearing in mind that no attempt has been made to provide for necessary and self-evident exception."[17] The RCAF took a major step toward defining itself as a separate and distinct institutional entity. For many years, the regulations rather than a statute governed RCAF discipline.

The Royal Canadian Navy, on the other hand, sought closer interaction with the Royal Navy in the disciplinary sphere. The Admiralty recognized that the Naval Discipline (Dominion Forces) Act of 1911 and the legislation in the dominions bringing it into effect had done "nothing to make the R.N. and the Dominion forces one navy, or to make the members of the different navies amenable to the Courts Martial convened by the authorities of another Navy."[18] Although a single disciplinary code existed in the Naval Discipline Act, dominion authority remained the fundamental principle. The Royal Canadian Navy, like the Australian and New Zealand navies, was responsible for its own organization and administration under Canada's Naval Service Act.[19] The large numbers of British naval personnel seconded to or temporarily under RCN control complicated matters. In January 1920, Royal Navy ratings, awaiting passage to Bermuda aboard HMCS *Niobe,* refused an order from a Canadian petty officer to scrape paint work and were then charged with disobedience.[20] Since Great Britain's judge advocate of the Fleet was unsure how far Canadian jurisdiction extended to persons who were not members of the RCN, the ratings were released without a court martial or summary trial. At a conference in the Colonial Office on 12 March 1920, representatives from the Naval Service of Canada requested some way to make such personnel amenable to Canadian naval discipline.[21] Although the Admiralty drafted a suitable provision with the concurrence of Canadian naval authorities, a revised naval discipline bill never came before the British Parliament because the Admiralty considered the timing inopportune. The problem, however, refused to go away.

Instances of British officers and ratings committing breaches of service discipline in Canada continued to raise the question time and again. As a compromise, the Admiralty finally allowed the Naval Service of Canada, with the judge advocate of the Fleet's sanction, to treat British naval personnel as Canadians by giving them equivalent RCN rank.[22] In theory at least, Canadian naval authorities became responsible for application of the disciplinary provisions of the Naval Discipline Act within their sphere of jurisdiction. Whether this arrangement was reciprocal for Canadian warships acting or operating in conjunction with the Royal Navy remained ambiguous. At a court martial of a British naval lieutenant, a convening authority excluded Canadian officers from sitting as members, even though an amendment to the *King's Regulations and Admiralty Instructions* made clear that they were eligible and required to perform such duty.[23] Canadian participation was still too much of a chance for senior Royal Navy officers concerned about upholding the legality of proceedings. The legal position was made more exact when the Admiralty forwarded a warrant to the senior officer of the Canadian Naval Service allowing the convening of courts martial for trial of Royal Navy officers and ratings when circumstances demanded.[24] For all intents and purposes, the Royal Canadian Navy was placed on the same legal footing as the Royal Navy.

The introduction of the National Defence Act slightly modified the ad hoc arrangement worked out between the Naval Service of Canada and the Admiralty. After the statute's enactment, Orde rather than the judge advocate of the Fleet in London reviewed courts martial and advised on legal matters pertaining to the RCN.[25] The work was not too onerous because the number of naval courts martial in any given year was small. Under the austerity regime of William Mackenzie King's Liberal government, Canada's navy was reduced to a force of two destroyers, one on each coast, and a personnel limit of 500 officers and other ranks. Orde recommended that in regard to the Canadian Naval Service, the minister of national defence be vested with the same powers, duties, and functions as the Admiralty possessed under the Naval Discipline Act and the *King's Regulations and Admiralty Instructions*.[26] An order-in-council to this effect was promulgated in January 1926. Ultimate review and confirming authority for all courts martial in the RCN now belonged to the minister of national defence.

Due to the small size of Canada's interwar navy, court martial procedure predominantly followed that of the British. In 1922, the Admiralty issued an updated memorandum for the guidance of officers sitting on courts martial, judge advocates at trial, and accountant officers required to pass promotion examinations on the subject.[27] The memorandum covered the Naval Discipline Act and other statutes, naval court martial regulations, regulations for disciplinary courts, instructions for framing charges, order of procedure and recording of proceedings, as well as applicable forms. Orders-in-council regarding the Canadian, Australian, and New Zealand navies were inserted after a section with the 1911 Naval Discipline (Dominion Naval Forces) Act in the memorandum.[28] The Admiralty also sought out the views of the dominions on proposed amendments to naval court martial procedure. In response to a query from the deputy minister, Orde simply stated that "bringing the procedure of both naval and military courts martial into line is extremely desirable."[29] The navy held a certain advantage over the other two services with the training of specialized officers in legal work.

The paymaster and accountant branch of the Royal Navy, and by extension the Royal Canadian Navy, handled most naval court martial work and other legal business. Promotion examinations for this branch required a knowledge of the *King's Regulations and Admiralty Instructions,* the Naval Discipline Act and court martial procedure, the Merchant Shipping Act, and international law.[30] After the Dominion government closed the Royal Naval College of Canada to save money, the Admiralty accepted cadets from Canada for instruction in Royal Navy establishments. Under special entry, candidates who chose the accountant branch followed a structured training and career progression.[31] Accountant officers were generally qualified as judge advocates and advisors to captains or convening officers for confirmation of sentences after six years of experience in naval court martial procedure. Until more Canadians qualified as accountant officers, the RCN used Royal Navy paymaster commanders and lieutenant commanders seconded from the Admiralty. This practical arrangement ensured that good quality legal expertise was available to a small navy otherwise unable to afford its own system of training and instruction in naval law.

The JAG was less confident about affairs within the Canadian militia. When military authorities handed out summary punishments in a case involving the severe whipping of a trooper named Bowen in the Royal Canadian Dragoons on 4 February 1924, the attorney general of Ontario intervened and charged seven soldiers with assault. For perhaps the first time in Canada during peacetime, Canadian military law attracted a great deal of attention from the press; and the incident soon gained widespread prominence. The Department of National Defence was quick to downplay any suggestion of problems with discipline in the militia, but the matter was now out of its hands. On 19 February 1924, the seven soldiers appeared before a judge in a Toronto police court. Trial before a civil magistrate prevented the military from hiding the significance of the case as more sordid details became known. Court testimony confirmed newspaper reports that Bowen had been dragged from his bed and whipped in the middle of the night after a kangaroo court in the barracks. Given the case's high public profile, the JAG personally attended the judicial proceedings in Toronto as an observer. Although acknowledging the damage to the Canadian militia's prestige with the public, Orde tried to find a positive side to the case and stated that the convictions at least showed "the public at large and the troops that civil law was supreme, and that the mere fact that a person was a soldier did not permit him to act in any way differently than would be the case were he a civilian."[32] For Orde, the highly publicized case was one of many signs that discipline was deteriorating within the militia because of insufficient knowledge of military law among officers.

Military law received too little coverage in current militia training. Lack of money and limited instructional time restricted the frequency of courses at provisional and permanent military schools. Suggestions were put forward for introduction of correspondence courses in certain theoretical subjects, such as military law.[33] Officers then could study at home at their own pace and according to their own time schedule. While perhaps not the preferred choice, the method was better than no instruction at all. In the meantime, the adjutant general issued a circular letter on recent changes in the Army Act and their effect on the Canadian militia.[34] Instruction at the military schools scarcely kept up with new developments. A militia staff course that Sherwood Lett attended in Vancouver in late 1924 used Colonel Otter's now somewhat dated guide as a reference for lectures on the Militia Act, military law, and aid to the civil power.[35] It was essential for professional officers to study and read continuously. To be successful in the military law component of the promotion examinations, permanent force officers were required to be familiar with the *Manual of Military Law* and the militia's *Regulations and Orders*. Regular practice using the most current editions of these books and old examination questions facilitated a mastery of military law.[36] Many officers failed to devote enough time to extracurricular study. Finding considerable illegalities and irregularities while reviewing courts martial and courts of inquiry, Orde observed that "the knowledge of military law and the provisions of the *King's Regulations* relating to discipline possessed by officers of the Permanent Force is considerably below that which they possess in other military subjects."[37] The JAG agreed with the general staff that more systematic instruction in military law was needed.

The pressure of other duties, however, prevented Orde from pursuing plans for instruction in military law in the near future. The amount of work that the JAG performed in these years, at least comparable to that handled by a much larger staff several decades later, was absolutely phenomenal for a single individual. In addition to reviewing courts martial and courts of inquiry, Orde completely revised the KR&O for the Canadian militia, prepared new regulations for the clothing of the non-permanent active militia, drafted reports and submissions to the Privy Council, and responded to queries from the military districts.[38] Pension, pay, air force, and naval matters added to his heavy workload. Where practicable, Orde attempted to consolidate regulations and orders as much as possible: "Difficulties have been experienced, as a considerable amount of research is required to cull from the regulations all matters pertaining to detail, and steps are now being taken to simplify in a very drastic fashion the whole system."[39] Orde knew that more easily understood regulations and better knowledge or reference in military law meant potentially less work in the long run for the JAG.

At the suggestion of the deputy chief of the general staff, Orde spent several months during mid-1926 in London at the War Office to see first-hand the organization and activities of the British JAG office. The primary reason was to learn more about the way the British pursued instruction in military law. In a report to the deputy minister, Orde remarked on the differences between the Canadians and the British: the JAG in Great Britain was a civilian with separate civil and military departments underneath him, legal work of a quasi-military nature outside courts martial was referred to treasury solicitors, and officers from the JAG office gave regular lectures and demonstrations on military law.[40] All members of the British JAG office, whether civilian or military, were qualified lawyers. The civil department provided judge advocates at general and district courts martial and reviewed all convictions, whereas the Military and Air Force Department gave pretrial advice, took summaries of evidence, and furnished prosecutors for particular trials. Instruction in military law represented the principal function of the Military and Air Force Department since its inception in 1922.[41] The division of duties allowed the British to undertake comprehensive and systematic legal instruction throughout the British Army and Royal Air Force. For the overworked Canadian JAG, the arrangement seemed practical, logical, and perhaps adaptable to Canadian circumstances.

Upon his return to Canada, Orde requested the appointment of an officer to assist him in implementing a formal program of lectures and court martial demonstrations. His other work had precluded the JAG from providing any instruction in military law during the previous five years. "The normal duties of my office are such as to occupy the whole of my time," he wrote.[42] Orde's stated preference to have a serving officer with some legal training posed some difficulty. Only two officers in the permanent force – Captain Gerald Grant-Suttie and Captain Meredith Logan – possessed suitable legal experience to fill the position.[43] Grant-Suttie had served as a court martial officer in London and France during the First World War, but he had completed only two years of law school and had not attempted the bar examination. Logan, on the other hand, was a qualified lawyer, and the nature of the work appealed to him. When subsequently told that Logan was unavailable, Orde informed the deputy minister that "the additional instructional duties which this office is to undertake and which are urgently required make it essential that an officer with some legal training be procured."[44] As a temporary measure, Orde accepted periodic employment of officers from the permanent force to perform instructional duties, with the proviso that an officer with legal qualifications be appointed if the arrangement proved unsatisfactory.

Officers in the militia continued to commit many errors and irregularities during and after courts martial. In late 1926, revised rules of procedure introduced certain changes from the previous 1907 rules of procedure in the conduct, composition, and promulgation of courts martial.[45] Responsibility for making officers engaged in court martial work aware of these changes and military law in general rested with district officers commanding, but the lack of opportunities for specialized legal instruction complicated the task. Work was often left undone, even though ignorance of the law was no excuse. Major H.T. Cock, the general staff officer for Military District 13, told a military audience during a talk on discipline: "I am not a lawyer but I believe that obedience to the letter of the law, even though there is a clear breach of the 'Spirit,' or as we are not dealing with the liquor question, I will say 'intention,' that a man will not be convicted. In the service, however, the reverse is the case, if a man executes the letter of an order well knowing it is wrong, or if he being solid ivory from the neck up fails to use common sense, he is hardly, if ever, excused."[46]

Proper interpretation of the law required a sound working knowledge of the current rules and regulations, reinforced by constant practice. In December 1926, Orde held two mock courts martial at the Royal Military College of Canada "to illustrate the various forms of evidence given at a court-martial dealing with a simple military offence."[47] The practical method of instruction allowed officers to learn in a simulated true-life situation and highlighted common errors. Orde noted that "the type of mistakes and irregularities which occurred in Canada in connection with Courts Martial proceedings also occur in England."[48] Even in the most effective military justice system, errors inevitably occurred; the aim was to minimize them through education and awareness. Orde suggested that circulars be issued every six months under the adjutant general's signature, pointing out the most serious errors and irregularities at recent courts martial for the information of all militia officers.

In spite of the assumed usefulness of lectures, demonstrations, and circulars, courts martial in the militia and air force steadily increased. The number rose from 33 in 1925 to 53 in 1926 and 55 in 1927. This incremental trend worried military authorities and called for some innovation in legal instruction. Many officers complained that military law was dull and uninteresting "largely due to the fact that reading and studying of the Manual is irksome, and results in little benefit unless the student, during his reading, is continually applying the knowledge gained to the solution of concrete problems."[49] Standard lectures were little more than a repetition of the *Manual of Military Law* and were ineffective at imparting a good working knowledge of military law. Orde instead took students step-by-step through the trial process, highlighting the more important principles of military law and pointing out possible problems and pitfalls. Non-commissioned officers were required to know how to frame and lay charges properly, handle grievances, and maintain general discipline.[50] Officers, on the other hand, assumed most responsibility for the administration and application of military law. In promotion examinations, a situational approach was adopted for military law questions, for which officers needed to demonstrate an ability to reason out specific legal problems arising from the application of military law, framing of charges, conduct of courts martial, and confirmation.[51] Mere memorizing and rote learning of the regulations and manuals no longer guaranteed success. Captain Logan wrote a short article on British general courts martial between 1795 and 1820: "And having aroused interest in military law by this means, a study of the subject would be carried on by many of those who at the present time consider it dry and uninteresting."[52] The illustrations showed that military law dealt with real people and real-life situations.

Although the disciplinary situation was far from satisfactory, the JAG remained optimistic about the results of the limited time devoted to legal instruction. The number of courts martial in 1928, mostly involving charges of desertion and absence without leave, actually increased by almost fifty percent to 75.[53] Active efforts by commanding officers to deter crime through district courts martial and the frequency of soldiers and airmen electing trial by court martial instead of accepting summary punishment mostly accounted for the increase. Aware that education in military law needed time to show results, Orde asked the adjutant general to keep the courts martial in perspective:

> As you are aware, during the past few years a large number of Courts Martial contained numerous irregularities indicative both of a lack of knowledge on the part of the officers composing the Court and a lack of care on

> the part of the District Headquarters responsible for reviewing the Proceedings prior to confirmation. In all these cases I have made it a practice to write to the District concerned commenting very fully on the irregularities etc. which the Proceedings of a Court Martial disclose, the intention being that my comments and remarks will be forwarded by the District Headquarters to all officers concerned for their information and future guidance. These continuous efforts on the part of this office to improve the situation are at last producing some beneficial results, as the Courts Martial which have been reviewed during the past fiscal year indicate that not only have the officers composing the various Courts begun to have a proper appreciation of their important duties, but also that the District Staffs are taking greater pains in ensuring that the requirements of the law are complied with.[54]

The JAG achieved modest progress in increasing awareness of military law throughout the militia. For the benefit of district officers commanding, Orde prepared general notes on the application of the Army Act to the Canadian militia and court martial procedure.[55] Some interest was evident in the military districts. Major General William Griesbach, who included military law among six subjects he singled out for serious military study, emphasized the importance of study and reading for all officers because the worst murderer and criminal in the world, he asserted, was an ignorant military officer.[56] While a good knowledge of military law might not bring officers fame or fortune, conscientious study made them competent, responsible, and a credit to Canada by enabling them to recognize misconduct or negligence.

The JAG and senior officers were convinced that military law was a worthwhile subject. In his annual report for 1929, Orde stated that "there should be established a more comprehensive method of instruction in military law and court-martial procedure, together with improved facilities for the dissemination of advice on technical points connected therewith."[57] The appointment of an additional lawyer, previously postponed because of budgetary constraints, soon enabled the JAG to inaugurate specialized military legal instruction for the permanent force. In June 1929, the civil service commission assigned Colonel J.S. Rankin as an assistant departmental solicitor.[58] He assisted Orde with the enormous amount of detailed legal work referred to the JAG office. Shortly after Rankin's appointment, Orde expressed his intention to issue to the military districts "at regular intervals, say once a month, a set of four or five questions, each set dealing with some particular point in Military Law."[59] The questions, accompanied by explanatory memoranda, were to be answered by officers individually or in small syndicates and then returned to the JAG office for marking and correction. By this means, the JAG hoped to gain a fair idea of how much, or how little, military law permanent force officers actually knew.

For promotion and qualification, Canadian officers needed to demonstrate an intimate knowledge of the most current official publications on military law. During 1929, the War Office issued a new edition of the *Manual of Military Law* and a pamphlet on courts martial.[60] These publications quickly became the standard works for promotion examinations and everyday use within the Canadian militia. In a short review article on the 1929 *Manual of Military Law,* Captain Logan remarked that the "general arrangement has been improved, the style and print are clearer, and new references add interest and value to the text."[61] Canadian officers could now use current books to prepare more effectively and with greater success for promotion. Orde noted that most candidates had done poorly on the military law component of examinations in recent years. Syllabi for lectures on military law prepared by Logan left much of the detailed information to private reading in the manual and concentrated on main points regarding arrest, summary punishments, offences and punishments, courts martial, and aid to the civil power.[62] The 1929 edition of the British *Manual of Military Law* became the reference book of choice for most officers in the Canadian Armed Forces.

As much as possible, the JAG attempted to integrate instruction in military law with broader training and educational activities within the militia. In a detailed précis on military law and courts martial, Orde emphasized the importance of the subject for every officer:

> As the tribunals constituted under the Acts dealing with Military Law are made up of officers of senior rank down to junior officers, and officers of all ranks in the ordinary routine of military duty run into its provisions every day, it is essential that every officer should be absolutely familiar with this code of law, and as during wartime the ordinary officer who has to function on military tribunals as judge and jury is working usually at high pitch with other duties, the real and practically the only time an officer can make himself sufficiently proficient in this branch of his profession is during time of peace. To be proficient also involves study and continual re-study of the subject.[63]

Military law was not something that could be easily picked up later when the need arose. As part of the militia staff course, officers learned military law through correspondence courses and lectures during the winter months and then wrote a final paper in April before proceeding to the practical portion in camp during the summer.[64] The questions that Orde distributed provided the advantage of additional study and discussion.

Better instruction in military law remained a priority for mitigating acknowledged disciplinary problems in the militia. The successful results in the initial year led the general staff to ask the JAG to continue his instruction again the following year.[65] Orde and Rankin prepared suitable question papers and answers on military law with explanatory material. The first paper in 1930 focused specifically on tribunals and their relative jurisdiction and authority.[66] Officers worked through individual problems with the aid of the *Manual of Military Law* and other available books. Two authors of a recently published handbook on military law conceded: "The bent of the average officer is not bookish; it is practical. He wants to be told as plainly as possible not only what rules he is to follow, but the guiding common sense principles which underlie them."[67] The JAG's extra instruction came at a crucial time. A lack of funds, due to the throes of the Depression, forced many militia units to cut back on training to save costs.[68] The militia received even fewer opportunities for instruction in military law and discipline in the course of its normal activities.

Despite many obstacles in a peacetime armed forces under severe financial restraint, the JAG believed in the importance of military law for all officers and other ranks. Orde knew that teaching in military law would not receive the attention it deserved unless he took an active part in its dissemination. In the final analysis, the JAG was solely responsible for the administration of Canadian military law in general. And military legal instruction within the Armed Forces was one of his most important duties.

The entire legal position of the Canadian Armed Forces soon underwent a major transformation with enactment of the Statute of Westminster. As a result of imperial conferences in 1926 and 1930, the British government initiated steps to redefine Great Britain's constitutional relationship with the dominions into the British Commonwealth of Nations. In short, Canada and the other white dominions were offered self-autonomy. Significant changes for the Canadian Armed Forces included giving the Dominion Parliament power to pass laws extending beyond Canada's territorial boundaries and absolute authority to enact legislation from the date of the Statute of Westminster's commencement.[69] As well, the British proposed new legislation to allow visiting dominion forces in Great Britain and other parts of the British Commonwealth to maintain discipline in accordance with the laws of the dominion from which they came. Orde left Canada in early 1931 to attend the Imperial Defence College in London, and in his absence, Rankin served as DJAG.[70] Orde's presence in Great Britain kept the Canadian JAG abreast of the latest developments affecting the new legislation and freed him from the daily grind of his normal duties in Ottawa. Rankin was the channel for information back home and when the DJAG was asked for his assessment of the proposed British Act, he answered that the statute provided the "legal ground work for the effective operation of a Canadian contingent with a United Kingdom force, and if and when supplemented by analogous legislation passed by the Dominion of Canada, will afford a basic ground for the effective co-operation of all three services of United Kingdom and Dominion Forces."[71] To this end, an interdepartmental committee on the discipline of Armed Forces, chaired by John Read, legal advisor to the Department of External Affairs, was struck. The committee was to consider the Canadian legislation necessary to meet the changed conditions under the Statute of Westminster, which came into effect on 11 December 1931. Upon his return from London, Orde recommended amendments to the Militia Act to ensure continued application of the annual Army and Air Force Acts; he also recommended new legislation to allow visiting forces from Great Britain and other Commonwealth countries to remain subject to their own service codes while in Canada.[72] In cooperation with Orde and the Department of National Defence, the interdepartmental committee prepared bills for presentation to Parliament.

In spite of the opening afforded by the Statute of Westminster, the Canadian Armed Forces continued using British statutes modified by existing Canadian legislation. During a meeting at the Dominions Office in London on 16 March 1932, General Andrew McNaughton, Canada's chief of the general staff, expressed a "desire for cooperation" and asserted that Canadian forces "were His Majesty's forces equally with the Forces of the United Kingdom."[73] The Canadians suggested only minor alterations to wording and phraseology in the imperial Visiting Forces Act. In April 1933, the Canadian Parliament passed its own Visiting Forces (British Commonwealth) Act to govern command and disciplinary relationships between Canadian forces and other forces from the British Commonwealth.[74] Henceforth, Canada exercised complete authority over the application, supervision, and review of discipline and military law among its Armed Forces deployed at home and abroad.

Owing to the unsettled legal position of the RCAF under the new Aeronautics Act, the interdepartmental committee's other draft bills were set aside. Orde viewed the proposed legislation as temporary anyway "pending a comprehensive review of the legislation relating to the Naval, Military and Air Forces of Canada, with the ultimate object of covering the whole situation in a comprehensive code which, irrespective of the form it may eventually take, will have to be done before many years pass."[75] Although McNaughton also favoured a common service code covering all three services, lack of a proper statutory basis for the RCAF postponed matters. In 1936, Orde again reiterated the need for some resolution of the problem through reintroduction of the interdepartmental committee's previous bills or the drafting of a new National Defence Act for all three services; he acknowledged, however, that the latter entailed "considerable magnitude, and would demand the uninterrupted attention of at least one legal draftsman with considerable clerical assistance for a number of months, a matter which, having regard to the volume of normal Departmental work, I could not suitably undertake."[76] A distinctly Canadian service code, common to all three services, was deferred for the time being. Beyond the JAG and the chief of the general staff, the issue generated little interest. Even with the Visiting Forces (British Commonwealth) Act in place, the Canadian services still applied the British Army, Air Force, and Naval Discipline Acts. There was no precursor in the 1930s to Canada's National Defence Act of 1950. The changed circumstances under the Statute of Westminster required the teaching of new subjects in military law in Canada.

Despite severe financial stringency, the Canadian militia managed to impart some knowledge of military law during its limited training and educational activities. Instruction in theoretical subjects was generally cheaper and easier than practical or field exercises. Officers usually bought their own books, and lectures or demonstrations were given as time and space permitted. Notes from the militia staff course in 1932 explained the powers of commanding officers and company commanders, various aspects of courts martial, and offences.[77] Instruction stressed military law's practical applications. During an address on military law and aid to the civil power to the Alberta Military Institute, Major D.E. Cameron from the University of Alberta's COTC contingent urged "every military man to study common law with a view to understanding the protection offered by the law and be able to distinguish between civil and criminal liability."[78] A good knowledge of the law was an officer's best means to avoid civil prosecution if he overstepped his authority under military law. The military districts established provisional schools at convenient locations for officers to attend courses leading to qualification or promotion.[79] The role of the permanent force was to provide instructors to the non-permanent active militia. At provisional schools in Calgary and Esquimalt, Donald MacLauchlan from the Calgary Highlanders Regiment attended lectures on rules of evidence, punishment powers of officers commanding and company commanders, discipline, and military law.[80] The *King's Regulations and Orders for the Canadian Militia* and the 1929 *Manual of Military Law* remained the main reference sources. Captain R. Townshend-Stephens, a former AJAG at the War Office, also published a book in 1933 to help officers more easily understand the official military law manual.[81] Through reading and attendance at lectures and courses, Canadian officers learned the fundamentals of military law as applied to the militia.

As he had done previously, the JAG took an active part in trying to increase general legal knowledge throughout the permanent force and non-permanent active militia. Orde directly advised district officers commanding on the confirmation of courts martial and other legal matters.[82]

The worst and most serious mistakes occurred at this level, and continuous effort was required to sustain any interest in military law. Other work had prevented the JAG's office from undertaking any comprehensive instruction in military law since 1930, and Orde feared "lack of this will, in all likelihood, be noticed when officers who have been appointed during the past two years, and who did not receive the instruction this office formerly gave, reach such seniority as will make them eligible to be detailed for Court Martial duty."[83] He always found time for some instruction when his other duties allowed. In lectures to the staff college preparatory course at the Royal Military College of Canada, Orde described the Statute of Westminster and its effect on the Canadian Armed Forces.[84] As Orde recognized, the effectiveness of military law relied upon keeping officers up to date on the most recent legislation and regulations. In September 1934, the JAG office issued a digest of opinions and rulings for general reference purposes.[85] This type of aid was useful if officers bothered studying their professional duties, but many in the small permanent force chose not to. During the Depression, military service offered stable, if not well-paid, employment until better economic times returned. In March 1934, more than half the captains and lieutenants who wrote promotion examinations failed in one or more subjects.[86] Military law, a detailed and complex subject, proved a particularly weak area for those officers without a serious interest in improving their professional competence.

Since no uniform progress in individual training was apparent, more specialized legal instruction seemed imperative. In late 1935, the JAG conducted advanced courses in military law and court martial procedure for officers in the permanent force and non-permanent active militia.[87] As with earlier instruction on military law within the Canadian militia, précis and questions were prepared on specific topics, and the answers were then marked in the JAG office. In 1936, the War Office issued a new edition of its pamphlet on court martial procedure.[88] Six sections covered preparation of a case for trial; convening of the court; duties of the president, prosecutor, and defending officer; and confirmation of proceedings. Canadian officers used the pamphlet on court martial procedure as a guide in conjunction with the 1929 *Manual of Military Law* and the *King's Regulations and Orders*. Orde chaired a committee established to redraft and revise the regulations for the permanent force and non-permanent active militia.[89] He strove toward definite improvements in the dissemination of military law within the Canadian Armed Forces.

Nevertheless, the amount and sophistication of legal instruction in Canada lagged far behind that in Great Britain. Wherever possible, military authorities detailed Canadian officers to attend courts martial, but Orde admitted that "the facilities for practical experience in Canada are in no way commensurate with those available to Officers of the Regular Army."[90]

The limited number of courts martial held in the small Canadian militia was an impediment. Beyond lectures on military law during the militia staff course, opportunities for practical application were few and far between.[91] Military legal instruction in Canada remained predominantly academic in nature. To prepare for higher command and promotion examinations, officers were merely encouraged to study and read the *Manual of Military Law* and the *King's Regulations for the Canadian Militia*.[92] Formal courses reinforced self-study in military law. In late 1937, the military law component of the advanced militia staff course included the powers of commanding officers, courts martial, rules of evidence, aid to the civil power, staff duties in connection with courts martial, the military's relation to the state and civil society, as well as discussion on the Statute of Westminster.[93] The scope of the course was admittedly broad. Major Barry Watson criticized the practice of cramming by many officers prior to final examinations and suggested spreading the course's theoretical portion over a two-year period.[94] The British, on the other hand, favoured more short courses of instruction in military law, targeted at officers with some previous experience in court martial work. In 1938, the British JAG's Military and Air Force Department conducted lectures and discussion groups with junior officers and captains in various commands to prepare them to act as court martial presidents.[95] Circulars explaining the purpose and interrelationship of the lectures were distributed beforehand. Unlike the Canadians, the British divided military legal instruction into manageable, intensive segments offered on a regular basis.

Orde's familiarity with British developments in military law, the continued reliance of the Canadian Armed Forces on the disciplinary provisions of British statutes, and general disinterest from Canada's Parliament and judiciary in military matters during the interwar period meant that Canadian military law remained heavily influenced by British proposals for reforms in the administration of military law. In March 1938, the War Office established a committee, chaired by Roland Oliver, to examine the entire system of courts martial under the Army and Air Force Acts with particular attention to a right of appeal to a civil judicial tribunal. Over the course of twenty meetings, the committee considered various memoranda and interviewed numerous witnesses with grievances or complaints against previous court martial convictions. Its final report stated that the existing system furnished

> a uniform machine which deals in the end with all cases of every degree of seriousness and affords the same standard of justice for everyone. It deals equally with offences committed in distant countries and at home. It works alike in peace and war. Very little reflection would bring home to the mind the sort of difficulties which must arise in the actual oral hearing of

appeals in cases from distant countries, or from the front in war-time, or where the Accused and the witnesses belong to a Unit which is under orders to go abroad.[96]

Although a formal appeal was unwelcome for the stated reasons, the committee recommended the reorganization of the British JAG office to give at least the perception of independence from the War Office and Air Ministry. The report suggested transfer of the Military and Air Force Department to a Directorate of Legal Services, responsible to the adjutant general and the air member for personnel. Oliver's committee, like Darling's previously, identified legal education for officers of all ranks as essential for the efficient administration of military law. The report recommended preparation of handbooks for each service to guide officers at courts martial, posting of legal officers to individual commands, and appointment of a dedicated officer in the proposed Directorate of Legal Services to undertake legal instruction throughout the army and air force. The Oliver Committee generally endorsed the operation of the military justice system at the time, while suggesting slight improvements to make it work better.

On 11 January 1939, the secretary of state for war established an interdepartmental committee, chaired by the British JAG, Sir Henry MacGeagh. The interdepartmental committee, composed of representatives from the War Office and Air Ministry and a former JAG in India, considered the recommendations of the Oliver Committee's report section by section.[97] While opposed to creation of a Directorate of Legal Services, MacGeagh's committee concurred with transfer of the Military and Air Force Department from Britain's JAG office to separate legal branches under the adjutant general and the air member for personnel. Centralizing legal officers in these branches, the committee stated, was preferable to their distribution within the commands. In regard to improved legal education for officers, MacGeagh's committee agreed with the Oliver Committee's conclusions by supporting appointment of a senior officer with a major or captain as an assistant to implement a comprehensive scheme of legal instruction with a special emphasis on rules of evidence and court martial procedure. Making more efficient use of legal officers already there instead of simply adding more staff was the main challenge. MacGeagh's committee recommended that promotion and other examinations in military and air force law be set and marked by legal officers without extra remuneration and suggested that the War Office's pamphlet on courts martial be amended and enlarged as a handbook. The interdepartmental committee strongly emphasized the importance of increasing overall legal knowledge among officers, especially in the Royal Air Force.

Strong objections from outside the War Office and Air Ministry deferred implementation of the recommendations from the Oliver and MacGeagh

Committees. From the outset, the Admiralty had refused to participate in any review of the military or naval justice system. Lord Stanhope, the Admiralty's first lord, viewed the Oliver Committee's proposals as "the first step on a very slippery slope, that of setting up an independent authority outside the control of the Service Department who would," he thought, "tend more and more as time went on to be the ultimate authority on matters of discipline."[98] The Admiralty argued that administration and review of service law properly belonged to service authorities. Application of army and air force solutions to an arguably different naval disciplinary structure seemed inappropriate. Stanhope feared that the Royal Navy "might be forced to adopt measures based on what seems ... to be a fundamentally unsound conception of the role of the judge advocate [of the Fleet]."[99] In the interests of the service as a whole, the Board of Admiralty occasionally acted differently from the advice of its retained civil solicitor, whose function remained purely advisory. Stanhope believed that it would become "very easy for a critic in Parliament or elsewhere to launch an apparently entirely reasonable attack upon a system which gives the Admiralty power to ignore a trustworthy legal opinion to the effect that there has been a miscarriage of justice."[100] The Admiralty was not the only interested party troubled by the proposed changes. The government of India took strong exception to Oliver's recommendation that the JAG in India, in his capacity as advisor on British military and air force law, should act as a deputy of the British JAG.[101] Historically, the JAG in India had developed along a different path, in no way subordinate or inferior to legal authorities in London.

The relevance of the recommendations by the Oliver and MacGeagh Committees to military law in Canada and organization of legal activities within the Canadian Armed Forces was not immediately apparent. As long as Canadian military law remained dependent on British statutes and official publications, changes or reforms in Great Britain necessarily had a ripple effect on the administration of military law in Canada. Still, the Statute of Westminster and indigenous defence legislation such as the Militia Act and the Naval Service Act gave the Dominion exclusive control over administering and disciplining its forces during the interwar period, at least within the territory of Canada. There were no public concerns or internal institutional rationales driving major reforms to Canada's military justice system. The Canadian services were small compared to imperial and other dominion forces, and the actual application of military law was correspondingly limited. The structural reorganization proposed for Great Britain's JAG office was inapplicable in Canada because Orde and Rankin were the only two full-time members in the JAG branch. However, Orde certainly shared the concern over poor legal knowledge among members of the armed services, as reflected by his considerable efforts at teaching military law during the previous two decades. The Canadian militia was not up to the same standard in its members' general knowledge of military law as the British Army, but was certainly further ahead than it might have been without Orde's guidance and instructional efforts. The minister of national defence's authority to confirm and review sentences from courts martial in all three services negated a formal right of appeal to a civilian judicial body; and, civilian supervision was firmly established over the Canadian Armed Forces. Canada's Department of National Defence may have shared some of the concerns expressed by the Admiralty, but the issue was not pressing for the time being. In due course, the outbreak of the Second World War shelved the Oliver Committee's recommendations for changes to military law and the military justice system. In late September 1939, the Lord Chancellor informed the War Office that he didn't "propose to raise Oliver Report problems for the duration" of the conflict.[102] Orde and Canadian military authorities only fully began to appreciate the serviceability of the Oliver Committee's recommendations with the dramatic and rapid expansion of the Canadian Armed Forces and their legal activities to meet the wartime emergency of total war on a world scale.

4
Total War

The Second World War furnished the first actual application of the new legal arrangements under the Statute of Westminster and the Visiting Forces Agreements. Although British statutes were still used for convenience' sake, the Canadian military exercised complete control over the administration and supervision of military, air, and naval law among its own personnel. The Canadian JAG office expanded to meet the disciplinary demands of greatly enlarged land, sea, and air forces, deployed at home and abroad. As an invaluable source of recruitment and legal expertise, the larger Canadian legal profession rose to the occasion. Separate legal establishments were founded in Great Britain for the Canadian Army and the Royal Canadian Air Force. Canadian legal officers handled matters related to courts martial, revised regulations and manuals, and prosecuted alleged atrocities committed against Canadian service personnel in the theatres of war. Although at least one of the services introduced a distinctly Canadian service code of discipline, a stronger sense of national identity from the wartime experience was not immediately translated into substantial changes to military law. The Canadian Armed Forces used modifications of British military law and manuals for the duration of the conflict.

In defence of the British Commonwealth, Canada's Parliament declared war against Nazi Germany on 10 September 1939. The government immediately began preparations to send Canadian troops to assist Great Britain. At the direction of the minister of national defence, an ad hoc committee comprising Reginald Orde, John Read, C.P. Plaxton from the Department of Justice, and Group Captain H. Edwards, director of air personnel, convened to examine legal and constitutional questions arising from deployment of Canadian naval, air, and military forces outside Canada.[1] The committee concluded that British and Canadian visiting forces agreements adequately covered discipline and administration within Canadian military and air forces acting together or in combination with British and other Commonwealth forces. Canadian authorities, however, insisted on complete control over Canadian forces on the principle of unity of command.[2] The cabinet authorized organization of a Canadian Active Service Force and called out the militia on active service within Canada. Several orders-in-council applied the Visiting Forces (British Commonwealth) Act and the War Measures Act to forces sent outside Canadian territorial limits. The Canadians consulted British authorities for specific deployments, such as including Canadian troops in an expeditionary force sent to the continent of Europe.[3] Well aware of Haig's experience with the Australians during the First World War, General Lord Gort, the British commander-in-chief, accepted Canadian autonomy in courts martial and matters of discipline by selecting a Canadian DJAG. Both legislatively and in practice, the Canadian military exercised jurisdiction over its own disciplinary affairs.

The JAG recognized the necessity for qualified legal staffs within the military districts in Canada to handle immediate wartime and reinforcement demands. Although technically on active service, soldiers who committed offences were tried at the direction of the adjutant general, either summarily or by district courts martial.[4] Field punishments were handed down only in exceptional circumstances. For a short time, the military authorities tried to adapt the peacetime disciplinary structure to the new conditions. But as courts martial and other legal business increased during 1940, AJAGs were appointed in certain military districts.[5] These officers were often older, practising civilian lawyers who were put in uniform for the war's duration. While some of them obtained experience in the First World War or the interwar militia, Orde was not above giving temporary senior rank where conditions and the background of particular candidates warranted.[6] He viewed legal ability as more important than military seniority. The AJAGs advised on questions of law, examined applications for district courts martial and summaries of evidence, acted as judge advocates at courts martial, and advised confirming authorities in the review of proceedings.[7] Orde assigned additional AJAGs, deputy judge advocates, and legal officers as work became heavier. In early 1941, commanders of active divisions within the Canadian Army in Canada and Newfoundland were empowered to convene and confirm general and district courts martial.[8] Legal staffs provided assistance and advice to these officers.

As the Canadian Armed Forces rapidly expanded, military authorities accepted many officers from civilian life who had little or no experience in court martial work. Since only general and field general courts martial required a judge advocate with legal qualifications, the JAG issued to district officers commanding a handbook and circulars on initiating, preparing, and conducting district courts martial.[9] Orde soon formalized the entire system. On 14 September 1942, Lieutenant Colonel L.H. Clayton became inspector of courts martial in Canada.[10] Clayton's function was to maintain overall uniformity and legality in proceedings submitted by the military districts. From 1943 onward, Orde detailed officers with legal qualifications for duty as permanent presidents and prosecutors at courts martial.[11] Like the AJAGs, these men were usually experienced civilian lawyers who had joined the active or reserve forces for patriotic or other reasons.[12] Orde's employment of available lawyers in the military districts was a practical and flexible way of ensuring the efficient administration of military law during a period of unprecedented growth in the Canadian Armed Forces.

The JAG office was housed at National Defence Headquarters in Ottawa and its duties expanded during the wartime emergency. Orde was promoted to brigadier on 6 June 1940.[13] Additional legal officers joined his staff to handle the growing and diverse matters referred to the JAG. Orde's office no longer came under the authority of the deputy minister, but instead became an independent component of National Defence Headquarters.[14] Urgent ministerial or Privy Council inquiries and timely review of courts martial demanded immediate action. Orde, who shifted legal officers around where the work was heaviest or to fill shortages caused by employment of officers on special duties, insisted on "clearing the maximum quantity of work on the day it [was] received."[15] The division of responsibilities generally corresponded to whatever particular specialization or experience individual legal officers brought from civilian life. On 30 August 1941, Henry Nolan, KC, a senior partner with the law firm of Bennett, Hannah, and Nolan in Calgary, became DJAG.[16] Wing Commander C.M.A. Strathy and Commander Duncan MacTavish, RCNVR, were subsequently appointed DJAGs for the air force and navy respectively. Promoted to the rank of colonel, Nolan acted as a sort of roving executive officer, thus freeing Orde from the pressure of considerable daily work.

By mid-1943, the exorbitant amount of work called for changes to the JAG office. Besides the general supervision of all legal activities of the Canadian Armed Forces within Canada and overseas, Orde also acted under a special arrangement with the British government as a deputy to the British JAG in respect of all British military and air force personnel in North America.[17] In this capacity, Canada's JAG collected and reviewed all court martial proceedings without reference to London. Orde proposed a new organizational structure for his office because "the time has now come where we should know where we stand instead of functioning on a species of hand to mouth basis as we have been doing for some four years, which in the circumstances, could not be avoided."[18] He created the post of vice judge advocate general (VJAG) and separated legal education, administration, and records into distinct divisions. DJAGs – two army, one navy, and one air force – directed sections dealing with courts martial, claims, leases, military, air force, and naval law, regulations, contracts, pensions, and other legal matters.[19] In addition to the legal expertise within his own office, Orde benefited from the active assistance of the larger legal profession in Canada.

The JAG cultivated a close working relationship with the Canadian Bar Association during the Second World War. At a meeting in Windsor during August 1942, the council of the Canadian Bar Association decided to undertake a definite war work program in cooperation with the Department of National Defence.[20] The American Bar Association had already organized such a program in the United States, and Canadian lawyers feared adverse publicity if they did not do the same. After consultation with Orde and provincial law societies, the Canadian Bar Association designated prominent civilian lawyers in each military district as honorary advisory counsel with whom AJAGs could consult.[21] The arrangement allowed military lawyers to obtain expert legal advice without referring to Ottawa. The Department of National Defence incurred no expense because the Canadian Bar Association and individual lawyers considered the service as their patriotic contribution to the war effort. In 1943, Kenneth Mackenzie, chairman of the Canadian Bar Association's Committee on War Work, suggested extending the scope of the program to include legal aid to members of the Canadian Armed Forces and their dependants.[22] Orde accepted the offer, but restricted assistance to soldiers who demonstrated financial need in legal cases of a strictly personal nature in no way related to disciplinary actions, criminal offences, or pay and allowance matters. Applications for legal aid were made to AJAGs or the JAG directly; the applicants, if accepted, were then referred to provincial representatives of the Canadian Bar Association who participated in the scheme.[23] Matrimony was by far the leading matter, with nearly three-quarters of legal aid cases referred from the Canadian Army Overseas involving divorce or annulment.[24] Employing civilian lawyers spared the services of military lawyers for other important work. In effect, Orde used the Canadian Bar Association as a convenient reserve of legal expertise for the JAG office throughout the Second World War.

As a result of the war, lawyers and serving officers focused their attention on military legal education. Legal instruction was built upon Orde's earlier efforts within the militia. On 28 November 1940, the Canadian Military Institute in Toronto offered lectures on military law by Major Wilfrid Heighington, KC, an instructor with the Osgoode Hall COTC contingent and a partner in the Toronto law firm of Johnston, Heighington, and Johnston; Heighington's lectures were part of a refresher course for the institute's members.[25] Interested officers were referred to official books on the subject. Besides the 1939 KR&O for the Canadian militia and the *Manual of Military Law,* the 1939 *Field Service Pocket Book* briefly dealt with discipline and courts martial; Canadian Army training pamphlets included sections on military law and interior economy; and a reprinted War Office pamphlet explained the rights of an accused in custody and under arrest.[26] Officers were encouraged to study military law through further reading in official and privately published books. Captain Percival Hayman, a British officer with considerable experience as a prosecutor, judge advocate, and instructor in military law and court martial procedure in the previous world war, remarked that "many men in the ranks of the Army to-day have quite a sound knowledge of the general principles of law, and in some cases an expert knowledge, and it behooves the junior officer to watch his step – to say nothing of senior officers as well."[27] Sooner or later, every officer encountered some complicated aspect of military law or discipline. Gale and Polden published standard texts on military law by Lieutenant Colonel Stephen Banning and Major Harold Shurlock.[28] Appearing in several revised editions, these books explained the Army Act and court martial procedure in a simple and easily understandable way for most officers and other ranks. Fitzherbert Coddington, another author, perhaps best summarized the importance of military legal education: "A sound knowledge of the relevant portions of the *King's Regulations* in particular, and of Military Law in general, will not directly enable a young Officer to kill the enemy or to win the war, but it *will* help him to be an efficient and respected member of his unit. He will know his rights, duties and powers, and those of others, so that he will neither overstep the mark himself nor allow others to do so – and this knowledge of the 'rules of the game' should materially smooth his path in daily life and toward promotion."[29] Military law was an essential and significant part of an officer's career, no matter how brief it may have been.

The most popular and commonly used handbook within the Canadian Army at the time was Lieutenant Colonel R.J.S. Langford's *Corporal to Field Officer.* Langford, who possessed an intimate knowledge of military law as former chief instructor for the Osgoode Hall COTC contingent and commanding officer of the Royal Canadian Regiment, included a chapter on the fundamentals of military law and discipline.[30] His small booklet became the unofficial textbook for many instructors teaching training courses. Lecture notes taken by Corporal J.W. Mickleborough during a course in 1944 duplicated Langford's definitions of military law and martial law almost word for word.[31] In 1941, Langford collaborated with Burrell Singer to write a more detailed book on military law for the general guidance of civilians, soldiers, and officers. As the two authors pointed out, ignorance of the law did not excuse anyone from the consequences of their actions, and in regard to a soldier, the contention was "not unreasonable, since great pains are taken to bring the law to his attention."[32] It was the duty of all officers and other ranks to stay informed about regulations, orders, and military law in general. The Department of National Defence reprinted extracts from the British *Manual of Military Law* covering offences and punishments, arrest, courts martial, evidence, offences punishable by ordinary law, enlistment, relation of soldiers and officers to civil life, aid to the civil power, the Army Act, rules of procedure, and forms of application for courts martial.[33] Faced with wartime shortages of the British manual, the Canadian edition of the *Manual of Military Law* was widely circulated throughout the Canadian Army. Unfamiliarity with published orders and readily available books was poor justification for non-observance of Canadian military and civil law.

The university contingents of the Canadian Officer Training Corps also undertook considerable military legal instruction. Notes on military law, prepared by Major Clarence Young at the University of Toronto, explained the purpose and sources of military law, relevant acts of Parliament, regulations, aid to the civil power, discipline, offences and penalties, arrest and military custody, military tribunals, investigation of charges, summary and minor punishments, as well as the principles of evidence.[34] The intended objective of the small booklet was to provide junior officers with a convenient means to understand military law within a short period of time and assist them with the official publications. Brooke Claxton, an associate dean of law at McGill University, published for a wider audience similar notes that he had prepared for lectures on military law to that university's COTC contingent.[35] The advantage of a legal academic with an appreciation of military matters writing such a work was readily apparent. Fully referenced with the *Manual of Military Law,* the *King's Regulations,* and the Canadian Criminal Code, Claxton's notes distilled military law into an understandable and usable form. COTC contingents at certain universities also issued publications with sections on military law to help officers and non-commissioned officers in reserve formations prepare for qualification and promotion.[36] For the duration of the war, qualified teachers and instructors gave lectures and wrote books on military law. The universities provided an academic rigour to instruction in military law that was lacking during peacetime.

The heaviest demands on military law were made abroad in the main theatres of war, particularly in Europe. In November 1939, Orde designated Colonel Percival Montague as DJAG at the Canadian Military Headquarters in London.[37] The appointment was calculated. Montague, a graduate of the University of Toronto and Osgoode Hall Law School, possessed considerable military and civil legal experience as assistant adjutant and quartermaster general for the 2nd Canadian Division during the First World War and puisne judge on the Court of the King's Bench in Manitoba since 1932.[38] Like Dennistoun's two decades before, Montague's judicial credentials afforded enormous prestige in British and Allied legal circles. Much of his time in London was devoted to attending luncheons and giving speeches at various functions.[39] Montague's duties and legal staff expanded proportionately to the size of Canadian forces in Great Britain. In late 1940, the JAG's department was separated from the adjutant general's branch at Canadian Military Headquarters.[40] Since Montague concurrently served in various capacities with the Canadian Army Overseas, Colonel William Anglin, KC, a prominent barrister from New Brunswick who served as Montague's AJAG, supervised daily activities in the legal department and issued instructions to legal officers. The staff mostly consisted of lawyers too old for active service at the front.[41] Subsequently promoted to major general, Montague intervened only on important matters of policy. On 20 December 1943, Montague was officially designated JAG for the Canadian Army Overseas, exercising all the duties, functions, and powers of the JAG in respect of military forces in the European war theatre.[42] Anglin duly became his DJAG. The arrangement allowed review of courts martial, claims, and other matters to be handled with little reference to Ottawa. Since the headquarters in London functioned as an advance National Defence Headquarters, Orde gave Montague virtual autonomy in legal affairs affecting Canadian military forces in Great Britain and on the continent of Europe.

Military law issues arose as Canadian troops in Great Britain prepared for eventual invasion of the European continent. Other Allied forces, forced into exile by Nazi occupation of their homelands, continued to apply their own disciplinary codes, including in some cases the death penalty and corporal punishment.[43] The presence of Canadian troops in Great Britain under the Visiting Forces (British Commonwealth) Act was not exceptional. British courts intervened when soldiers committed civil offences, but the Canadian military generally administered its own disciplinary system.[44] Some problems remained peculiarly Canadian. After defending a French Canadian private at a court martial, an officer protested that interviews had been conducted in English, which the accused could not understand, and asked if "a practice which he [did] not think [was] in accordance with the spirit of Military Law [was] being slowly developed in the Canadian Army (Overseas)."[45] Legal staffs subsequently prepared official French translations of the caution used before interviews and the Army Act.

Lack of adequate knowledge about military law in the recently expanded army was a major problem. Among the tasks facing legal officers was imparting some knowledge of military law to "the hundreds of untutored officers who serve in field formations."[46] The legal branch at Canadian Military Headquarters distributed the British "Green Book" on field general courts martial and offered help to assistant deputy judge advocates (ADJA) in lower formations. Captain W.B. Bredin, an officer from the review section, prepared a guide for presidents at courts martial and delivered lectures on summaries of evidence, preparation for trial, duties of prosecuting and defending officers, and various features of courts martial to both junior and senior officers.[47] Canadian legal officers repeatedly stressed uniformity in the administration of military law. When Anglin submitted draft notes on military law for the guidance of the Canadian Army Overseas – nicknamed the "Red Book" – to the staff college at Camberley for perusal, the British suggested avoiding legal phraseology or complicated words because many officers were "now coming from the ranks, and whilst being good soldiers, are not always fully educated."[48] After a visit to London, Orde sent Montague and Anglin fifty copies of the *Canadian Handbook on District Courts Martial* for reference purposes. Selected Canadian officers also attended courses on military law offered at British colleges and educational institutions.[49] Circulars and a digest of rulings and opinions, prepared by the legal staff at Canadian Military Headquarters, facilitated practical application of theoretical instruction. Summaries of evidence, often prepared incorrectly in applications for field general courts martial, received special attention.[50] Instruction in military law was the combined responsibility of legal officers at headquarters and legal officers in field formations.

Unlike the British, the Canadians kept legal officers decentralized at the divisional level. The Canadian Military Headquarters reviewed courts martial to allow legal staffs in corps and field formations more time for pretrial advice and "education of regimental officers in Courts-Martial matters."[51] The British, on the other hand, maintained legal officers in a pool for employment at designated court martial centres. When a British major general suggested a common pool of Canadian and British permanent presidents for the sake of greater uniformity in court martial sentences, Lieutenant Colonel Thomas Norris, KC, the Canadian DJAG at the 21st Army Group Headquarters, responded that "uniform or equal sentences are a very bad thing, as of course each case must be decided on its merits."[52] Not enough Canadian officers possessed sufficient experience and knowledge of military law to sit as permanent presidents at a court martial centre, and ADJAs and AJAGs performed many other legal duties beyond simply court martial work.

Even without formal sanction, the Canadian Army's integration into the 21st Army Group's organization and common application of the Army Act inevitably resulted in considerable working integration between British and Canadian legal staffs within the 1st Canadian Army.[53] The Canadians often consulted their British counterparts for advice or guidance on particular cases. In mid-1944, Henry MacGeagh commented on the relative success of the wartime arrangements: "The fact that we have got through nearly five years of war with little or no adverse comment from the House of Commons on the administration of Justice in the Services is surely some tribute to the efficiency of the present system and to the administration of the Staff, approximately 90% of whom are temporary and have had to be recruited and trained since the outbreak of war, and which had to cope with an Army and an Air Force which has increased in personnel from thousands to millions."[54] Lawyers on temporary service performed the bulk of the work. JAGs in both Great Britain and Canada resisted considerable pressure from the civil legal professions for immediate release of lawyers from wartime service.

British influence on Canadian administration of military law remained persuasive. A revised British "Green Book" was the standard reference for preparation and conduct of field general courts martial "to enable an offender to be brought to justice with the least possible delay."[55] Differences between the British and Canadians mainly concerned the question of flexibility in active operations. While acknowledging court martial centres might be useful in static situations, Norris preferred having legal officers in field formations on the move since "the comparative novelty of the Courts-Martial Centre as a piece of Canadian legal machinery – glittering as most novelties are – has proved to have blinded those concerned to the very many draw-backs which are entailed, and it will later be realized that the Courts-Martial Centre is not the panacea which is sought."[56] For reasons of time and distance, administration of military law was most effective at a lower level. In due course, the Canadian legal staff at the 21st Army Group's Headquarters prepared a small guide for commanding officers on Canadian military law and court martial procedure.[57] Publications with a Canadian emphasis differentiated Canadian discipline from British discipline. Practical necessity in the field accounted for such texts being introduced so late in the war.

During active operations in the Second World War, the maintenance of discipline within Canadian fighting forces sometimes demanded infliction of harsh penalties. Military authorities possessed a better appreciation of the psychological effects of combat and battle exhaustion on soldiers, but courts martial still handed down unduly heavy sentences, especially lengthy terms of imprisonment with hard labour for the offences of desertion or cowardice.[58] The treatment that a soldier received usually depended upon the operational situation and the attitude of individual commanding officers toward punishment of such military crimes. The number and frequency of field general courts martial varied widely from regiment to regiment.[59] Reinforcement policies and criminal behaviour may have partly accounted for discrepancies, but deterrence remained the overriding concern of military authorities in the application of military law. Some officers favoured the reintroduction of the death penalty as a solution to the problem of battle absenteeism.[60] Although still on the books for certain civil offences, death had been abandoned under considerable public pressure as a punishment for most military offences within British and Commonwealth forces by an amendment to the Army Act in 1930.

Canadian legal officers proved reluctant to implement death sentences. Unlike in the First World War, the chances of a convicted soldier's being shot immediately after confirmation were slight.[61] Death sentences occasioned considerable review from Canadian legal staffs in London and Ottawa. When a court martial in Italy communicated a sentence of death (subsequently commuted to life imprisonment) to Gunner L.J. Doyle, Montague advised that a 1918 British administrative instruction on the subject was no longer part of Canadian military law.[62] Canadian military authorities executed only one soldier in the field during the entire war. On 5 July 1945 at Avellino, Italy, a Canadian firing squad shot Private Joseph Pringle, an absentee soldier convicted by a general court martial on a charge of murdering another soldier.[63] Montague felt that the circumstances of this specific case did not warrant remission or commutation, as was done in all other sentences of death within the Canadian Army.

In contrast to the Canadian Army, the Royal Canadian Air Force gradually asserted control over discipline within its forces sent overseas. Although Canadian units and airmen actually served with the Royal Air Force, the Canadian air headquarters insisted that the relationship with the Air Ministry remain "one of close liaison, but not of subordination."[64] Questions of policy were referred through the Canadian High Commissioner in London to the minister for air at National Defence Headquarters in Ottawa. As DJAG, Montague initially supervised legal affairs for both military and air forces. Differences of opinion occasionally occurred between the British and Canadians on proper interpretation of the visiting forces agreements in respect of the RCAF.[65] The Canadian government, however, retained the power of confirmation over all courts martial involving the RCAF. During a visit to London in mid-1942, Brigadier Orde and Squadron Leader G.G. Morrow negotiated a new legal and disciplinary arrangement with the Air Ministry affecting RCAF and RAF personnel in Great Britain and Canada.[66] Shortly thereafter, a qualified legal officer arrived at the RCAF overseas headquarters. On 19 January 1943, an order-in-council vested Wing Commander J.A.R. Mason with the powers, functions, and duties of the JAG over RCAF units in Europe, Africa, and Asia.[67] The RCAF attained a degree of independence from military authorities in the administration of air force law. The War Office, on the other hand, turned down a request from the Air Ministry to establish a separate RAF legal department on the grounds that it "would re-open the old agitation for some new appeal machinery, which for the moment is dormant."[68] Canadian air authorities still worked closely with the British. Court martial warrants distributed to RAF units with Canadians serving in them were no longer necessary after March 1943.[69] The change brought the RCAF overseas into line with orders-in-council already covering the West Indies, British Guinea, and Newfoundland. In 1944, the air officer commander-in-chief of the RCAF overseas issued a warrant authorizing British commanding officers not below the rank of group captain to convene courts martial for trial under the Air Force Act as applicable to the RCAF, and to confirm resulting sentences.[70] By doing so, the RCAF maintained both its authority in the disciplinary sphere and its close working relationship with the British in support of air operations against the Axis powers.

In Canada, the RCAF devoted much attention to instruction in air force law and court martial procedure. At the beginning of the war, the main official books available to air officers were the 1924 *King's Regulations for the Royal Canadian Air Force* and the 1933 edition of the British *Manual of Air Force Law.*[71] Works from private publishers also appeared during the war. An anonymous Canadian officer prepared a guide, modelled upon Langford's booklet for the infantry, which included a chapter on air force law applicable to the RCAF.[72] Brief sections dealt with various aspects of discipline, arrest, powers of squadron and commanding officers, penalties, and courts of inquiry. In preparation for courts martial or promotion examinations, many Canadian air officers referred to Harold Shurlock's detailed question and answer book on air force law.[73] Legal officers attached to the JAG office gave periodic lectures and courses in air force law. Citing British practice and reasons of practicality, Orde refused to countenance a suggestion that the RCAF should create its own legal branch, separate from the JAG office.[74] RCAF legal officers instead formed a distinct section within JAG's larger structure. Orde allowed Wing Commander Strathy and his air force section to handle most disciplinary and court martial matters pertaining to the RCAF. After the Commonwealth Air Training Plan was introduced in Canada, air authorities prepared a précis on the legal status of British and Canadian personnel serving together, for the use of legal officers in various commands; they also produced a short summary of court martial procedure for the guidance of air officers.[75] Under the JAG's overall supervision, the RCAF assumed responsibility for the administration of air force law.

The deficiencies of the existing regulations became increasingly apparent with the progressive expansion of the RCAF. In April 1942, a committee chaired by Wing Commander E.B. Pitblado assembled at the RCAF station in Rockcliffe to revise and redraft the *King's Regulations (Air).*[76] Air authorities canvassed all directorates, air officers commanding, and commanding officers of air units in Canada and Newfoundland for comments and criticisms. *King's Regulations for the RCAF,* incorporating changes brought about by the Royal Canadian Air Force Act of 1940, were issued in early 1943.[77] Whereas the old regulations were outdated and confusing, the new regulations provided a firm basis for day-to-day administration and the maintenance of discipline. Under Orde's direction, Wing Commander Pitblado and RCAF legal officers also prepared a Canadian edition of extracts from the *British Manual of Air Force Law* with the latest amendments to the Air Force Act and rules of procedure.[78] The RCAF, to a greater extent than the Canadian Army, recognized the importance of staff and legal training. Eastern command headquarters detailed administrative and staff officers to assist commanding officers on matters of morale and discipline between August 1944 and January 1945.[79] During the Second World War, the RCAF made a serious effort to disseminate information about air force law through current regulations, official manuals, and tours of inspections.

Unlike the other two services, the Royal Canadian Navy remained outside the fold of the visiting forces agreements. Both the Admiralty and Canadian naval authorities desired "to have recourse only in necessity to the provisions of this Act, relying normally on the pre-existing arrangements for the relations of the several naval forces of the Empire."[80] The Canadians accepted the British theory of a common fleet under a single Naval Discipline Act. In fact, Canadian naval officers stressed the distinctiveness of the navy from the other services in its close relationship with the Royal Navy.[81] British and Canadian naval officers remained interchangeable on courts martial when ships from the two navies served together.

During the Second World War, the Admiralty and the Canadian minister of national defence for naval services issued commissions to individual flag officers authorizing courts martial to be convened within their respective area commands. Where a flag officer did not possess such a commission, RCN personnel were drafted to Royal Navy ships or establishments for trial before British naval courts, commonly with one or two Canadian members. It is, therefore, difficult to say whether surviving registers of courts martial and disciplinary courts for the RCN include all wartime courts martial, since some sailors were tried under British jurisdiction.[82] Available records disclose a variety of offences committed in the naval service during the Second World War, including disobedience, striking superior officers, absence without leave, desertion, hazarding or stranding ships, indecent assault, theft, drunkenness, and fraud. The Royal Navy generally tried the same types of charges by courts martial or disciplinary courts.[83] Under the Naval Discipline Act and the *King's Regulations and Admiralty Instructions,* captains of ships and commanding officers at naval establishments wielded extensive powers of summary punishment. For the most part, legal prosecution and punishment were viewed as measures of last resort after all other sanctions and encouragements had been exhausted. The navy's divisional system put sailors "in the habit of obeying orders without question and without hesitation, since to fail to do so might some day be disastrous."[84] In ships at sea, deviant and criminal behaviour was seldom tolerated. Canadian naval officers in busy wartime ports, such as Halifax, also convened disciplinary courts for merchant sailors.[85] Although courts martial and formal legal proceedings were less frequent in the Royal Canadian Navy than in the Canadian Army and the Royal Canadian Air Force, legal officers were assigned to oversee the application and administration of naval law.

Small naval legal staffs were established in response to wartime demands. Beginning in 1940, naval reserve officers who had legal qualifications joined the JAG office. Promoted from lieutenant to lieutenant commander, Duncan MacTavish, a prominent Ottawa lawyer with the law firm of Gowling, MacTavish, and Watt, became an AJAG in May 1941.[86] He and other lawyers belonged to the legal section of the RCNVR's special branch. On 1 May 1942, the chief of the naval staff appointed Paymaster Captain Marc Cosette, RCN, as deputy judge advocate of the Fleet. Although not a qualified lawyer, Cosette dealt with matters relating to courts martial, disciplinary courts, boards of inquiry, and punishment warrants. The exact relationship between the deputy judge advocate of the Fleet and the JAG was left rather ambiguous.[87] The navy probably regarded Cosette's position as subordinate to the judge advocate of the Fleet in London since he was never a deputy of Canada's JAG. Instead, Orde appointed MacTavish as his DJAG (Navy) in December 1942. Lieutenant (N) William Chipman served as AJAG and Lieutenant (N) Philip Hurcomb became MacTavish's assistant. The DJAG (Navy) and his staff worked in the Naval Service Headquarters "making noises like JAG's."[88] MacTavish's physical separateness gave the illusion of independence, but Orde, as in the case of the RCAF, never condoned a detached RCN legal branch. While sometimes disagreeing with the JAG on certain legal points, both Cosette and MacTavish consulted Orde about complications arising from naval courts martial or disciplinary courts. The arrangement existed because Orde delegated the bulk of work associated with the disciplinary side of the RCN so that the JAG's office could cope with the ever-increasing demands placed upon it. In late 1945, Hurcomb was designated judge advocate of the Fleet after Cosette's retirement and MacTavish's demobilization with the rest of the wartime lawyers.

Like so many other fields of activity, the RCN gave as much notice to instruction in naval law and court martial procedure as permitted by wartime exigencies and the rapid expansion of the tiny Canadian naval force into a fully fledged navy. Lack of proper secretariat and administrative staffs resulted in complete reorganization of the Naval Service Headquarters in 1940. The RCN's paymaster and accounting branch accepted probationary paymaster sub-lieutenants directly from the volunteer reserve divisions. A lecture on naval law and articles of war in the RCNVR syllabus of training stressed the positive aspects of the naval justice system: "Our discussion of Naval Law should not leave any impression that the Naval Discipline Act and *King's Regulations and Admiralty Instructions* contain only restrictions and punishments. Nothing is further from the truth. Impartial justice is meted out with fairness to all. In short, they are very human regulations, based on long experience and great understanding. Under them life in the Service can be carried on with happiness and contentment, coupled with a comfortable feeling of security."[89]

Wartime pressures necessarily restricted the scope and amount of legal instruction. Since there was insufficient time for new officers to acquire the full range of expertise required of accountant officers, a certain amount of specialization occurred "with the result that knowledge of all regulations and particularly discipline and court martial procedure have been neglected."[90] As the operational and personnel situation stabilized, naval authorities attempted to correct the deficiency. Make-up courses at the accountant training school located at HMCS *Cornwallis* covered deprivation of good conduct badges, offences and punishments, desertion, naval courts martial, disciplinary courts, and boards of inquiry.[91] After successful completion, accountant officers returned to ships and naval establishments to assume responsibility for courts martial and training of junior officers.

The overall legal knowledge of those involved in the administration of naval justice was crucial. Some wartime naval officers in the executive, paymaster, and special branches were practising lawyers in civilian life.[92] They drew upon formal legal training and previous experience in the law in the application of naval justice. Nonetheless, the vast majority of naval officers relied mostly on lecture notes and available reference books. In addition to official publications, Canadian naval officers commonly consulted wartime editions of a book by Paymaster Captain Arthur Duckworth, RN, which presented "to the naval officer at the outset a bold outline of court-martial procedure from beginning to end."[93] Canadian and British procedures were almost identical. In fact, Naval Service Headquarters obtained papers for Part II of the examinations for the rank of paymaster lieutenant commander, which included naval and court martial procedure, from the Admiralty and returned them for marking to the Royal Navy's supply and secretariat school, HMS *Demetrius,* at Whetherby, Yorkshire.[94] Nevertheless, the RCN perhaps went further during the Second World War than the other two services in drafting distinctly Canadian disciplinary regulations.

This anomaly was more by accident than by design. At the outbreak of the war, the RCN was subject to the British *King's Regulations and Admiralty Instructions* of 1938 and various Admiralty Fleet orders.[95] Regulations and instructions for the permanent component of the RCN had been issued in 1937. Revised editions incorporating various amendments then appeared in 1940 and 1942.[96] The RCN's regulations were not as comprehensive as those for either the Canadian militia or the RCAF. As with separate regulations for the Royal Canadian Naval Reserve and Royal Canadian Naval

Volunteer Reserve, a chapter on discipline within the RCN regulations merely applied the Naval Discipline Act and the *King's Regulations and Admiralty Instructions* to Canadian naval personnel.[97] Consequently, Canadian naval officers generally referred to the latter for courts martial and other disciplinary matters. The Naval Service Headquarters issued a Canadian reprint of the British *King's Regulations and Admiralty Instructions* in January 1942.[98] Since this publication was in no way adapted to Canadian circumstances, the secretary of the Naval Board was made responsible for producing completely new Canadian naval regulations.

After some false starts, the secretary of the Naval Board decided that the job required an appointed revision committee. It was similar in nature to the recent committee that undertook revision of the RCAF regulations.[99] Naval Service Headquarters established the Regulations Revision Committee on 15 November 1943, with Commander Horace Read, RCNVR, as vice-chair. Directly responsible to the minister of national defence for the naval service, this committee canvassed the directorates and the navy as whole for suggestions on how to improve the regulations governing the RCN. In order to provide better statutory authority for the proposed regulations, Parliament passed the Naval Service Act in August 1944.[100] This legislation and its accompanying regulations superseded the Naval Discipline Act and the *King's Regulations and Admiralty Instructions*. The Regulations Revision Committee attempted to finish the regulations before 1 July 1945.[101] Printing delays and last minute amendments, however, prolonged the process. Consequently, the new *King's Regulations* for the government of the RCN were not actually promulgated until after the end of the war.[102] The Naval Service Act officially came into effect on 7 September 1945. The Royal Canadian Navy was the first of the three Canadian services to fall under the disciplinary provisions of wholly Canadian legislation rather than British statutes.

At the end of the war, the JAG and Canadian legal officers also became involved in war crimes trials for offences against members of the Canadian Armed Forces. Even before rumours of German atrocities during the Normandy campaign reached Canada, the cabinet had established an interdepartmental war crimes advisory committee, which included members from the Department of National Defence and the JAG office.[103] Canadians aspired to an active part in the investigation and prosecution of war crimes. In London, a war crimes investigation unit under the direction of Lieutenant Colonel Bruce Macdonald, a lawyer from Windsor and former president of a war crimes court of inquiry at SHAEF (Supreme Headquarters Allied Expeditionary Force), examined 171 cases of alleged improprieties against Canadian service personnel.[104] Canada and other Allied countries worked through the United Nations War Crimes Commission. Anglin and service authorities consulted closely with Vincent Massey, the Canadian representative on the commission and Canada's high commissioner in London.[105] The British attorney general and treasury solicitor drafted a royal warrant for convening war crimes trials in British-occupied Germany. At a meeting with Massey and Macdonald, David Maxwell Fyfe suggested that the Canadian government could, under the British royal warrant but with a court composed of Canadian officers, prosecute Kurt Meyer, former commander of the 12th SS Panzer Regiment and a suspect in the killing of Canadian soldiers in Normandy.[106] The Canadians decided against the offer and asked instead for a copy of the draft royal warrant through the Dominions Office. Using the British royal warrant as a model, Macdonald, Strathy, and Wing Commander E.R. Hopkins drafted Canadian regulations for the trial of alleged war criminals.[107] An order-in-council brought the regulations into effect on 30 August 1945. Thus Canadian war crimes trials in occupied Germany took place under Canadian law and regulations.

Only a small number of the cases investigated by Canadian legal officers actually proceeded to trial. Canadian military and air force authorities held several war crimes trials in Aurich, Germany during late 1945 and early 1946.[108] All prosecutions involved the murder and mistreatment of Canadian soldiers and airmen. Despite a skilful defence by Lieutenant Colonel Maurice Andrew of the Perth Regiment, a Canadian military court convicted Meyer for his responsibility in the killing of eighteen Canadian prisoners of war at his field headquarters in the Abbaye d'Ardenne, and sentenced the SS general to death.[109] Even with an apparent conflict of interest from his earlier investigations, Macdonald headed the Canadian prosecution team in the case against Meyer. After consulting with Orde and Massey, Major General Chris Vokes, the confirming authority, commuted Meyer's sentence to life imprisonment.[110] The air officer commander-in-chief, Air Marshal George Owen Johnson, felt no such mistaken pangs of conscience after subsequent trials. During March and April 1946, the RCAF convicted and executed four Germans: Wilhelm Jung, Johann Schumacher, Robert Holzer, and Walter Weigel.[111] Wilhelm Ossenbach and Johann Nietz, two other Germans convicted of crimes against Canadian air personnel, served terms of imprisonment in Germany. Both men submitted numerous pleas for clemency to the Canadian government.[112] On the advice of air authorities and Orde, all petitions were turned down outright.

Over the course of 1946, Canadian occupation forces and legal staffs quickly withdrew from Germany. After talks with the Canadian high commissioner, British authorities assumed responsibility for the custody of Canadian prisoners and prosecution of further Canadian war crimes cases.[113] Canadian authorities reserved the right to consider appeals, presumably in close consultation with the British. On 20 January 1949, British authorities hanged two former members of the 12th SS Panzer Regiment, Bernhard Siebken and Dietrich Schnabel, after their conviction by a British military court for the execution-style killing of three wounded Canadian soldiers at Le Mesnil Patry in Normandy during the summer of 1944.[114] The pair undoubtedly deserved their punishment, but more senior German commanders, equally implicated in outrageous crimes against Canadian service personnel, escaped prosecution. Wilhelm Mohnke, an SS armoured commander who was almost certainly personally responsible for the massacre of more than 200 Canadian soldiers, was never brought to trial because he was in Soviet captivity at the end of the war.[115] The Canadian government, sensitive about its relations with the new Federal Republic of Germany, repeatedly declined to ask for his extradition. Meyer, Mohnke's compatriot in arms, was released on 7 September 1954 after serving only part of his life sentence at Dorchester penitentiary in New Brunswick and the Allied National Prison in Werl, West Germany.[116] Despite numerous pleas from Canadian veterans and the regiments involved, Germans involved in improprieties against Canadians and never brought to trial in the immediate postwar period escaped deserved punishment or acknowledgment of their crimes.

Recent efforts by a war crimes section within the Department of Justice have focused almost exclusively on the extradition of alleged war criminals from Canada for trial elsewhere, usually in Eastern Europe, rather than reopening existing cases of alleged acts against Canadian soldiers. Documentary evidence to support such prosecutions was strong, but the political will was not forthcoming and ambitious lawyers within the Department of Justice, more often concerned about their individual careers, perceived no eminence in the Canadian cases. The Department of Justice was content to pursue war crimes cases with no immediate relevance to Canada, other than that particular immigrants might have entered the country under false pretences. The whole enterprise was little more than a ruse to convince the public that the Canadian government was truly serious about the prosecution of war crimes after embarrassing findings by a commission of inquiry in 1986.[117] Meanwhile, Wilhelm Mohnke remained free in Germany without the worry of prosecution for his despicable crimes. Where was the justice for the Canadian soldiers murdered by the SS in Normandy during that summer of 1944? The Canadian government's promise of a tough stance on war criminals rang hollow in the case of Wilhelm Mohnke.

The experience with war crimes in the Second World War demonstrated the importance of a good knowledge of military law among senior Canadian officers and the vital importance of prompt prosecution. Vokes allowed sentimentality to cloud his judgment in the Meyer case; Johnson, on the other hand, knew the law well and recognized the gravity of the offences against RCAF aircrew. To be effective as a deterrent, the punishment of war crimes required timely prosecution and severe penalties. The victor's justice meted out was harsh but appropriate for persons who flouted the recognized customs and rules of war. The murder of Canadian service personnel warranted the death sentences passed by Canadian military courts. By not executing Meyer or prosecuting Mohnke, the Canadian Armed Forces failed to punish serious military crimes in the proper way. Failure to do so sent the wrong message to individuals who behaved callously and ruthlessly on the battlefield, contravening all existing law and custom relating to the conduct of war.[118] Clearly, the determination to reproach atrocities and misconduct faded with the passing of time and memories. Thus the best opportunity to prosecute war crimes was immediately after a conflict, not forty or fifty years after the fact. Otherwise, effective prosecution or punishment could not be guaranteed. War crimes trials constituted a new and novel assignment for Canadian military lawyers, most of whom remained engaged in administrative or military justice work.

A major task for Canadian legal authorities was the review of outstanding courts martial sentences against Canadian service personnel arising from the Second World War. Shortly before the end of hostilities, the cabinet informed members of the three services that a general amnesty at the war's termination was not in the public interest.[119] Officials feared the adverse effect such an amnesty might have on the maintenance of discipline if soldiers believed that they could commit military crimes or misbehave with virtual immunity. In retrospect, the concern probably had some justification. On V-E day, Canadian service personnel went on a drunken rampage of looting in Halifax, for which a royal commission assigned much of the blame, deservedly or not, to the port's naval commander, Rear Admiral Leonard Murray, RCN.[120] The JAG dealt with the aftermath of the Halifax riot and demobilization disturbances of a similar scale affecting the Canadian Army in Great Britain. Where appropriate, naval and military authorities convened courts martial for the prosecution of individual offenders or ringleaders. In November 1945, the minister of national defence established a courts martial review board, with Justice John Keiller MacKay of the Supreme Court of Ontario as chairman and Major General Thomas Louis Tremblay and Colonel Nolan as members.[121] The three men examined all courts martial sentences of penal servitude, imprisonment, and detention over ninety days handed down to service personnel in and out of Canada and made recommendations to appropriate military authorities whether particular cases required mitigation, commutation, remission, or suspension of sentences. Orde also ruled that the minister of national defence retained authority under the Army and Air Force Acts to remit sentences from previous courts martial.[122] In this way, Canadian service personnel in prison for wartime offences were gradually released into civil life.

The Canadian Armed Forces wound down their legal activities overseas. After the reduction of the Canadian Military Headquarters in London toward the end of 1946, British authorities issued instructions for the return of deserters or absentees apprehended in Great Britain, Germany, and Austria so "that the soldier may be tried on his arrival in Canada."[123] A general pardon for these truants was not implemented until the new National Defence Act was introduced in June 1950. The Canadian Armed Forces and the JAG office faced new conditions and new enemies in the immediate postwar period.

5
Under the National Defence Act

After the Second World War, the Canadian Armed Forces retained a far larger legal establishment than in previous peacetime. Military lawyers oversaw administration of military justice within the three services. As the JAG challenged a proposal from the chief of the general staff for partial civilianization of the military's legal office, a National Defence Act and uniform regulations applicable to all three services were prepared at the direction of the minister of national defence. Canadian authorities closely watched reforms to military law in the United States and Great Britain. A commission of inquiry also convened to examine disciplinary problems within the RCN. Canadian troops deployed during the Korean War and in Western Europe as part of Canada's contribution to NATO came under the new disciplinary code's provisions. Cold War demands and alliance commitments kept the Canadian Armed Forces at inflated force levels. Promotion examinations constituted the main means of ensuring that officers possessed sufficient knowledge of military law after Canadian service colleges and universities stopped teaching the subject on a formal basis. Amendments to the National Defence Act and a single set of service regulations resulted from the unification of the Canadian Armed Forces in 1968.

The JAG office was placed on a fixed personnel basis in the immediate postwar period. Considerable reorganization and reductions in staff accompanied the demobilization of Canada's large wartime Armed Forces.[1] Lawyers on temporary service in the military returned to civil law practices. Orde retained legal officers to handle matters arising from the war and various legal aspects of the Armed Forces, but he underestimated the volume of work that would be referred to his office.[2] In addition to his normal disciplinary and court martial duties, the JAG administered legal aid, served legal documents on service personnel, screened applications for inventions and patents, oversaw application of the Militia Pension Act as president of the Pension and Claims Board, approved contracts, provided lectures on military law to the Royal Military College of Canada and schools of instruction, drafted regulations and orders-in-council, and on 31 August 1947, became director of estates. Orde found that "it was barely possible to keep pace with the work which had to be performed."[3] In October 1946, the JAG office consisted of Orde, two DJAGs (one army and one air force), nine AJAGs (five army, one navy, three air force), two legal officers (one army and one air force), one administrative officer, and nine service lawyers (five army, three air force, one navy) at National Defence Headquarters and various commands.

Since the workload showed no signs of abating, the JAG sought increases to his staff. Orde asked Major General Ernest Geoffrey Weeks, the adjutant general, for additional qualified legal officers, irrespective of service affiliation.[4] After a visit to Western Canada, Orde decided to proceed with integration of legal services for the army and air force in several commands and districts. His request for an AJAG in Alberta, however, was turned down. When the War Establishments Committee suggested using legal officers in the supplementary reserve or civilian lawyers on a fee basis instead, Orde replied that his experience with some 300 legal officers during the war "indicated beyond doubt that in respect of any legal services, a legal officer who does not measure up to the desired standard, is a liability rather than an asset and frequently gets the army into more trouble than would be the case if his advice had not been sought."[5] What seemed economical in the short term sometimes proved expensive in the long run. Difficult and complicated questions, Orde argued, continually arose in the districts and commands, and officers commanding required the best legal advice available.

Although Orde clearly preferred military lawyers, existing arrangements were clearly unsatisfactory. Court martial and other legal work often required legal officers to travel enormous distances within their areas of jurisdiction. Squadron Leader G.W. Brown, the AJAG in Vancouver, had trouble coping with even routine work since it simply piled up while he was working in such far-away places as Whitehorse.[6] Without additional assistance from some other source, regular legal officers could not administer military justice effectively. Time and geographical constraints worked against them. Orde was reluctant to employ legal officers from the primary or supplementary reserves because not all of them were willing to interrupt civilian law practices for military work. Consequently, military lawyers in the regular force were viewed as more convenient and dependable. Orde's leeriness toward reserve officers created a dilemma since trained and experienced replacements were not available in emergencies or in times of rapid expansion such as war. The response of so many Canadian lawyers to the call to arms during the Second World War perhaps convinced him that they would do the same in any future conflict.

Orde's attitude was peculiar because the postwar Canadian Army placed a great deal of emphasis on the training of its reserves, especially in regard to military law. In an address to the Canadian Officers Club and Institute in Toronto on 22 October 1946, Major General Chris Vokes declared: "There is only one Canadian army and The Reserve Force is its most important part."[7] To a large extent, the army returned to the pre-war relationship between the permanent force and the militia. The active force furnished training and administrative staffs to assist commanding officers and their subordinate officers undertake necessary instruction in reserve units.[8] A qualifying course at the Royal Canadian School of Infantry for senior non-commissioned officers in the reserve force included four instructional periods over separate days on the Army Act, arrest and investigation of charges, fines, forfeitures, stoppages, and redress of grievances, as well as the framing of charges.[9] Further periods of instruction at the local headquarters of individual units reinforced formal courses. A lecture on military law for junior officers noted that the subject was "a very big one and requires very steady study because the *Manual of Military Law* is not easy to understand and is not a very popular book."[10] Officers and soldiers required practical instruction because regulations alone were insufficient.

Since all officers required a good knowledge of military law, army authorities requested additional reference materials. The director of military training distributed a series of study papers on military law, prepared at the Canadian Army Staff College in October 1948.[11] Individual précis dealt with military law in general, offences, arrest and summary trial, taking of evidence, courts martial, courts of inquiry and boards of officers, as well as completion of relevant forms. As a supplement to official regulations and manuals, study papers on military law became suggested reading for officers working toward qualification or promotion.[12] The Canadian Army still remained closely tied to British military law. For instance, there was only one military law–related question on the lieutenant's qualifying examination in 1949: "The Army Act is an Act of the British Parliament. Under what authority are its provisions applicable to the Canadian Army?"[13] Continued and sustained instruction ensured an adequate knowledge of military law within the reserve components of the Canadian Army.

The JAG expressed more concern about recruitment and retention of competent military lawyers within his own office. The availability of legal officers with considerable professional and service experience from the war proved a mixed blessing. Pressing work demands and the limited number of personnel allowed Orde to keep only the most experienced officers with the ability to perform specific tasks immediately. Younger, less experienced officers were demobilized, and the Armed Forces made few efforts to attract recent graduates from law schools. Orde belatedly realized that the time would eventually arrive, "possibly in the not distant future, when it [would] be difficult to obtain replacements and adequately trained officers."[14] At the time, no junior legal officers were groomed or trained to fill higher positions of responsibility. Orde expressed some doubt whether promotion and pay prospects were sufficient to attract young lawyers into the JAG office, which was "in effect a law firm whose sole clients are the Department of National Defence, the three armed services, and the Defence Research Board."[15] Low attrition among senior ranks frustrated aspiring captains and majors, who were always tempted to leave the Armed Forces by the allurements of private law practice or other civil employment.

The idea that the JAG office constituted a self-contained establishment was a legacy of the Second World War, when the temporary employment of civilian lawyers closely resembled a large law firm. Unfortunately, this separateness was simply not sustainable with much reduced numbers. The JAG office was not a law firm, but part of the larger Canadian Armed Forces. Although Orde had earlier convinced the Chiefs of Staff to keep his office on a service basis, Canadian legal officers were in reality lawyers in uniform rather than soldiers with formal legal training. Lack of opportunities for advancement inside and outside the military legal hierarchy resulted in dissatisfaction and stagnation. To avert a possibly unfavourable situation, Orde asked the Chiefs of Staff to increase the JAG office's authorized personnel establishment.[16] The matter was duly referred to the Personnel Members Committee and the Defence Council for consideration.

Despite the true nature of the problem, Orde stoutly defended the military character of the JAG office. At a meeting of the Defence Council on 17 June 1949, Lieutenant General Charles Foulkes, chief of the general staff, stated that the best solution was to bring civilian lawyers into the JAG office at rates of pay prevailing in the public service commission.[17] Civilian lawyers demanded less in regard to promotion since employment in other government departments was a viable option. Foulkes still saw a need for some military lawyers, and he recommended automatic promotion to the rank of major after a definite period of time. The chief of the air staff suggested that the Personnel Members Committee examine the whole matter before any changes were made to the JAG office's constitution or operation. A memorandum from the JAG argued strongly against assignment of civilian lawyers because "they would inevitably attempt to exercise some sort of legal control just as civilian Treasury officers exercise a limiting financial control."[18] Although most legal officers in the last war were civilian lawyers on temporary service, the JAG contended that only lawyers in uniform possessed the necessary knowledge of service law, organization, and traditions within the Armed Forces to provide a nucleus for future expansion. While perhaps pertinent for courts martial and disciplinary matters, the argument ignored the fact that a great deal of the work performed in the JAG office corresponded to comparable civilian legal activities. As Foulkes asserted, civilian lawyers could do such tasks just as well as, or better than, military lawyers.

Since the Chiefs of Staff approved a recommendation that officers with legal qualifications be allowed to serve until they were fifty-five years old, the Personnel Members Committee compared career prospects between the JAG office and other service branches. The director of army personnel favoured a policy of rotating younger legal officers from the JAG office into corps or staff employment, but he asserted that existing legal officers were not suitable, either by training or through experience, as general-purpose staff officers.[19] None had attended staff college, their advanced ages precluded a normal career progression, and each knew little about the Armed Forces outside his own chosen specialization or particular field of legal expertise. The suggestion that JAG officers should receive some sort of preferential treatment in regard to promotion was an anathema to both the army and the navy. Military authorities worried that such a step might create an unwelcome precedent for other specialists and professionals, such as military doctors. Extension of the compulsory retirement age merely represented a way to compensate legal officers for otherwise limited career and promotional possibilities. Largely through Orde's persuasive arguments, the Chiefs of Staff and the Personnel Members Committee accepted the status quo. The JAG office remained on a strictly military basis for the indefinite future. The drafting of the new National Defence Act placed an added burden on Orde and his military lawyers.

The driving force behind the introduction of a common disciplinary code for all three services was the minister of national defence, Brooke Claxton. Claxton had served in Mackenzie King's cabinet as minister of health and welfare during the latter part of the world war and reluctantly took over the defence portfolio on 12 December 1946.[20] As a veteran of the First World War and part-time lecturer for McGill University's COTC contingent, Claxton possessed some familiarity with military matters. His small booklet on Canadian military law was still regarded as one of the best sources available on the subject. Although given a strong mandate from the prime minister to economize and consolidate the activities of the Department of National Defence wherever possible, Claxton was also a reformer. He sought to eliminate waste and duplication of effort in order to make the Canadian Armed Forces more efficient and stronger.

The main impetus for revamped defence legislation came from Claxton's desire for organizational reform and economy, reinforced by the recent wartime experience. Unlike Orde and McNaughton fifteen years before, Claxton provided the political will to make a single National Defence Act a reality. Not all officers in the three services welcomed the effort, but they recognized that Claxton was serious about a common Canadian disciplinary code and substantial reforms to military law. The sturdy minister squared off against entrenched interests within National Defence Headquarters and the individual services. As a first step, Claxton established a committee consisting of Elmer Driedger from the Department of Justice, senior officers from the three services, and JAG officers to draft a new disciplinary code for the Canadian Armed Forces.[21] Much of the actual work was done within the JAG office under Orde's supervision. Daily meetings over the course of many months covered virtually every aspect of the proposed bill.[22] After consulting with service members, military lawyers redrafted contentious sections. Claxton maintained a close hand in the committee's progress through weekly meetings to discuss concerns or problems that required his personal attention. His legal background and intimate knowledge of Canadian military law proved indispensable.[23] As one of the most able ministers of national defence in the history of Canada, Claxton took an active interest in the reform of military law. The resulting defence bill, which went through eleven complete redrafts over the space of three years, was testimony to the strength of his convictions. During the process, Canadian officials followed coinciding revisions to military law in other countries, in particular the United States and Great Britain.

In the aftermath of the Second World War, the United States undertook a comprehensive review and consolidation of its defence legislation. Various committees, panels, and study groups of civilian and military legal experts examined specific aspects of US military law and its application.[24] Considerable support existed within the civilian side of the US military bureaucracy for further unification of the US services, especially in the military justice sphere. In 1948, the US secretary of defense, James Forrestal, appointed a committee to integrate the services under a uniform code of military justice, modernize defence legislation in order to inspire more public confidence and better protect individual rights of soldiers, and update wording and legal phraseology in existing statutes.[25] Like Claxton in Canada, Forrestal was the mover behind major reforms to US military law. He took a personal and active interest in the endeavour and provided the political clout to ensure that the proposed changes were carried through.

The committee comprised officers from the army, navy, air force, marine corps, and coast guard, as well as a number of leading civilian legal experts, under the direction of an assistant general counsel for the US Department of Defense, Felix Larkin. Larkin's committee recommended uniformity across the services in terms of offences, trials, rules of procedure, other rank representation on selected courts martial, and creation of a civilian court of military appeals to review sentences and findings. After extensive amendments by Congress, a statute incorporating the uniform code of military justice was approved on 5 May 1950. Preparations began on a manual to explain and expand upon the new disciplinary code to the armed services.

American officers, of all ranks or professional levels, had traditionally relied upon manuals derived from the statutes and regulations in the practical application of military law.[26] These handy books included almost everything an officer needed to know about military law between one cover. The US Department of Defense distributed a manual for courts martial under President Harry Truman's signature, in effect from 31 May 1951.[27] In the uniform code of military justice and its accompanying courts martial manual, the United States possessed a modern disciplinary code applicable to all its armed services and the means to disseminate information about military law throughout the US armed forces. Although Canada's Department of National Defence closely watched the major changes to military justice in the United States, British example, for historical and practical reasons, remained overwhelmingly persuasive.

Given the nature of Canada's involvement in the Second World War and the coming conflict in Korea, Canadian military law continued to draw inspiration from reforms to the structure and administration of military justice in Great Britain. At the time, the Canadian Armed Forces still used predominantly British equipment and trained to British standards. Although approval in principle had been reached in 1939, the War Office decided that the Oliver Committee's recommendations be reviewed in light of experience with courts martial and discipline during the recent world war.[28] The British JAG wished to include all three British services on a new committee, but the Admiralty declined to participate. The first lord, Sir John Lang, hoped "to avoid having a formal examination of the Naval system by such a Committee, by a willingness to prove that careful consideration will be given to any recommendation of your Committee which might affect the Administration of Justice in the Navy."[29] The Admiralty still held serious reservations about changes to the existing naval disciplinary system and the position of the judge advocate of the Fleet. Although naval officers attended as observers, the committee remained confined to administration and application of military law within the British Army and the Royal Air Force. Like the previous Darling and Oliver Committees, the new committee included senior officers from the War Office and Air Ministry, interested members of Great Britain's Parliament, and a judge appointed by the Lord Chancellor as chair.

The Army and Air Force Courts Martial Committee, chaired by Justice Wilfrid Lewis, adopted a wide scope in the course of its deliberations. The War Office's terms of reference specifically allowed the committee to examine the desirability of a formal appeal from the findings and sentences of courts martial, the punishment powers of courts martial and commanding officers, and appropriate scales of punishments. It held thirty-seven formal meetings, interviewed thirty-seven witnesses, and considered more than 200 submissions. In a lengthy final report on 18 April 1948, the Lewis

Committee recommended making the JAG directly responsible to the Lord Chancellor, the formation of separate departments for legal services in the army and air force, the establishment of a higher court martial appeal court to hear appeals on points of law only, and better legal aid before and during trial.[30] To preserve the impression of independence in the review of military justice, Lewis and his colleagues advocated the reinforcement of delineated military and civil legal staffs within the British JAG office. While acknowledging that military law was predominantly administered by officers without formal legal qualifications and little experience before civil courts, the committee gave less attention to better military legal education, an area so strongly emphasized by the previous Darling and Oliver Committees. The report instead suggested employment of members with legal qualifications on general and district courts martial, an oral right of appeal against convictions, and creation of a pool of permanent presidents in peacetime. Although comprehensive in many matters of structure and form, the Lewis Committee report undervalued the importance of legal education among all officers in the proper functioning of military law.

Despite this obvious shortcoming, Canadian authorities were anxious to learn more about the Lewis Committee's recommendations. Canada's high commissioner in London approached the War Office through the Commonwealth Relations Office "to see a copy of the report as they [the Canadians] are at present introducing legislation in their Parliament which involves court martial procedure and feel that there is much to be said for harmonizing Canadian procedure to that of the United Kingdom."[31] British officials met the request, but a similar query from New Zealand led to the British House of Commons publishing the report as a parliamentary paper, prior to full consideration by the Army Council and the British cabinet. Canada, therefore, obtained foreknowledge of the Lewis Committee's findings before an interdepartmental committee, chaired by Albert Napier, met to examine the steps necessary to bring specific recommendations into force.[32] The British privately worried that the resulting Canadian legislation might adopt features of the report later considered objectionable by the British government; but there is no evidence to suggest that Orde or Claxton ever intended to blindly follow the Lewis Committee's recommendations. Claxton's parliamentary assistant, Lieutenant Colonel Hughes Lapointe, and Group Captain W.W. Bean travelled to London to learn more about the organization of Britain's new Ministry of Defence and recent developments in British defence legislation.[33] But the National Defence Act and organization of Canada's JAG office eventually differed in many fundamental respects from those in Great Britain. The Lewis Committee's report was instead no more than a helpful guide from which the Canadians adopted the recommendations they liked. As the Canadian Armed Forces had done in the case of the United States, they drew upon British experience and expert opinion in the absence of any comprehensive public review of courts martial or military law in Canada. It was not ideal, but Claxton recognized that neither the general public nor his own political party was interested in such an endeavour at the time.

Sit-down strikes aboard three Canadian warships in quick succession during early 1949, however, compelled the minister of national defence to appoint a commission of inquiry to probe the disciplinary situation in at least one of the Canadian services. Sailors on Canadian warships had refused to perform duty on previous occasions, but never before had so many joined such demonstrations of mass insubordination in so short a period of time.[34] The Department of National Defence was reluctant to describe these breaches of service discipline as mutinies, preferring instead the more euphemistic term "incidents." Claxton asked the commission of inquiry, consisting of Rear Admiral Edmond Rollo Mainguy, Louis de la Chesnaye Audette, and Leonard W. Brockington, to examine the circumstances behind each of the events and recommend specific improvements.[35] W.N. Wickwire, a prominent lawyer from Halifax, served as chief counsel for the commission, and Commander Hurcomb was assigned as assistant counsel. Travelling to both coasts, the commissioners heard testimony from 238 witnesses and accepted numerous papers and submissions.[36] In stark contrast to the present-day Somalia inquiry, the Mainguy Commission was a model of speed, efficiency, and economy. The three commissioners delivered a critical final report in October 1949, less than eight months after the last incident.

The Mainguy Commission identified several major areas of concern within the RCN. Disciplinary problems on HMCS *Magnificent,* HMCS *Athabaskan,* and HMCS *Crescent,* the commissioners contended, were largely due to organizational and personnel problems within the navy as a whole. Aggravated by the RCN's rapid wartime expansion and overwhelming British influence in officer training, a gulf had developed between Canadian officers and the lower deck. Treated in an arbitrary fashion and denied formal channels to air grievances, many sailors lost confidence in their superior officers; the reluctance of individual commanding officers to punish misbehaviour or insubordination when discontent accumulated only encouraged collective action. The result was a virtual breakdown of the divisional system on some Canadian warships. Cataloguing the various factors behind the incidents, the report recommended better training and educational opportunities for officers, more honesty in recruiting, improved living conditions and amenities for the lower deck, increased emphasis on a distinctly Canadian naval tradition, and reinvigoration of the divisional system.[37] The Department of National Defence was receptive to the Mainguy Commission's criticisms. In response, naval authorities ordered welfare committees established in all Canadian warships and fleet establishments "to provide a full opportunity and the proper machinery for free discussion between officers and men of items of welfare and general amenities within the ship or establishment."[38] The scope of subjects for discussion before these committees was left virtually unrestricted. Faced with an adverse report on its disciplinary regime, the RCN promptly adopted corrective and preventive measures to reduce the likelihood of similar occurrences in the future. The first and most difficult step was acknowledging that a serious problem existed within the service.

As the RCN considered and implemented the main recommendations of the Mainguy Commission's report, another committee in Great Britain examined the administration of justice under the Naval Discipline Act. Officers within the Royal Navy had followed the deliberations of the Lewis Committee with some interest, particularly the suggested right of an appeal from court martial convictions.[39] The Admiralty faced growing political pressure for uniformity across all three British services. The Lord Chancellor asserted that the existing naval disciplinary system worked "fairly well in practice, but there was no doubt it was wrong in principle."[40] From a legal point of view, a formal appeal was preferable to review in secret by service authorities. The board of Admiralty favoured an entirely new committee rather than simply a reconvened or reconstituted Lewis Committee so that members could "start their investigations of the naval field with fresh minds."[41] The first lord exercised considerable discretion in nominations to the committee. His short list included former civil and service members from the Admiralty who were not overly critical of the Royal Navy's disciplinary system and members of Parliament with experience in naval court martial and civil criminal procedure. The Lord Chancellor appointed Justice Sir Gonne St. Clair Pilcher as chair. Stressing the distinctiveness of its own disciplinary system, the Admiralty made a concerted effort to direct and control the Pilcher Committee's conclusions.

To a limited extent, the Admiralty was successful in this endeavour. Pilcher's presence gave the impression of unbiased investigation, but the hand-picked committee was never as judgmental or disparaging of existing arrangements as either the Lewis Committee or the Mainguy Commission in Canada. Amended terms of reference allowed Pilcher's committee to examine both the naval court martial system and powers of summary punishment afforded commanding officers under the Naval Discipline Act. Pilcher and his colleagues held twenty-five meetings, interviewed twenty-four witnesses, and accepted memoranda and letters from interested parties. In a report issued on 20 February 1950, the committee recommended changes to the constitution of naval courts martial; advanced training and practical experience in legal matters for supply officers; clarification of the duties of the judge advocate, prosecution, and defending officers; and right of appeal to an independent appeal tribunal – preferably on a service basis – on questions of law and finding.[42] To some extent, the Pilcher Committee merely reiterated the Lewis Committee's recommendations as they applied to the naval context. The committee had been forced upon the Royal Navy in the first place, and the Admiralty possessed absolutely no desire to go any further.

British naval authorities had already initiated steps to improve specialized legal education within the Royal Navy. From 1946 onward, officers from the supply and secretariat branch were encouraged, through full and partial subsidies, to train and qualify as barristers. And junior officers were selected to work for a specified period of time with the deputy judge advocate of the Fleet or in the chambers of civil counsel. The aim was to have at least one supply officer with legal qualifications in each command. After a further sixteen meetings, the Pilcher Committee produced an additional report, which recommended certain changes to the system of summary punishments.[43] These included procedural refinements, extension of the right by leading ratings to elect trial by court martial, and more attention in training establishments to the long- and short-term consequences of punishments. An official in the Admiralty's naval law branch, however, noted that the Pilcher Committee found "no quick way of recommending a simplification of this complicated system."[44] Summary punishments were still the main means of enforcing discipline within the Royal Navy. The Admiralty established a committee, responsible to the Board of Admiralty, to provide final decisions on proposed amendments to the Naval Discipline Act as a result of recommendations in the Pilcher Committee's two reports.

As the Pilcher Committee completed its work, the British government formed an interdepartmental working party to consider the reports from the Lewis and Pilcher Committees. This work was largely a continuation of the earlier interdepartmental committee, and Albert Napier again acted as chair. Members included the Treasury solicitor, the JAG, the judge advocate of the Fleet, and representatives from the War Office, Air Ministry, Lord Chancellor's Office, Admiralty, and Ministry of Defence. The working party considered four major areas of concern: a higher appeal court, assignment of permanent presidents to important courts martial, unanimity of findings, and other rank representation on courts martial for trials involving other ranks.[45] Since the Lewis and Pilcher Committees differed in certain respects, the function of the working party was to harmonize or decide upon specific recommendations. Napier and his colleagues were not averse to differences between the services if ministers "were prepared to defend the differentiation," but they viewed an appeal to a combined services appeal court or the Judicial Committee of the Privy Council as the preferred course of action. The working party urged against appeal to a higher civil court. Although the working party favoured a special bill covering all three services to bring the recommendations into effect, the Admiralty was in no position to proceed before fully considering the Pilcher Committee's second report and consulting further with Commonwealth nations who were still using the Naval Discipline Act.[46] Consequently, the Napier working party decided that the other two services should submit their respective bills to Parliament separately. Revised Army, Air Force, and Naval Discipline Acts subsequently incorporated recommendations from the Oliver, Lewis, and Pilcher Committees.[47] While interesting for the elucidation of general military law issues, the effect of these British deliberations on Canada became largely academic once the National Defence Act superseded British defence-related statutes.

By late 1949, the Department of National Defence was ready to introduce a single National Defence Act covering all three Canadian armed services. After the minister of national defence, his parliamentary assistant, and the deputy minister, Charles Mills Drury, scrutinized a bill submitted by Orde and the drafting committee, the Department of National Defence gave its final approval. Since Claxton wanted the new legislation passed as expeditiously as possible before the current session of Parliament neared completion, the defence bill was presented to the Senate first rather than to the House of Commons. In a rare appearance for a cabinet minister, Claxton provided a full explanation of the intent and purpose of the proposed legislation before its second reading on 8 November 1949.[48] The defence bill was duly referred to the Senate's Standing Committee on Banking and Commerce, which carefully examined its sections and made certain amendments. Claxton encountered greater difficulty in the House of Commons with his arguments for a committee to consider the proposed National Defence Act because the Conservative opposition wanted a standing committee on defence established, similar to one that already existed in the United States.[49] Claxton preferred the British practice of parliamentary committees with no fixed function. Although the Senate passed the amended bill on 8 December 1949, Parliament was prorogued two days later.

Claxton reintroduced the amended defence bill in the next parliamentary session. In describing the purpose of the bill on 23 March 1950, the minister of national defence stressed that "all provisions governing the armed services of Canada will, for the first time, be found in a statute enacted by the Canadian Parliament, representing the Canadian people."[50] The new National Defence Act, which replaced no less than seven separate British and Canadian statutes, was the largest piece of legislation before the House of Commons in the previous forty-six years. Although the Conservatives still pressed for a permanent committee on defence, Claxton requested the establishment of a special committee to consider the defence bill and two other related bills. He stressed that the legislation was more than just a simple consolidation. Changes included a single Code of Service Discipline, uniformity in the administration of military justice, right of appeal from the findings and sentences of courts martial, abolition of field general courts martial, and provision for retrial upon discovery of new evidence.[51] Having lost the earlier round in the House of Commons for the formation of a permanent defence committee, the Conservative defence critic expressed his party's willingness to cooperate with the Liberals on a special committee after the bill passed first reading.

The Special Committee on National Defence examined the proposed National Defence Act in considerable detail and made suggestions for improvement. The committee, which included many members of Parliament with previous military or wartime service, elected as chair Ralph Osborne Campney, one-time private secretary to the prime minister, secretary to the minister of trade and commerce, and former chairman of the National Harbours Board. Under Campney's direction, the special committee considered the defence bill clause by clause "in as reasonable a time as possible."[52] Over the course of thirteen meetings, the special committee questioned several witnesses, including Drury, Commander Hurcomb, and Brigadier William Lawson, who replaced Orde as JAG in May 1950. Lawson had practised law in Toronto with the law firm of Lucas and Lucas between 1934 and 1940 before joining the JAG office as a career officer. In the House of Commons, Claxton paid tribute to Orde's thirty years of service as JAG and described the defence bill as "a lasting monument to his own achievement and work."[53] The special committee generally clarified particular points rather than making wholesale changes to the proposed legislation. For the most part, parliamentarians sought to protect and increase the rights of the individual under military law.

Although not all proffered amendments were acceptable to the Department of National Defence or the three services, the National Defence Act benefited from the special committee's considered opinion. The bill passed third reading in the House of Commons on 7 June 1950.[54] Coming before the Senate, the bill again went to the Standing Committee on Banking and Commerce, which returned it without amendment. The defence bill passed third reading in the Senate on 20 June and received royal assent on 30 June 1950.[55] Implementation of the National Defence Act's provisions awaited completion of new regulations for the three armed services.

Canadian authorities prepared the regulations on a tri-service basis. While a service advisory group was revising the Canadian Army's militia regulations in early 1947, Lieutenant Colonel L.W. Sharpe proposed that a start be made on drafting a volume applicable to all the services "on the Legal side, particularly the discipline angle."[56] In view of the work then proceeding on the National Defence Act, the JAG took note of the suggestion. The Regulations Revision Advisory Committee, composed of the vice adjutant general, the deputy air member for personnel, and the judge advocate of the Fleet, estimated, on the basis of previous experience with wartime regulations, that complete revision of the regulations would take at least eighteen months and suggested formation of a Regulations Revision Committee of experienced officers from the three services to work under its direction.[57] Two officers previously engaged in drafting the defence bill, Wing Commander Jack Hollies and Major W.J. Strachen, became senior members of the Regulations Revision Committee for the air force and army respectively. At a meeting on 26 July 1949, Orde decided that a working committee within the JAG office would draft the disciplinary sections of the regulations in close consultation with the Regulations Revision Committee.[58] Although issued separately for each service, the regulations were to be as uniform as possible, with the same format and structure.

The coexistence of different committees essentially performing the same work was not without problems. The Regulations Revision Committee criticized the JAG committee's inclusion of verbatim extracts from the National Defence Act in the body of the draft regulations "which must necessarily result in confusion, particularly in time of war when the Services must expect an influx of officers with only a minimum of service training."[59] As Hollies emphasized, the regulations needed to be as simple and clearly understandable as possible.

Once completed, individual chapters were forwarded to the Revision Regulations Advisory Committee for approval. Last minute amendments to the defence bill in the House of Commons delayed final drafts for the disciplinary chapters in volume two. At a meeting on 31 August 1950, the Personnel Members Committee approved establishment of a tri-service regulations office, headed by a civil servant named H.J. Jackson, to prepare amendments and distribute explanatory material for the regulations after dissolution of the Regulations Revision Committee. Serving officers received a preview of the National Defence Act and the draft regulations during a course at the Canadian Army Staff College between 29 November and 6 December 1950.[60] The adjutant general advised commanding officers on the best means of disseminating knowledge about the new disciplinary code, but noted that the regulations still required formal approval. The draft regulations received endorsement from the Chiefs of Staff in February 1951, and departmental officials forwarded them to James Francis, the Privy Council Office's legal advisor, in an attempt to accelerate the final process. Claxton submitted the regulations for the Royal Canadian Air Force, the Royal Canadian Navy, and Canadian Army to the governor-in-council on 28 March 1951.[61] Defence officials had hoped to issue the published regulations by 1 July 1951, but printing delays and a contracted firm's failure to deliver binders on time postponed the effective date to

1 September. The JAG wanted an additional month to allow enough time for legal officers from his office "to assist in familiarizing the forces with the regulations."[62] Claxton, however, was eager to bring the disciplinary provisions of the National Defence Act and the regulations into effect without delay because Canadian forces were now deployed on active service in Korea.

Canadian troops went to Korea under the auspices of the United Nations. On 25 June 1950, North Korea sent a large invasion force over the demarcated 38th parallel into South Korea. The UN Security Council, at the behest of the United States, called upon member states to provide assistance in deterring this aggression. Canadian warships sailed to eastern Asia and the RCAF committed its sole long-range transport squadron. On 7 August 1950, Prime Minister Louis St. Laurent announced the recruitment of a Canadian Army Special Force, which subsequently formed the basis for the 25th Canadian Infantry Brigade. Over the next four years, 21,940 soldiers served with various military units in Korea and a reinforcement group in Japan.[63]

Canadian military authorities encountered a significant number of disciplinary problems with the Canadian Army Special Force. The adjutant general, Major General Wilfred Macklin, attributed a high level of military crime and absences without leave to "the overall lowering in the class of men being enlisted into the Active Force since the start of the Korean Incident."[64] Eager to fill quotas and under pressure from Claxton, officials accepted many men with objectionable backgrounds and little previous military training. As a result, Canadian soldiers committed numerous offences against service discipline and the Korean civil population.

The most regrettable incident involved the 2nd battalion of the Princess Patricia's Canadian Light Infantry Regiment, the first Canadian formation to arrive in Korea. After three weeks of heavy combat, the battalion went into reserve for two weeks of rest just north of Chip-Yong-Ni.[65] Lieutenant Colonel J.R. Stone, the unit's commanding officer, declared 17 March 1951 a regimental holiday to honour the birthday of Lady Princess Patricia Ramsay, the honorary colonel of the regiment. As a special privilege for the occasion, other ranks received a generous issue of beer and access to a large bowl of gin and fruit juice. After drinking heavily all afternoon, Private Glen Blank, Private Alan Davis, Private Donald Gibson, and several other soldiers departed in a jeep to visit a bawdy house in the nearby area of Chung Woon Myon.[66] Several miles from camp, the drunken group came across a farmhouse that they mistook as their point of final destination. The Canadians discovered not prostitutes but a farmer, several South Korean officers and soldiers, and two young women, one of whom was a sister of one of the officers. Instead of leaving, the Canadian soldiers began threatening and abusing the occupants.[67] After declining repeated proposals for sex, the women were punched in the face and dragged off, one into an adjoining room and the other to a veranda. When the South Korean soldiers tried to intervene, they were beaten senseless at gunpoint. Only the extremely intoxicated state of the Canadian soldiers prevented full completion of the rapes. Following some taunting from Gibson, Blank threw a grenade from the courtyard into the main room, killing two Koreans and seriously wounding the remainder. The Canadians fired several rifle shots into the house before jumping into their jeep and leaving the scene.

Canadian military authorities only slowly realized the extent of the atrocity committed. Responding to complaints from local South Korean officials, military police questioned the participants. Confessions were not easy. Canadian soldiers admitted being at the farmhouse, but they denied any active part in the attempted rapes or murders. Nonetheless, Blank, Gibson, and Davis were placed under arrest. An information release on 1 August 1951 declared that the three soldiers faced murder charges.[68] Colonels A.G. Chubb, C.B. Ware, and W.C. Dick arrived from Ottawa to preside over separate general courts martial in Seoul, South Korea's capital city. Military judges convicted Blank of manslaughter on 28 August, Gibson of attempted rape on 31 August, and Davis of attempted rape on 3 September.[69] Defending officers convinced the courts that the absence of intent, the drunken state of the soldiers, and doubts about exact identity justified the lesser charges. Although given lengthy sentences of imprisonment, all three men were released within a year of being returned to Canada.[70] Those implicated in the disreputable business at Chung Woon Myon escaped deserved punishment because military authorities were embarrassed to have soldiers incarcerated in civilian prisons for crimes in the field. Once the immediate need of providing a deterrent for other soldiers contemplating such behaviour was fulfilled and the general public lost interest, the Department of National Defence quietly returned the disgraced soldiers back to civilian life as quickly as possible. Contrary to assertions by some senior officials in today's Department of National Defence, the tragedy in Somalia was not the first time Canadian soldiers committed serious crimes against civilians during a United Nations operation.

Besides the high-profile Chung Woon Myon trials, Canadian military legal staffs handled a variety of work involving courts martial and other related matters. As AJAG for all Canadian forces in Korea, Major J.T. Loranger exercised the powers, duties, and functions of the JAG in the Korean operations.[71] He headed a small legal detachment at the brigade level for investigations, trial and prosecution work, and advice on review of courts martial. After 1 September 1951, all courts martial were held under the disciplinary provisions of the National Defence Act and the new regulations.[72] Canadian soldiers were now subject solely to Canadian defence legislation. During late 1951, Lawson accompanied Claxton on a visit to Korea to examine personally the state of discipline and functioning of military justice there.[73] The JAG conferred with unit commanders and legal officers in the field. Approval was eventually attained for the formation of a standing court martial establishment with permanent prosecuting officers, but no provision was made for defending officers because "as in the Second World War there will be sufficient lawyers on regimental duty who can be made available to defend on the request of an accused."[74] The number of courts martial involving serious offences in the field was significant. Between 1951 and 1954, the Canadian Army Special Force held upward of sixty courts martial, two of which passed sentences of death.[75] The majority of charges involved murder or attempted murder, violence against superiors, drunkenness, and theft. The outcomes of the cases generally followed the same pattern. Soldiers received stiff sentences at courts martial in the theatre of operations, but substantial remissions or mitigation took place after return to Canada.[76] The trend provided a strong argument for serious civil offences to be tried by civil courts in Canada rather than courts martial. During the Korean conflict, situation remained instrumental in the application of Canadian military law.

Disciplinary problems also arose among the troops who were in Europe as part of Canada's NATO contribution. Western leaders worried that the Soviet Union might take advantage of the hostilities in Korea by invading Western Europe. The NATO countries started the buildup of conventional forces and after Eisenhower became president of the United States, tactical nuclear forces in the region to deter possible aggression. Canada sent an air division and an infantry brigade group to France and West Germany. Under the NATO Status of Forces Agreement signed in London on 19 June 1951, the Canadian Armed Forces exercised broad jurisdiction over civil-related offences committed by Canadian service personnel.[77] Where crimes involved the person or property of a foreign national, courts in host countries often intervened. Canadian legal officers in Germany received permission from Canada's attorney general to seek advice from German civil lawyers on a fee basis for matters arising from the 27th Canadian Infantry Brigade.[78] Since the Canadians occasionally asked the local police or judiciary to waive prosecution, offenders also came before courts martial instead of foreign civil courts, even in serious cases. On 5 March 1954, a Canadian military court handed down a sentence of death against Private G.E. Mitchell, a soldier from the 2nd battalion of the Princess Patricia's Canadian Light Infantry Regiment, on a charge of murder for stabbing a woman he mugged on a street in Iserlohn.[79] Many of the problems encountered in Korea were repeated in Germany because the Canadian Army, in the rush to fulfil the NATO commitment, re-engaged many of the same soldiers. The result was a string of injurious crimes against civilians in host European countries.

The majority of cases, however, involved more common disciplinary offences. Charge cards disclose that RCAF personnel, in particular, liked to fly planes low and drive cars fast. Punishments usually involved varying terms of detention or monetary fines. After a visit to Europe in 1955, Lawson also proposed legislation to make dependants and accompanying civilian employees amenable to Canadian military law, especially in regard to charges resulting from motor vehicle accidents and drunk driving.[80] The largest Canadian presence was at military bases in West Germany. In 1959, Canada signed a supplementary agreement with the Bonn government in respect of foreign forces stationed on German soil.[81] This bilateral arrangement formalized the rather inconsistent and obscure situation under the NATO Status of Forces Agreement. The Germans granted the Canadian Armed Forces almost carte blanche authority to try Canadian personnel and related persons for crimes committed in West Germany. Under mobilization planning, the JAG earmarked two detachments to provide legal services for Canadian forces in Europe.[82] Since the National Defence Act extended criminal jurisdiction to forces deployed overseas, offences normally tried by civil courts in Canada came before courts martial. The lengthy Canadian presence in Germany during the Cold War made the practice almost routine for Canadian legal staffs. Over a period of time, the Canadian Armed Forces became accustomed to handling serious civil crimes by courts martial instead of civil courts.

The trial of soldiers for serious criminal offences by court martial made review by an independent judicial body especially important. The National Defence Act allowed a formal right of appeal from court martial convictions against both finding and sentence, and established a Court Martial Appeal Board consisting of Justice J. Charles Alexander Cameron, a puisne judge of the Exchequer Court of Canada, as chair and four other members: Bernard Morris Alexandor, Duncan MacTavish, Louis Audette, and Leonce Plante.[83] While service authorities automatically reviewed all court martial convictions, appeal to the Court Martial Appeal Board required application by the accused within a set time period. Appeals were not encouraged, but simplified forms at least made the process relatively easy.[84] Although ostensively civilian, the Court Martial Appeal Board remained strongly sympathetic to a military viewpoint. MacTavish, as mentioned previously, was the RCN's wartime DJAG, Alexandor was an AJAG in the RCAF between 1940 and 1946, and Audette served as a member on the Mainguy Commission. Other members soon joined the Court Martial Appeal Board: Justice A.G. MacDougall, a county court judge for Carleton; George Arthur Addy, a long-time militia officer and commanding officer of the University of Ottawa's COTC contingent; Melville Burgoyne Kennedy Gordon, commander of Ottawa's reserve force garrison; and Leonard Brockington, Audette's colleague on the Mainguy Commission. Reginald Orde, Canada's former JAG, subsequently became a member.

In September 1959, an amendment to the National Defence Act replaced the Court Martial Appeal Board with a Court Martial Appeal Court. During the next decade, a disproportionate number of members of the court possessed some sort of military background and previous experience in the administration of military law: Joseph Thorson, John Kearney, Thomas Grantham Norris, Angus Alexander Cattanach, Kenneth Gibson Morden, Louis McCoskery Ritchie, Arthur Louis Thurlow, George Eric Tritschler, Camilien Noel, Yves Bernier, Roderick Kerr, and Allison Walsh. It must be acknowledged that many of these men went on to distinguish themselves in the legal profession and on the bench after participating in the Armed Forces during their younger years, but their presence called into question the objectivity of the "civilian" Court Martial Appeal Court. Did officers and soldiers during the 1950s and 1960s receive a fair hearing upon appeal to a judicial body comprising such members? The available evidence is far too incomplete to make definite conclusions. Still, a reluctance to overturn or alter previous convictions appeared particularly prevalent in marginal cases where some measure of doubt existed. Whether consciously or unconsciously, members of the Court Martial Board or Court more often than not sided with the Armed Forces in appeals. Thus Canada's court martial appeal system gave the impression of independence and unbiased justice, but the Armed Forces still retained a great deal of influence.

Less pretence of impartial justice was made in regard to summary punishments. Under the previous Army and Air Force Acts, the maximum summary punishment that commanding officers could hand down was restricted to twenty-eight days' detention after proper investigation. For the sake of uniformity in the three services, the National Defence Act extended the maximum to ninety days.[85] Naval authorities firmly argued that the higher maximum sentence was imperative on warships because facilities for convening courts martial were limited. The Canadian Army and the Royal Canadian Air Force, therefore, received the same summary punishment powers as the Royal Canadian Navy.[86] Army and air force officers quickly appreciated the convenience of this form of punishment and tried many offences that had previously necessitated courts martial in a summary fashion.

The result was a progressive decrease in courts martial as the Canadian Armed Forces remained at unprecedented high levels for peacetime. In 1950, the 47,185-member Armed Forces held 249 courts martial; by 1959, the numbers were 120,412 and 49; and in 1964, they were 120,781 and 28. The most substantial decline took place in the army as officers liberally exercised their new-found powers of summary punishment, sometimes inappropriately and arbitrarily. Since summary punishments were not recorded in any systematic fashion, exact numbers are unknown, but many officers viewed their increased powers to inflict summary punishment as an easy way to avoid courts martial. The lack of formality and structured review in the application of summary punishments encouraged abuse and inequality.

The JAG was sensitive to this state of affairs. In early 1957, Lawson expressed concern over the substantial number of serious charges being tried summarily rather than by court martial and felt that because of "a lack of an appreciation of the principles of justice on which a trial should be conducted, a man may be sentenced to a long period of detention without a fair trial."[87] He suggested granting accused, irrespective of rank, the right to elect trial by court martial when commanding officers intended to impose sentences over thirty days' detention. Non-commissioned officers already possessed that privilege. As Lawson asserted, neither the US nor the British services (with the exception of the Royal Navy) furnished commanding officers with such sweeping powers of summary punishment. In fact, the trend was in the other direction – toward further limitation of such powers and increased judicial review corresponding to that available in the civilian world.[88] The JAG believed that his proposal took care of a glaring area of potential criticism of the military justice system and that the total number of courts martial in the Canadian Armed Forces would not necessarily increase.

The Personnel Members Committee opposed changes to the military justice system and referred the matter to the Defence Council. The Chiefs of Staff decided at a meeting on 19 March 1957 that existing arrangements were adequate because the services had no complaints and the policy saved a great deal of administrative work. The military, however, did not have the final word. The Canadian Bill of Rights, enacted by Parliament in August 1960, required the Canadian Armed Forces to make amendments to the National Defence Act and the QR&O pertaining to restrictions on summary disposal of certain offences and to provide greater access to trial by court martial.[89] The Canadian Bill of Rights guaranteed the fundamental freedoms of all Canadians to have a fair trial, protection against arbitrary detention or incarceration, and access to counsel. Whether service authorities welcomed the changes or not, Canadian soldiers, airmen, and sailors received better protection of their individual rights under military law. The Canadian Bill of Rights vindicated Lawson's earlier warnings. Canadian military law needed to stay abreast of legal developments in civil society. Otherwise reform would be forced upon the Canadian Armed Forces, perhaps not to their liking.

Despite the existence of the Court Martial Appeal Court and service review, the JAG and service authorities understood that keeping officers and other ranks well informed about their rights and responsibilities under military law was the best safeguard against injustice in courts martial and summary punishments. In an article in the Canadian Army's service journal, Macklin declared that officers ignorant of the QR&O could "hardly be said to be fit to hold Her Majesty's Commission."[90] All three services carried out professional development in educational establishments and training centres. The study of military law was part of the broader process of making officers and other ranks more proficient and capable members of the Armed Forces. Each armed service issued small guides or pamphlets dealing with aspects of discipline and the related subject of leadership.[91] These reference sources were not as comprehensive as the earlier wartime pamphlets and treated military law in an elementary fashion. Those interested in learning more about specific aspects of military law were encouraged to read the QR&O for that particular service. Unlike the US and British militaries, the Canadian Armed Forces issued no dedicated manual to explain the fundamentals of Canadian military law and the National Defence Act to service personnel. Without official sanction, some Canadian officers consulted the latest edition of the British *Manual of Military Law,* issued in three parts between 1956 and 1958.[92] While perhaps useful on certain questions of international law, the manual contained no references to Canadian military law, and was now, in effect, based on the law of a foreign country. Having moved beyond its previous colonial status, Canada was now a free and independent nation.

Why was a manual of Canadian military law never prepared? Service authorities appear to have considered the QR&O, kept up to date with amendments, sufficient for the purpose. The history of military law in general and the laws and customs of war were dealt with authoritatively in available British or US manuals. An interservice committee on joint training periodically issued manuals and pamphlets on law-related topics, such as the treatment and conduct of prisoners of war after capture.[93] But service personnel remained ignorant about the distinctly Canadian development of military law. No training manual explained Canadian military law in a systematic or comprehensive fashion.[94] This oversight was perhaps excusable in the larger Armed Forces, but few legal officers even knew who the first JAG was, how the JAG office evolved as an institution, or what historical rationale motivated defence legislation in Canada. An occasional lecture or address by retired legal officers, such as Reginald Orde, were often the sole sources of information.[95] In other words, the JAG office relied upon oral history to sustain its collective identity. Those responsible for the administration of Canadian military law focused on the mechanics of the military justice system and application of the regulations.[96] Not surprisingly, a great deal was lost over time, to the detriment of subsequent generations of JAG officers.

A working knowledge of military law among all officers was still the core of Canada's military justice system. Competitive qualification and promotion examinations guaranteed a minimum level of expertise in the regular and reserve forces of each service.[97] At every rise in rank, officers were expected to demonstrate a more detailed knowledge of the regulations and the application of military law in practical situations. In 1959, the military law paper for the Canadian Army's lieutenant to captain qualification examination asked specific questions based on eight situational narratives.[98] To prepare for the test, candidates studied questions distributed by service authorities. Legal officers in the commands also gave lectures on various aspects of military law.[99] Success in examinations generally depended on the amount of time the individual officer devoted to study and his ability to think logically and provide correct solutions under the pressure of time constraints. Although unpopular, competitive examinations were an effective means of ensuring a uniform and broad knowledge of military law among officers at every rank. The process was cumulative; exposure to military law started early and became continually greater throughout an officer's career.

Not everyone met the required standard. Only about sixty percent of officers who wrote the Canadian Army's militia staff course examination in 1959 passed the paper on military law.[100] The examining board concluded that the main cause was a lack of familiarity with the QR&O. Unless forced to study, officers generally avoided military law entirely until they were asked to defend an accused or they became a member of a court martial or board of inquiry. Sufficient familiarity with military law was important because officers were also required to instruct subordinates. The militia training program for young soldiers included six periods on military law and the National Defence Act, taught by platoon commanders.[101] A sure way to learn military law thoroughly was to teach it to others. Promotion examinations and the instructional role made military law a key element of military life. Between 1960 and 1962, over eighty-five percent of candidates who wrote the Canadian Army's lieutenant to captain qualification examination passed the military law paper.[102] Officers could not advance in the Canadian Armed Forces without a good knowledge of the subject.

Promotion examinations assumed added significance with changes to the curriculum at Canadian services colleges. In September 1948, the Department of National Defence had established a joint education and training program for the three services at the Royal Military College of Canada in Kingston and Royal Roads Military College in Victoria. A French-language military college opened along the same lines at Saint John, Quebec, in 1952. The services colleges offered a course of academic and military studies that prepared prospective officers for careers in the three services. Military law was originally one of the professional subjects taught to cadets by service instructors from each service.[103] Air force cadets learned military law with an air force emphasis, whereas the army and navy tailored instruction to their particular service milieus. Unlike the US Military Academy at West Point, the Royal Military College of Canada never established a separate department of law, but instead placed military law under the Department of Military Studies.[104] Instruction in military law became more tri-service in nature after the Regular Officer Training Plan (ROTP) was introduced in 1952 and the Department of Military Studies was reorganized in subsequent years.

Every cadet learned the basics of the National Defence Act, rules of evidence, and court martial procedure. Although a shortage of copies of *QR&O* made instruction difficult at times, commandants viewed military law as an important component of military studies at the services colleges. Yet instruction in military law virtually ceased when a reduced course of military studies was inaugurated in 1959.[105] To become a recognized degree-granting educational institution, the Royal Military College of Canada placed greater emphasis on academic subjects and curtailed military content in the overall program. Military law was a convenient area to cut because cadets took the subject during practical training in the summer and later on in their careers. For the sake of uniformity, the other two colleges followed the RMC's lead. Military law was not taught at Canadian services colleges in any systematic or extended way from 1960 onward. Canadian military law has virtually disappeared from the curriculum at the Royal Military College of Canada, unlike at the US military colleges, where constitutional and military law is still taught to cadets to the present day.

The decision to stop teaching military law at Canadian services colleges coincided with the progressive elimination of military law and military studies as subjects for study at Canadian universities. One by one, COTC contingents at individual universities closed down. Many universities had been reluctant to grant academic credit toward degrees for military courses taken through the COTC. Consequently, military studies remained marginalized within university communities. In the anti-war and anti-military climate of the 1960s, the COTC experienced extreme difficulty in just attracting students into military courses. After the COTC contingents ceased operating, university students still entered the Armed Forces through the ROTP, but military-related courses were taught during the summer months or after graduation.

Under these conditions, military law never gained a secure foothold in Canadian law schools. US law schools, however, under pressure from the US Armed Forces during the mid-1950s, offered a limited number of courses on military law and related subjects.[106] The draft and strong regular officer training corps at the universities made the American situation somewhat different from the Canadian; but resistance always existed among legal academics toward accepting military law as a legitimate academic subject. Unlike other types of law, military law was based on regulations and orders for a legislatively structured organization rather than on case law or legal opinions.[107] Military law was practical in its application, served primarily the interests of the Armed Forces, defied neat categorization, and to those unfamiliar with its background, appeared archaic. Canadian legal academics shared many of the same prejudices as their American counterparts. An occasional graduate student may have pursued a military law-related topic, but Canadian law schools refused to accept military law as a subject worthy of study in their undergraduate programs.[108] Professors who could teach military law were scarce, and interest among the student population was low. Consequently, the curriculum of most Canadian law schools excluded military law. The fact that prospective lawyers might become involved with military law, either as members of the Armed Forces or as legal counsel in administrative or disciplinary matters, was overlooked. Responsibility for teaching military law rested predominantly with the Canadian Armed Forces.

Despite the resistance of legal academics toward military law, the Canadian Armed Forces increasingly relied upon Canadian law schools as their primary source of trained lawyers. For several years, the JAG office had met its requirements with lawyers entering the Armed Forces from civil practice and summer employment of officers from local commands and units. Naval officers with legal training joined the JAG office after the RCN's supply branch focused more on the supply than the secretariat side of its work.[109] Under Brigadier Lawson, DJAGs represented the services: Colonel W.M.W. Shaw for the army, Group Captain Harold A. McLearn for the air force, and Captain (N) J.P. Dewis for the navy. Officers from the three services served as AJAGs, deputy judge advocates, assistant deputy judge advocates, and legal officers.[110] Vacancies opened as the JAG office expanded, older legal officers retired, and the supply of serving officers interested in legal work dwindled. During 1960, no new applications were received for available positions, and Lawson requested appointment of public service commission solicitors as a temporary expedient.[111] E.F. Coughlin, William McClemont, and F. Power served in the JAG office as civilian officers in the property and estates sections. Orde's earlier concern about civilian lawyers exercising some sort of controlling influence proved unfounded since they merely freed up military lawyers for other work. Lawson appointed Group Captain Hollies to the new position of chief judge advocate in early 1961.[112] The Canadian Armed Forces made concerted efforts to recruit recent law school graduates into the JAG office. Increased opportunities for foreign employment provided one obvious attraction for young lawyers. In addition to duty with Canadian forces in Germany and France,

Canadian legal officers were increasingly employed with United Nations peacekeeping forces.[113] Military lawyers found themselves posted to a variety of exotic and foreign locations around the world. Legal officers handled disputes with local authorities, negotiated contracts, advised commanders, and administered military law among deployed troops.

The Canadian Armed Forces also extended military assistance to developing nations in Africa. After a Commonwealth conference in 1961, military lawyers from the JAG office joined Canadian training teams sent to Ghana, Nigeria, and Tanzania. For a short time, Wing Commander S.L. Howell served as Ghana's deputy attorney general.[114] The Canadians filled training and administrative positions until African officers gained sufficient knowledge and expertise to handle such duties in a competent manner. Since some of these countries were new or aspiring democracies, military law and the relationship of the Armed Forces to civil society received special consideration.[115] Legal officers proffered Canada's experience with its National Defence Act and military law as a model for the Africans to emulate, without the taint of neocolonialism.

Despite the common British colonial background, cultural differences existed between Canada and the Commonwealth African countries. For example, a Canadian officer posted to Ghana's military academy asked a prosecuting officer not to call cadets "boys" during trials for minor offences.[116] Living and working in places like Ghana and Tanzania made a lasting impression on many Canadian legal officers and provided personal contacts with lawyers in foreign armed forces. Squadron Leader Peter Partner drafted Tanzania's National Defence Act, framed appropriate regulations and a code of service discipline, and trained the country's JAG-in-waiting.[117] A thorough grounding in military law assumed added significance because African militaries actively intervened in the politics of these developing countries. Tanzania's People's Defence Forces supported one-party rule until the early 1990s; Ghana's army staged military coups in 1966 and 1982; and Nigeria's military forces seized power from a civilian government in 1983. Whether Canadian tutoring left any lasting impact on the way African militaries behaved or organized themselves remains an open question. The training teams withdrew as greater emphasis was placed on bringing foreign officers to Canada for training, and as Canada's military assistance program was phased out in the early 1970s.[118] Besides possibly making contributions to the internal stability and security of the developing African countries, legal officers returned to Canada with a better appreciation of Canadian military law in a comparative context. While they were away, the Canadian Armed Forces underwent restructuring and unification.

Major changes to Canada's military had been in the offing for some time. The prospect of nuclear war with the Soviet Union predominated in Canadian and North American defence arrangements. Claxton's successors

Ralph Campney and George Pearkes (the latter coming in after the Conservatives came to power) redefined the roles of the militia to include training in national survival.[119] In the event of nuclear attack, the Department of National Defence intended to form mobile columns for re-entry into Canadian cities and target areas. The powers to be conferred on military forces were tantamount to martial law.[120] Soldiers were to console frightened and sick survivors, control crowds and refugees, and protect private property from looting. Training in military law at the unit level emphasized disciplinary control over troops, summary disposal of charges, and duties in aiding the civil power.[121] In the apocalyptic environment of nuclear disaster, military commanders on the spot had permission to exercise considerable authority, including using force against or shooting persons who eschewed military or government orders. Instructional periods in the block syllabus for the training of recruits and non-commissioned officers in the Canadian Army sought to "ensure that the candidate understands the legal requirements and implications of a proper military order, as well as the penalties for disobedience."[122] Military law provided the justification for drastic actions in times of extreme national emergency and possible nuclear catastrophe.

In 1964, the minister of national defence, Paul Hellyer, undertook a comprehensive review of defence policy to fulfil an election promise by Lester Pearson's minority government. A white paper reaffirmed Canada's commitment to NATO, North American defence, and peacekeeping, but emphasized increased flexibility and mobility.[123] According to the recommendations of a ministerial committee chaired by Brigadier E.R. Suttie, the militia was supposed to be a force-in-being for reinforcement of the regular force. Nonetheless, years of neglect and the sojourn into national survival training resulted in the decline of the militia as any sort of effective combat force. Hellyer, inspired by the experience with the white paper and a critical report by the Glassco Commission on government organization, went ahead with plans to completely reorganize and unify the Canadian Armed Forces.

Although primarily another step toward further economy and efficiency, unification of Canada's Armed Forces brought corresponding changes to military law. In August 1964, the separate Chiefs of Staff were combined into a single position with Air Chief Marshal Frank Miller as the first chief of the defence staff. The appointment was a prelude to the elimination of the three formal services and creation of an integrated headquarters under one chain of command. A bill introduced into Parliament by Hellyer at the end of 1966 sought amendments to the National Defence Act to implement reorganization and simplify or clarify the Code of Service Discipline.[124] Hellyer quietly removed the main opponents to the proposed changes among the senior ranks of the services through forced retirements and resignations. General Jean Allard, a more amenable and compliant French Canadian officer, replaced Miller as chief of the defence staff.[125] Parliament passed Hellyer's bill on 8 May 1967, and amendments to the National Defence Act were proclaimed into law 1 February 1968. Consolidated QR&O for the unified Canadian Armed Forces were prepared in consultation with the JAG.[126] Legally, the Canadian Armed Forces were now a single entity with a common Code of Service Discipline and single regulations for all ranks. Instruction during 1968 covered persons subject to military law, jurisdiction of civil courts, conduct of courts martial and summary trials, responsibilities of officers assisting accused, operation of civil law, and redress of grievances.[127] With unification, Hellyer brought Claxton's earlier reforms in Canadian military law to a logical conclusion.

Unification necessitated only limited changes to the legal activities of the Canadian Armed Forces. Military lawyers already functioned on a tri-service basis and were interchangeable as the work required. The JAG office exemplified what could be achieved in terms of efficiency and economy on a combined-service basis. Unlike other senior officers, Lawson accepted the rationale behind Hellyer's drive toward further consolidation. The JAG supported integration and provided the minister of national defence with powerful ammunition for use against critics before Parliament's Standing Committee on National Defence.[128] Hellyer appreciated the loyalty of Lawson and his military lawyers throughout the long and at times bitter unification struggle. Like the rest of the Armed Forces, legal officers adopted common ranks and wore the same uniform. After Lawson retired from the post of JAG at the compulsory age of sixty on 20 February 1969, Harold McLearn became JAG with the rank of brigadier general. Colonel Dewis and Colonel James M. Simpson were his DJAGs, Colonel H.G. Oliver replaced Hollies as chief judge advocate, and AJAGs functioned in regions throughout Canada as well as at bases in Soest and Lahr, West Germany. The JAG office, Canadian military law, and the Canadian Armed Forces as a whole underwent many tribulations in the decades following unification.

6
A Gradual Slide

An incremental erosion of capabilities and professional standards characterized the Canadian Armed Forces from the early 1970s to the ill-fated deployment in Somalia. Considerable refinement took place in the content and interpretation of military law, but serving officers and soldiers actually learned less in theory and practice. Legal officers trained other lawyers instead of general officers after a structured self-study and professional development system replaced promotion examinations. As Canadian military lawyers increasingly specialized, international law received an ever-greater emphasis within the JAG office. When the Canadian Charter of Rights and Freedoms required changes to the administration of military justice and imposed greater accountability upon the Canadian military, many officers responded with a mixture of suspicion and contempt. The Canadian Armed Forces made few attempts, either through published manuals or through formal instruction, to explain how the new legislation improved rather than hindered military law. Service personnel instead entered dangerous operational situations without a sound knowledge of their duties, responsibilities, and rights under Canadian military and civil law. Ignorance was a contributing factor to the disgraceful conduct by Canadian soldiers in Somalia.

The slow decline of the Canadian Armed Forces as a well-trained and professional institution began under the Liberal government of Pierre Trudeau. National defence was a low priority for the charismatic prime minister, who appointed a series of lacklustre ministers to head the department. At best, Trudeau treated the Canadian military with a mixture of indifference and contempt. Despite Hellyer's stringent economies with unification, Léo Cadieux, Trudeau's first choice as minister of national defence, imposed a three-year spending freeze on the Armed Forces and made drastic cuts in personnel.[1] With rampant inflation and further demands from the cabinet for economy in government departments, the Canadian Armed Forces lost ground. As part of a new direction in Canadian foreign policy, Trudeau also placed greater emphasis on sovereignty protection in addition to the military's traditional roles in NATO, North American defence, and peacekeeping; a white paper on defence ranked the commitments in that order of precedence in August 1971.[2] In spite of the new defence review, budgetary constraints still dictated the extent of Canada's defence policy. The Canadian military was called upon to do more with fewer resources.

To save money, the military and civilian sides of National Defence Headquarters amalgamated in 1972. A management review group that was commissioned to study structural problems within Canada's Department of National Defence recommended the organizational change. The powers of the deputy minister increased in the administrative and operational spheres at the expense of the chief of defence staff.[3] Military officers and civilian public servants became interchangeable in the higher echelons of the military bureaucracy. On the advice of the JAG, the JAG office was excluded from the reorganization.[4] Despite what critics have claimed of the arrangement, problems with the integrated National Defence Headquarters appear to have arisen from lack of proper accountability among civilians rather than an overriding civilianization or bureaucratization of senior military officers. The exact relationship between the two groups remained too ambiguous. When things went right, civilians accepted the praise, but when things went wrong, those in uniform usually took the blame. The pattern proved remarkably consistent over the next two decades.

The real problem was the lack of civilians in the right places. Unfortunately, frustration among military officers, who were already reeling from the fast pace of unification, coalesced into resistance toward any suggestion of more civilians or civilian influence at National Defence Headquarters.[5] A fact that is often ignored is that civilian public servants have played an active and important part in the administration of Canada's Armed Forces and formulation of defence policy almost since Confederation. Civilian control over the military is a cornerstone of a democratic society. As a perceptive commentator remarked on the US military's experience, professional soldiers could not "return to a golden age of isolation that never existed."[6] The integrated National Defence Headquarters did not introduce civilians into the process, but merely provided opportunities for more interaction between military officers and public servants already there. Civilian input was both necessary and beneficial. The Department of National Defence failed to delineate respective responsibilities in any legal or binding manner through amendments to the National Defence Act or some other legal instrument. Military officers stayed in posts where qualified civilians would perhaps have been more appropriate. In particular, the JAG office continued to be staffed mainly with military officers within National Defence Headquarters.

Military officers chosen as JAGs served much shorter tenures than their immediate predecessors. Contrary to the assertions of certain writers, the change owed more to the seniority and mature age of the most suitable candidates than to any deliberate attempt to open advancement opportunities within the Canadian military's legal branch.[7] Both Orde and Lawson were relatively young at the time of their respective appointments. McLearn, on the other hand, had been a DJAG since 1949 and assumed the higher post only at the age of fifty-eight, a mere two years before his compulsory retirement. On 13 August 1972, James Simpson became JAG with the rank of brigadier general. Simpson had joined JAG's ranks as a RCAF officer in the mid-1950s, worked his way up through the legal hierarchy, served abroad for a short time, and acted as senior legal advisor under Lawson before becoming DJAG. Simpson represented a newer generation of military lawyer. He was among the first legal officers within the Canadian JAG office to take a special and sustained interest in the international law of armed conflict.[8] During Simpson's term as JAG over the next four years, substantial changes took place in training, recruitment of legal officers, and the structure of the Canadian military's legal branch.

Instruction provided by lawyers in the JAG office progressively shifted away from maintaining a minimum standard of knowledge throughout the Armed Forces to specialized legal training for other JAG officers. In the previous decade, military legal instruction had been the responsibility of the chief judge advocate and his assistants, who offered courses on legal subjects to newly appointed or prospective commanding officers.[9] Students were divided into study syndicates with military lawyers as discussion leaders. This instruction was in addition to lectures and mock trials carried out by AJAGs for the benefit of local units in the various regions. As long as promotion examinations existed, teaching duties were accepted as a necessary, if somewhat mundane, part of a legal officer's normal work. Many military lawyers prepared notes and materials when called upon to give lectures, but comparatively few published these for a broader audience.[10] The quality of teaching usually depended upon the interest and dedication of individual officers. Colonel H.G. Oliver, Hollies' successor as chief judge advocate, and Lieutenant Colonel James Fay, the deputy chief judge advocate, trained junior JAG members in summary trials and the duties of legal officers at courts martial.[11] These seminars and lectures formed part of a syllabus prepared within the JAG office. Fay, who later completed a master's thesis on Canadian military law at Dalhousie University, ran a short primer course in May 1973 for new JAG members recruited over the previous two years.[12] Most military lawyers also attended an annual conference, held almost every year in Ottawa since Lawson's time as JAG, to hear military and civilian guest speakers. The JAG office devoted considerable time and resources to developing its own in-house expertise.

Making sure legal officers stayed in the Armed Forces long enough for the JAG to take full advantage of their training and experience posed a growing problem. As older officers retired, the JAG recruited lawyers through a direct entry scheme to fill its requirements, fixed at forty-four officers for 1973-4. Some recruits came from private law practice, whereas others were fresh out of law school. As was common in JAG branches in the US armed services, many of these new recruits viewed their time in the Canadian Armed Forces as a short period of stable employment to gain practical experience and earn money until a better opportunity came along. With a few notable exceptions, the majority requested release after completion of their initial engagement. As a result, the JAG continually trained legal officers revolving in and out of the office with little direct benefit to the Armed Forces over the long term.

Dissatisfied with the situation, Simpson decided that the JAG office needed a more stable source of recruitment. In August 1973, the Treasury Board approved funding for a military legal training plan, similar to those already in place for dental and medical officers, up to the 1978-9 fiscal year.[13] The legal plan accepted only currently serving officers in the regular force or the reserves. Activated in September 1974, the military legal training plan allowed "officers to obtain subsidized legal training at accredited Canadian law schools, for subsequent service as legal officers on the staff of the Judge Advocate General."[14] There was still no guarantee that such officers would not leave the Armed Forces once a further obligatory service commitment of six years was completed, but legal officers with previous military backgrounds were usually more inclined to stay in uniform longer. By 1975, five officers in the military legal training plan had completed first year at the law schools of major Canadian universities and were expected to graduate in 1977.[15] A candidate selection board, chaired by Simpson, met on 22 April 1975 to choose five more officers from thirty-two applications. As intended, the military legal training plan increased the number of career officers within the JAG office. Yet the effort sowed the seeds for a return to the promotional stagnation and limited career prospects of the late 1940s. More legal officers remained in the Armed Forces longer with fewer chances for advancement beyond lieutenant colonel rank or employment outside the JAG office.[16] Simpson eventually confronted the same problem as Orde had. Either the JAG office had to expand during a time of peace or job satisfaction had to be found in other ways. A combination of both inevitably took place.

Internal pressures rather than external needs largely accounted for the growth of the JAG office during these years. Simpson appointed, in addition to the positions then existing, separate directors of law for the areas of international law, advice, legislation, regulation and orders, property, military justice, claims, as well as pensions, estates, and finance. To a large extent, the new posts merely formalized a system that had previously existed on a less structured basis. The appointments, however, represented a definite increase in status for the selected legal officers and created sectional interests within the JAG office based upon particular areas of expertise. Military lawyers were rotated as much as possible to enable them to gain a broad range of knowledge and experience in all directorates, but legal officers increasingly identified with one field of law or another. Creation of separate directorates encouraged further specialization.

Some work proved more popular and exciting among legal officers than other work. International law provided opportunities for travel to foreign countries for conferences or workshops, and military justice often involved interesting and complicated criminal matters. Legislation, claims, training, and pensions – arguably more important activities for the Armed Forces as a whole – demanded the largest amount of time within JAG's office and rarely took legal officers outside Ottawa. The classic dilemma developed where those who performed the most detailed and necessary work received less recognition than colleagues in other, more interesting, fields. As the Canadian Armed Forces participated in peacekeeping operations under the auspices of the United Nations, international law became a viable career choice within the JAG office. Some Canadian legal officers began to call themselves international lawyers rather than military lawyers. The specialists gradually gained preference in advancement over the generalists.

The appointment of John Patterson Wolfe as JAG on 10 November 1976 reflected the increased emphasis on international law within the Canadian military's legal office. After active service in the Second World War, Wolfe had re-enlisted in the Canadian Army during the Korean conflict, completed law school at night at the University of Manitoba, and then joined the JAG office's international law section in 1954.[17] He assisted in negotiations for West Germany's entry into NATO, helped draft Tanzania's defence legislation, served as legal advisor to an international commission of control and supervision in Vietnam, and became deputy head of the Canadian delegation to the diplomatic conference for revision of the Geneva Conventions. Wolfe championed Canada's active involvement in reform of the international law of armed conflict to meet modern conditions.[18] His busy schedule of international conferences and speaking engagements continued while he was JAG. He attended UN conferences on the restriction of conventional weapons and revisions to the law of the sea. Leading by example, Wolfe created an environment within the JAG office for international law to flourish.

Wolfe's frequent absences from Ottawa meant that the other duties of JAG were often delegated to his immediate subordinates. Colonel G.L. Waterfield was DJAG, Colonel Frank Karwandy became DJAG (advisory), and Colonel Robert L. Martin filled the combined post of DJAG and chief judge advocate. Less than eight years after unification, three DJAGs once again existed in the JAG office. Pressure for the additional posts mostly came from within the JAG office rather than from the demands of legal work emanating from the Armed Forces. In response to the Canadian military's tougher policies on drugs and alcohol from the mid-1970s onward, courts martial increased in total number, but remained within manageable levels for a peacetime Armed Forces. The number of courts martial was certainly far less than that which Lawson's far smaller JAG establishment had handled in the early 1950s. The reasons for expansion were almost wholly institutional rather than operational. More higher-status positions increased upward mobility from lower levels, lessened dissatisfaction among senior legal officers, and encouraged officers to stay in the Armed Forces longer. Despite modest increases in pay bringing the level closer to public service commission rates, the Canadian Armed Forces experienced difficulty retaining well-trained and educated members with skills easily transferable to civilian employment.[19] Military lawyers represented such a group. During periods of low unemployment, the civilian sector placed pressure on the military's personnel resources. Interesting work, further education at the graduate level, and travel compensated for limited promotion, pay, and advancement prospects within the JAG hierarchy. Fields of legal endeavour that did not offer such attractions became sidelined within the JAG office. Instruction in military law was an obvious casualty of overspecialization and lack of interest among military lawyers.

Major changes in training and professional development within the Canadian Armed Forces facilitated the JAG's diminished participation in the education of general officers in military law. During basic officer training, all candidates took an introductory course in military law, arrest and custody, charges, summary trials, courts martial, and the Geneva Conventions.[20] Study of the National Defence Act and regulations was then required at each additional rank level. Candidates coming directly from the universities or elsewhere generally started with the same amount of knowledge as ROTP graduates because the Canadian services colleges taught little military law beyond occasional lectures on military ethics, the Geneva Conventions, or conduct during capture. As an alternative, the cash-strapped Canadian Armed Forces experimented with directed self-study courses, a less formal means of instruction based on uniform course materials prepared beforehand and distributed to students to work through at their own pace. Mobile Command used a study module on military law with some success in its professional development training program to give junior officers "an understanding of the special body of law and regulations governing the Canadian Forces and of the individual officer's responsibility for their application and administration."[21] A study package explained the purpose of military law, referred the reader to relevant sections in the QR&O and the National Defence Act, and included appendices covering the soldier's legal status in aid to the civil power as well as helpful practice questions. Correspondence-type courses seemed an economical and convenient way to teach professional knowledge that was previously covered in the theoretical portions of the promotion examinations. The Canadian Armed Forces was enthusiastic about the potential of directed self-study.

Faced with spiralling personnel costs and a high rate of failures, Canadian service authorities decided to replace promotion examinations entirely with a new training system, which incorporated self-study modules and attendance at formal courses later in an officer's career. In 1975, the Department of National Defence instituted the Officer Professional Development Program (OPDP), comprising a series of self-study modules in six subjects.[22] With some exemptions, every regular force officer commissioned after 31 December 1970 was required to complete the OPDP self-study modules. Military law was the focus of OPDP 4 in the first half or basic level of the OPDP. Additional lectures during courses at the staff school, the land forces command and staff college, the staff college, and the National Defence College focused on rules of engagement, the Geneva Conventions, and the various aspects of the international law of armed conflict. It was mistakenly assumed that officers became involved with complicated legal work only at relatively senior ranks.

Whereas the previous promotion examinations were cumulative in the expected knowledge of military law, the OPDP gave a concentrated dose early in an officer's career. But no adequate reinforcement took place after the officer completed the self-study module. And the incentive to learn the subject-matter thoroughly diminished once service authorities allowed students to consult the QR&O during the written examination of OPDP 4. Moreover, no corresponding increase in difficulty level compensated for the open-book nature of the test. During peacetime, opportunities for practical application of military law within the Armed Forces were infrequent, and the QR&O were consulted on rare occasions. Although the OPDP was expected to furnish a knowledge base throughout an officer's career progression, most officers quickly forgot whatever they had learned in the self-study module. Furthermore, the OPDP's military law component was prepared with almost no advice from JAG; the original study materials were neither comprehensive nor updated with subsequent improvements to the dynamic and ever-changing content of military law. As thousands of officers passed through the OPDP, the military law module proved increasingly flawed and outdated. Serious efforts to revise its subject-matter were not attempted until 1996, when the JAG expressed concerns about legal training of Canadian Forces personnel after the events in Somalia.[23] In respect of instruction in military law, the officer professional development system proved inferior to the established training and education system that it had replaced.

Despite obvious shortcomings in the new system, the Canadian Armed Forces extended self-study training methods to the reserves. After years of neglect and no clear sense of mission, the militia struggled for mere survival.[24] The naval reserve was better organized under Maritime Command, and a small air reserve came under a reserve officer with brigadier general rank after formation of Air Command. The reserves still attracted a disproportionately large number of teachers and students. A reserve officer university training plan, introduced in 1968 to replace the university naval training divisions, Canadian Officers Training Corps, and university reserve training plan, provided for training with reserve units during winter and at various locations under responsible commands during summer. Overall participation in the reserves continued to plummet. As part of a larger restructuring and revitalization plan in 1977, Mobile Command introduced the Militia Individual Training and Career Profile (MITCP) and revised content in the militia and command staff course, the successor to the old militia staff course at Fort Frontenac in Kingston.[25] The dual-pronged training program provided a logical qualification progression from lower to higher rank in the militia, distinct from the regular force.

Under MITCP, officers completed fourteen individual training blocks through courses or self-study before proceeding to the staff course. After several years of experience with the system, at least one Canadian officer involved in the program was reluctant to declare MITCP a success or a failure, but he noted that home study was an unmitigated disaster because the workload from block to block was uneven and reference materials were almost non-existent.[26] Of all the theoretical subjects, military law was perhaps the least liked. The QR&O were too detailed and complicated. Only a unit guide and a manual on the Geneva Conventions, both soon made out of date by two additional protocols in 1977, dealt with legal subjects in any extended fashion.[27] Militia officers received a poor grounding in military law with MITCP alone.

To provide a partial solution, the Canadian Armed Forces encouraged reserve officers to complete the OPDP on a voluntary basis. As the US-inspired Total Force concept gained more currency within the Canadian Armed Forces, pressure was placed on the reserves to train to the same standard as the regular force so that reservists could fulfil operational commitments with minimal extra training time. Militia soldiers served with UN contingents in the Middle East and augmented the 4th Canadian Mechanized Brigade Group in West Germany.[28] Nevertheless, the Total Force idea always worked better in theory than in practice. Without legislation to protect civilian jobs for the time spent away during training and deployment, the use of reservists on any prolonged basis was unsustainable. Even the Total Force's most stalwart supporters accepted this reality. MITCP instead provided a uniform and measured professional standard among officers in the reserves in case of possible future need. In theory at least, the criteria closely approximated those in the regular force as much as possible.

Professionalism was a buzz-word within the Canadian Armed Forces during the 1970s. Unification and integration had torn military officers away from their previous service identifications and traditions. Dressed in drab green uniforms, they were now organized by function under the equally colourless name of Canadian Forces (CF). The exact effects of this drastic change were still unknown. Knowledgeable analysts worried about loss of ethos and cohesion within the Canadian officer corps.[29] A new sense of identity and professionalism appeared to be needed to fill the vacuum left by unification. What differentiated military service from other forms of employment? No one had ever satisfactorily answered that question in Canada. To construct a theoretical concept of military professionalism, the Canadian Armed Forces borrowed from leading American and British writers, such as Samuel Huntington, Morris Janowitz, and John Hackett.[30] Their conclusions, however, never neatly fitted the Canadian context. Most Canadians maintained their long tradition of indifference and lack of understanding concerning the reason why Canada required armed forces.[31] Canada had made significant military contributions during past conflicts, but it was not a militaristic country. An article in the command and staff college's journal cited apathy among the general population, government, and a large number of serving officers as the greatest impediment to Canadian military professionalism.[32] The Canadian Armed Forces served a society that generally showed little consistent interest in military matters. Without any clear ethos, Canada's military slowly fell behind the United States and other Western nations in professional training and education of military officers.

Although numerous departmental and external studies discussed problems with officer professional development, the Canadian Armed Forces implemented few major changes. In 1969, the Officer Development Board, chaired by Major General Roger Rowley, had issued a report recommending a clearer definition of the "military ethic" in Canada and better educational standards (at least a university degree) for career officers.[33] The report's initial reception was favourable, but it remained on the shelf indefinitely until the financial and political climate improved. Unlike the US military after the debacle in Vietnam, no urgent need for reform inspired the Canadian Forces. Canadian officers grumbled about the supposed negative effects of unification and civilianization, but few recognized that they constituted part of the problem.[34] Influenced by current trends in the social sciences, the military curriculum at Canadian services colleges stressed the development of leadership and management skills. Lieutenant

Colonel John Eggenberger, head of the RMC's Department of Military Leadership and Management, tried to distil these somewhat elusive concepts into a formula of set variables.[35] The Canadian military's new-found infatuation with sociology and psychology redirected the focus of military education and generally caused more uncertainty. One observer complained that the Canadian Forces produced well-adjusted generalists rather than professional military thinkers.[36] Professionalism became another empty catch-word for a generation of Canadian officers lacking a strong sense of military ethos or attachment.

The deficiency was noted in a comprehensive review of the postunification Canadian Armed Forces. On 15 March 1980, a task force submitted a final report that summarized concerns and perceptions surrounding unification.[37] Specific recommendations included structural reorganization, some decentralization, increased input from the operational environments, and reintroduction of distinctive service uniforms for Maritime Command and Air Command. A review group formed to consider the task force's report observed "that the Forces have not been taking sufficient account of the need for individual service members to comprehend personally, to their own satisfaction, what the Forces are doing and why, or what their own role in them is."[38] The failure was attributed to weaknesses in training and education. The review group recommended a thorough examination of existing training manuals, study materials, and curricula, as well as preparation of a written statement on military ethos, to be approved by the chief of the defence staff.[39] A perceived crisis in leadership called for a renewal of military values throughout the Canadian Armed Forces. Lieutenant Colonel Charles Cotton, a military sociologist, suggested "a short ethical code about how members of the military ought to behave and about what their basic beliefs should be."[40] The simple statement of core values was to apply to every member of the Canadian Forces, from the most senior to the lowest ranks and stressed basic ethical guidelines rather than institutional concepts. Cotton expressed concern about the inward focus of Canada's military and its alienation from civilian society, a trend that he termed the "beleaguered warrior syndrome."[41] Many officers, particularly those involved in the operational sphere, blamed the military's ills on external civilian influences instead of the serious problems with training and professional standards identified by the review group. As discontent accumulated within the Canadian Forces over their own operational and organizational shortcomings, the new Charter of Rights and Freedoms provided a convenient scapegoat.

The Canadian Armed Forces received the Charter of Rights and Freedoms and its almost inevitable legal challenges to the Canadian military justice system with a great deal of apprehension. In 1980, the Supreme Court of Canada had heard an appeal from Private R.C. MacKay against a military conviction by court martial on a narcotics charge.[42] Although Canada's highest court declined to apply the Canadian Bill of Rights fully to the National Defence Act in its ruling, MacKay's case appeared to establish a precedent for more appeals from convicted soldiers, who were either dissatisfied with earlier military verdicts or trying to overturn decisions of the Court Martial Appeal Court. Thus defence officials were already concerned about greater scrutiny and criticism from the civilian judiciary in regard to military justice when Parliament passed the Constitution Act and introduced the Canadian Charter of Rights and Freedoms (the Charter) in 1982. The Charter went further than the Canadian Bill of Rights in guaranteeing fundamental legal, equality, and language rights for all individuals as Canadian citizens, including fairness in criminal and penal matters before the courts. In theory at least, members of the Canadian Armed Forces enjoyed the same basic rights and freedoms as the general populace in a free and democratic society, subject to certain reasonable limits prescribed by the National Defence Act and other legislation. For example, individuals who voluntarily enlisted in the Canadian Forces relinquished some rights and liberties, such as membership in trade unions, trial by jury, and freedom of movement while on duty. Section 11(f) of the Charter referred specifically to trial by military tribunal under military law. While obvious exemptions were made for the peculiarities of military service, the Charter opened up additional opportunities for civilian judicial input into the application of Canadian military law.

The nature of the Charter and its exact effect on the Canadian Forces generated much debate, both inside and outside the Canadian military establishment. On the one hand, the advent of the Charter seemed to signal a massive shift in government power from elected representatives to the judiciary, in which the courts became the highest law-making power in the land, perhaps even superior to Parliament. The judiciary, it was argued, would inevitably use this new-found power to regulate the Canadian Forces according to its own interpretation of the Charter. How could civilian judges, obsessed with civilian notions of individual rights and removed from the concerns of running an efficient military organization, possibly understand the rationale behind a separate military justice system? Military law existed to ensure discipline and obedience in an institution whose main purpose was to destroy and kill in defence of the national interest. On the other hand, the Charter represented little more than a vehicle for reform to ensure that the organization and administration of the Canadian Forces matched the concerns of the democratic society that it served and depended upon for resources to maintain military effectiveness. In spite of the judiciary's elevated role, Parliament still retained ostensive control and review over defence through the auditor general, various parliamentary standing committees, and the minister of national defence's ultimate responsibility to the cabinet and Parliament as set out in the National Defence Act.

The military was not immune from social pressures and developments in the rest of Canadian society, and the Charter certainly increased awareness within the Armed Forces about the legal remedies available to service personnel in seeking redress from military decisions. Although defence officials worried that judges would immediately wade into affairs that the Armed Forces held as sacrosanct, increased judicial review mostly entailed procedural changes to bring military law more into line with ordinary criminal law.[43] The Charter held the Canadian Forces and its military justice system to the same legal standard now pertaining in the rest of Canada. In enforcing more procedural fairness for defendants before courts martial or summary trials, the improved legal regime enhanced and strengthened the functioning of military law. Why should military personnel, as Canadian citizens and defenders of the nation, not receive the same protections and rights under the law as other members of society? Military law, as with law in general, needed to be dynamic and open to change in order to stay relevant in the current world and inspire public confidence.[44] Duty and law required the Canadian Forces to accept without question the new constitutional arrangements; the Department of National Defence was in exactly the same position as any other branch of the federal government. The Charter was part of Canadian law, and it was not the military's place to question why. Given the inconsistent attention from Parliament toward defence matters, the judiciary was in the next best position to assess the military's ability to meet the requirements of public trust.

Interpretation of the Charter, as applied to the Canadian Forces, fell mainly to the Court Martial Appeal Court in appeal cases. This civilian appeal body had undergone substantial changes in size and composition since the late 1960s, as a result of reforms in the larger federal court system. Administrative restructuring and decentralization created a demand for more judges across the country. By 1982, forty judges from the Federal Court of Canada and other superior courts of criminal jurisdiction appointed by the governor-in-council belonged to the Court Martial Appeal Court. Fewer and fewer of its members possessed direct military experience. Patrick Morgan Mahoney, a former member of Parliament and a judge on the Federal Court of Appeal, replaced Hugh Gibson as chief justice. Unlike the earlier days of the Court Martial Appeal Court, the Canadian military could no longer count on the presence of friendly judges because the enlarged court ensured greater rotation of individual members from case to case. Drawn from all walks of life, the new judges represented a range of different perspectives, viewpoints, and backgrounds. Barbara Joan Reed, a judge with the Trial Division of the Federal Court of Canada, became the first woman appointed to the Court Martial Appeal

Court. The court grew to fifty-five judges in 1986. The additional members ensured that the concerns of the wider civil society were well represented. The Court Martial Appeal Court finally became, as it was originally presented to the public at large, a truly civilian body of appeal for convictions from courts martial in the Canadian Armed Forces.

Despite the change in membership, the Court Martial Appeal Court exercised considerable circumspection in its decisions. The number of appeals in the years immediately following the introduction of the Charter increased relative to the total number of courts martial.[45] While appellants who used Charter arguments most likely expected some empathy from civilian judges, the Court Martial Appeal Court still allowed, either partially or completely, only a small percentage of appeals. The Court Martial Appeal Court proved reluctant to question the military's claim that some ordinary civil offences were by their nature detrimental to military discipline.[46] Canadian judges applied what came to be known as the "military nexus test," an inferior imitation of the US service connection test, to determine if the Canadian Forces retained jurisdiction in particular cases.

On the whole, the judiciary in the late 1980s and early 1990s was reluctant to intervene in Canada's military justice system. Ruling judges repeatedly declined to formulate precise guidelines advising when and why the military nexus test actually applied in particular appeals. More often than not, the Court Martial Appeal Court decided in the military's favour. For instance, appeals involving drug offences generally satisfied the military nexus test because the Canadian Forces insisted that regardless of whether a direct military connection was present, the use and distribution of drugs constituted behaviour in opposition to military duty and discipline.[47] Under military law, such offences received much more severe punishments than was common under civil law. The Court Martial Appeal Court sent back cases for retrial to give military authorities another opportunity to correct deficiencies; but it seldom overturned convictions unless a glaring injustice was done. Through application of the military nexus test, the Court Martial Appeal Court supported continued application of military law under the National Defence Act, at least in partial accord with the Charter.

In fact, while critical of apparent problems and limitations with military law, civilian judges upheld the legitimacy of a separate military justice system in a landmark decision by the Supreme Court of Canada in 1992. Under the National Defence Act, a dissenting vote on the Court Martial Appeal Court allowed an unsuccessful applicant further appeal to Canada's highest court. Such outcomes were rare, but a strong dissenting opinion in a case involving Corporal Michel Généreux, a soldier convicted by a general court martial on charges of possessing narcotics for the purpose of trafficking, provided an opening to the higher court. The Court Martial Appeal Court had previously declared the standing court martial unconstitutional under the Charter, and Généreux's appeal raised similar concerns about the judicial impartiality and independence of the general court martial.[48] The significance of the case was recognized at the time. Military lawyers feared that legal challenges threatened to undermine Canada's entire military justice system by possibly striking down one of its oldest and most important legal instruments. Although a majority of judges held that the general court martial as then constituted violated in some ways the right of an accused to a fair trial under the Charter, the Supreme Court of Canada recognized the existence of a separate military justice system "to allow the Armed Forces to deal with matters that pertain directly to the discipline, efficiency, and morale of the military."[49] In a lengthy judgment, Chief Justice Antonio Lamer reviewed the history and purpose of military tribunals in order to suggest proper limits on their jurisdiction and application. Although somewhat chastened, the military justice system survived its strongest assault in the post-Charter legal environment. Canadian military law emerged stronger than ever.

Military lawyers in the Canadian Forces quickly read into the Supreme Court's decision justification for the creation of an elaborate legal machinery to support a separate military justice system. Janet Walker, a warrant officer with a degree from Osgoode Hall Law School, interpreted the Généreux case as a demise of the military nexus test.[50] Military justice, she argued, was in no way inferior to its civilian counterpart, but merely different because of the military's unique function and role in society. The question involved fairness, or at least its perception, for those persons who fell under the jurisdiction of military law. Disparities between the civilian and military contexts left many opportunities for criticism of military justice, unless some structure was introduced to examine issues of fairness and impartiality.

The Department of National Defence amended the National Defence Act to establish an independent military judiciary within the Canadian Forces, which a selected reading of the Généreux decision subsequently endorsed. Legal officers were designated military trial judges and worked in a separate division at arm's length from command influence within the JAG office. While definite conclusions about the relative worth of such an innovation were premature, it was hard to see how the number of courts martial in any given year after 1992 could have possibly justified, much less sustained, an independent military judiciary in the Canadian Forces with full-time military trial judges. Nonetheless, the JAG office became committed to the buildup of a formal military justice apparatus, regardless of its ever increasing complexity and demands on personnel and branch resources.[51] Whether an independent military judiciary was an appropriate or even affordable solution to the legal challenges posed by the Charter was less important than the JAG's desire to support a separate military justice system, for which a large establishment of specialized military lawyers was required. Unwilling to concede any more authority than was absolutely necessary to the civilian judiciary, the Canadian Forces adopted a wholly extravagant and superfluous system of military trial judges for the relative size of armed forces in Canada and number of offences brought before military courts. Prudence and practicality were sacrificed for legal meticulousness.

The Charter resulted in both negative reactions and definite improvements within the Canadian Forces. Some officers objected to changes to the existing status quo on the grounds that any relaxation of military discipline promoted potential disorder and anarchy within the military organization.[52] The interests of the Armed Forces as an operational and combat-ready institution, they argued, always took precedence over the individual. Military service was not a "nine to five" occupation, and a direct connection existed between discipline, efficiency, and operational readiness. Through a series of four study packages, a revitalized military indoctrination program attempted to replace civilian values with supposedly military ethics and self-discipline.[53] Even though arguably conservative by nature, the Canadian Armed Forces often displayed a limited capacity for social reform. Functional bilingualism was the official policy within the Canadian Forces; between 1980 and 1990, the Department of National Defence spent $500 million on training in the two official languages.[54] Canada's military also worked to include groups previously excluded from certain military service. Following enactment of the Canadian Human Rights Act, which prohibited gender as a basis for discrimination, the Canadian Forces conducted several Service Women in Non-Traditional Environments and Roles (SWINTER) trials between November 1979 and October 1985.[55] Although highlighting the added complexity with mixed gender units, the SWINTER trials showed that the integration of females into previously male-only trades and occupations was feasible. A parliamentary committee, established to consider the impact of the Charter and equality rights, recommended complete integration of women across the full range of jobs in the Canadian Forces so Canada could "be in the vanguard in promoting full equality for men and women in the armed forces."[56] Citing concerns about operational effectiveness if women joined combat units, military authorities were in no rush to implement such sweeping changes, but outside pressure meant that they could not ignore the matter much longer. In September 1986, a task force headed by Brigadier General A. McLellan was created within the Canadian Forces to explore the ramifications of the Charter on the military's activities, devoting special attention to women and homosexuals.[57] In the final analysis, the Charter task force's conclusions hardly reflected an institution ready to embrace forward-looking ideas on social change and equality between genders wholeheartedly. Although willing to accept increased participation of women in non-traditional support roles, the Canadian Forces adhered to its previous policies of exclusion. New Combat Related Employment of Women (CREW) trials were proposed but the Canadian Human Rights Commission became concerned about the legality and constitutionality of further trials and formed a tribunal to consider the question in detail. A tribunal ruling on 20 February 1989 subsequently forced military authorities to expand the number of fields open to women, to be implemented fully within ten years in all military occupations and units except service on submarines.[58] Three years later, the Canadian Forces lifted its restrictions on homosexuals prior to the hearing of a lawsuit by Michelle Douglas, a lesbian forced out of the Armed Forces because of her sexual orientation. The chief of defence staff acknowledged that the military's ban on homosexuals was unconstitutional under the Charter. Whatever the personal views of individual service members, the Canadian Forces comprised a team of individuals working together, irrespective of gender and other differences. Canadian military and civil law supported equality of opportunity for all individuals. Actual assignment depended upon the standards for specific occupations or trades, training, and the backgrounds of individual soldiers. Women and homosexuals could fight for their country just as well as heterosexual men.

Unfortunately, the rationale behind the significant changes brought about by application of the Charter remained poorly understood within the ranks of the Canadian Forces. For old die-hards, judicial challenges to court martial convictions, women in erstwhile masculine occupations, and official approval of homosexuality only confirmed the impression that Canada's once proud military institutions were suffering a slow death. It had all started with unification, and the Charter was simply driving nails, one by one, into the coffin. This misperception gained increasing currency in the absence of official publications or manuals to explain that the reforms actually served to improve operational effectiveness and make most efficient use of available personnel resources. Military officers needed to harness social change for the benefit of the Armed Forces, not fear it as an incipient threat.[59] The message was never made clear within the Canadian Forces because the training and educational system was deficient.

Senior officials in the Department of National Defence tried to address the enduring problems with professional development. On 10 June 1987, General Paul Manson, the chief of defence staff, commissioned a study of the future officer corps, focusing on the recruitment, education, and training activities needed "to provide the very special high quality leadership the Canadian Forces will require in an era of great technological and sociological change."[60] Familiarity with military law, the National Defence Act, and the Charter was a prerequisite for every professional officer. A phase one report of the officer corps study emphasized the importance of a sound ethical framework, leadership skills, and solid professional education.[61] Learning was a continual process, and officers needed a proper balance of training, education, and experience at various points in their careers. Whether the existing officer professional development system met these requirements to the fullest extent possible was still doubtful.[62] The training system in the Canadian Forces concentrated too much on the means of instruction rather than the quality and quantity of information that officers and soldiers ultimately learned. Greater use of computers added a new dimension to self-study, but content in courses and study packages remained virtually unchanged since the mid-1970s.[63] A self-imposed intellectual stagnation impaired the Canadian Forces. How could an officer be expected to stay current in military law if instructional and reference materials failed to cover or keep up with the Charter and its application to the military justice system? As in so many other areas, Canada lagged ten years behind the United States and other NATO countries in appreciating the legal problems within its Armed Forces. International law received marginally better coverage because of sustained interest within the JAG office.

During the 1980s, the international law of armed conflict and human rights gained more attention from Canada's military lawyers. Frank Karwandy replaced Wolfe as JAG in November 1982, and Robert Martin assumed that post in November 1986. Both were competent service lawyers, but were largely unknown outside the Armed Forces. The JAG office continued to expand and specialize with the appointment of additional directors of law. Lieutenant Colonel J.S.A. DesRoches was the director of law responsible for training. Instruction mostly involved seminars and courses for JAG's legal officers, with occasional lectures on legal subjects at the staff college, the military colleges, or in the commands. Major William Fenrick moved from international law to the training slot after DesRoches became the AJAG in Halifax. Having decided that a graduate degree in history held limited future career prospects, Fenrick had completed law school in Nova Scotia and then joined the JAG office on a full-time basis in February 1974. He specialized in international law and almost single-handedly managed the field after superseding Major J.D. Chenier as director of international law in 1978.[64] Fenrick's appointment to training entailed far-reaching consequences for the direction and emphasis of subsequent legal instruction within the JAG office.

In terms of energy and conscientiousness, Fenrick took his position as director of law/training seriously. Unlike most other military lawyers in Canada, he found time in his busy schedule to write articles for academic journals, law periodicals, and service magazines. The JAG office published the first issue of its own *JAG Journal,* modelled upon the US Army's *Military*

Law Review, under Fenrick's editorship in 1985. Distributed to law schools across Canada, the journal represented one of the few sources on Canadian military law available to the larger legal profession. At Fenrick's invitation, Leslie Green, a professor of political science at the University of Alberta and a leading authority on the law of war, lectured on numerous occasions to JAG officers in Ottawa.[65] Although instruction remained predominantly oriented toward legal officers, the JAG office also prepared reference materials for distribution within the Canadian Forces. A series of twenty-five articles on various aspects of the law of war proved "useful as a guide for the preparation of local programs of instruction."[66] Most training materials during this time featured some sort of international law dimension. With Green's assistance, Fenrick revised the second draft of a large manual on the law of armed conflict in 1986 "to provide authoritative guidance to members of the Canadian Forces, particularly to legal officers engaged in advising commanders, on the customary and treaty law applicable in armed conflict."[67] Binding provisions in the Geneva Conventions legally required the Canadian Forces to make known the provisions of the law of war to all its members through legal advisors and manuals. Nonetheless, problems with translation into French, lack of money, continuous changes to the law of war, and Canada's pending ratification of the two additional 1977 protocols to the Geneva Conventions delayed publication of the international law of armed conflict manual on an official basis.[68] The momentum for further instruction and revisions was lost once Fenrick returned to his previous position as director of international law. Lieutenant Colonel D.B. Murphy, the new director of law/training, adopted a more balanced approach to legal instruction. International law was still important, but it was no longer the highest priority.

During this time, the JAG office put forward proposals to establish its own school to train military lawyers. The inspiration came mainly from south of the border. Each of the three main US services maintained separate legal branches and educational institutions.[69] The US Army's JAG office, which contained thousands of lawyers in its active and reserve components, advertised itself as the largest law firm in the world. The Americans took a serious interest in military law and devoted considerable resources to professional and legal training of service lawyers. As either guest speakers or students, Canadian military lawyers visited the US Army's JAG school on the grounds of the University of Virginia at Charlottesville, the naval justice school at Newport, Rhode Island, and the US Air Force JAG school in Montgomery, Alabama. The curriculum at US military legal schools was similar to that at civilian law schools but with a military emphasis. Besides pursuing standard courses, American military lawyers pursued further postgraduate studies in specialty fields such as military criminal jurisdiction, international law, and administrative law without going outside the Armed Forces.[70] As well, the US Army's JAG school granted an accredited master's degree in military law. Several Canadian military lawyers chose this option, and others completed advanced law degrees at Canadian, US, and European universities. Although not absolutely required, legal officers generally studied some current aspect of military law or the law of war.

Attendance at civilian universities gave military lawyers valuable exposure to the wider field of law, but legal academic expertise in military matters remained limited, particularly in Canada. Most Canadian law schools still regarded military law with a certain amount of derision and suspicion. In this unwelcome environment, the JAG office naturally preferred its own educational institution along the same lines as the US JAG schools. A suggestion was even put forward that prospective military lawyers might complete a bachelor of law degree at the Canadian JAG school without attending a civilian law school. The idea was never fully developed because authorities at a higher level decided against the entire proposal on budgetary grounds. It was just as well since the number of military lawyers in the Canadian Armed Forces was probably not sufficient to sustain a US-type JAG school over the long term. A JAG school remained little more than a dream that Canadian legal officers occasionally indulged in.

A contributing factor to the unviability of a dedicated school for Canada's military lawyers was the JAG's relatively small and undeveloped reserve. The US JAG branches could justify their schools because the number of reservist lawyers equalled or was greater than the number of active service lawyers on courses. The United States frequently used reservist lawyers in a variety of legal and related activities at home and abroad.[71] In comparison, the JAG office in Canada appeared reluctant to accept reservist lawyers as equals to regular force lawyers. The same prejudices from Orde's day still lingered: reservist lawyers were too civilian, lacked necessary proficiency in the intricacies of military law, and were not always available when needed. For a long time, it was just easier and more convenient to use military lawyers from the regular force; the limited number of disciplinary offences within the peacetime Canadian Forces encouraged that practice. The JAG felt no urgent need to recruit more lawyers from the larger legal profession into the reserves because the situation remained manageable. The reservists in the JAG office mainly comprised lawyers with a particular interest or background who happened to come along or regular force JAG officers placed into the primary and supplementary reserves after retirement. When time, money, and outside employment permitted, reservist officers attended courses, seminars, and the annual JAG conference in Ottawa. The director of law/training made serious efforts to increase or maintain professional and specialized legal knowledge among the small number of reservists. An occasional reservist lawyer was called out on an operational assignment, but the majority practised in or near the urban areas of Canadian cities and towns. Geographical dispersement, work commitments, and time constraints complicated the proper training of reservist lawyers.

The lack of a large and serviceable reserve of military lawyers resulted in certain drawbacks for Canada's JAG office. Reservist lawyers possessed a broad range of legal expertise and experience, either unavailable or too expensive to develop in the Canadian Forces.[72] With some additional training, they fulfilled operational commitments or deployed in situations of national emergency. Reservist lawyers also provided invaluable contact with the legal profession and the business community. Besides leaving a large talent base virtually untapped, the JAG office, in its timidity to extend its ranks to more civil lawyers, partly accounted for the continued isolation of military law from the mainstream of Canadian law. Despite Canada's experience with uniformed lawyers in both world wars, many JAG members were unwilling to admit that in some respects, reservist lawyers were superior to career legal officers in the regular force. A proper mixture of reservist and regular military lawyers was essential for carrying out the JAG office's many and varied tasks. The reserves represented relatively inexpensive force multipliers. The unique problems associated with using reservist lawyers were sometimes complicated and trying, but the potential benefits made the effort more than worthwhile. The JAG office's failure to develop its reserve component fully was a squandered opportunity.

The JAG office's subdued acceptance of reservist lawyers proved embarrassing as the Department of National Defence realized that the reserves represented a valuable and economical asset. A white paper issued by Brian Mulroney's Conservative government in 1987 stressed the importance of efficient reserve forces and promised to allocate more resources to this side of the Canadian Forces.[73] Canada was almost unique among the NATO countries in having a regular force that was larger than its reserves. Declining budgets and soaring costs had created a significant commitment-capability gap within the Canadian Forces, and the Total Force concept seemed a cheap and effective way to address Canada's defence needs. In July 1988, a reserve personnel integration planning team was established to study personnel policies in the regular and reserve forces with the goal of further integration.[74] In the absence of job protection legislation, the Department of National Defence formed the National Employers Support Committee to convince civilian employers to give reservists more consideration in such matters as unpaid leave and benefits. Despite moderate pay increases, the reserves remained vastly underpaid. In a report on Canada's land forces, a Senate committee recommended full pay parity between the reserve and regular forces.[75] Better remuneration and benefits were important attractions for professionals such as lawyers. Brigadier

General Martin and his office devoted more thought to the JAG reserve in terms of recruitment and training, but the collapse of communism in the Soviet Union and the end of the Cold War removed many of the assumptions on which the 1987 white paper had been based. The Canadian Forces and the JAG office adjusted to different roles and challenges in a new strategic environment.

Military lawyers deployed with Canadian troops in the Persian Gulf as Canada's contribution to the coalition forces collected in Saudi Arabia against the military forces of Iraq's Saddam Hussein. Iraq had invaded neighbouring Kuwait on 2 August 1990.[76] With the strong backing of the United States, the United Nations declared the invasion a clear act of aggression and invited Western nations to send forces to evict Iraqi military forces from Kuwait. Canadian warships, a squadron of CF-18 fighter planes, and a field hospital arrived in the war zone, but Canadian armour and infantry remained in Europe and Canada.[77] The small number of Canadian troops in the field and the shortness of the conflict allowed the recently appointed JAG, Commodore Peter Partner, to meet operational commitments through his office's existing establishment. Five legal officers – a minimum of three in the Middle East theatre at any one time – provided advice on disciplinary and administrative matters, legal aid, contracts, civil affairs, and rules of engagement.[78] The Korean War was the last time the Canadian Armed Forces had been involved in active combat operations, and a certain amount of relearning was required. Canadian and coalition forces carefully considered the legal aspects of prisoners of war, legitimate means of warfare, and aerial attacks against military and civil targets.[79] Serious doubts about training and logistical support, however, left most of the Canadian Armed Forces sidelined back at home. Fortunately, the Gulf War made few insurmountable demands on the JAG office's organization, and the small reserve of military lawyers in Canada was never tested. It most likely would have failed with a larger Canadian deployment in a longer war.[80] Legal officers from the regular force proved adequate for the limited Canadian commitment in the Persian Gulf.

In conjunction with Canadian peacekeeping operations in the former Yugoslavia, JAG lawyers also became involved in the investigation of alleged improprieties by members of Croatian, Serb, and Bosnian paramilitary forces. The conflict was a nasty civil war between different ethnic groups. Reports in the media about massacres, murders, and sanctioned rapes coined the new term "ethnic cleansing"; the level of barbarity had not been seen in Europe since the Second World War. On 6 October 1992, the United Nations established a commission of experts to examine violations of the Geneva Conventions and humanitarian international law within the territory of the former Yugoslavia in anticipation of prosecutions before an international criminal tribunal. Commander Fenrick, as one of JAG's most experienced and knowledgeable officers in the law of war, was appointed to the commission of experts and served as rapporteur on legal issues and on-site investigations.[81] On the advice of Fenrick and Barry Mawhinney, from the Department of External Affairs, Canada offered the services of a team of military lawyers and military police to undertake investigations in the field.

Lieutenant Colonel Kim Carter, JAG's director of international law, headed the Canadian war crimes investigation team. During three separate missions, Carter and her team examined a mass grave site near Vukovar, interviewed rape victims in Sarajevo, and exhumed bodies at Ovcara and Packrac Poljana.[82] These activities took place in the midst of fighting between the warring sides and with occasional resistance from local authorities. The experience left a lasting impression. Lieutenant Colonel J.C. Holland, a JAG veteran from the Gulf War and a later director of law/training, described his time in Croatia as exciting.[83] The high level of specialized knowledge in international law within Canada's JAG office was the legacy of Wolfe and Fenrick. Ironically, as the Canadian war crimes investigation team worked in the former Yugoslavia, Canadian soldiers were committing serious breaches against the Geneva Conventions and Canadian military law in Somalia.

In retrospect, Canada probably should have not sent troops to Somalia. The already large commitment to peacekeeping operations in the former Yugoslavia overstretched the limited capacity and resources of the Canadian Forces, particularly in the key area of infantry. The Department of National Defence relied on reservists and other groups normally not employed in peacekeeping to meet operational requirements. Why was the Canadian Airborne Regiment, a specially trained combat unit, sent to Somalia? Since the mission was ostensively for humanitarian relief purposes and enjoyed strong support from the United States and the United Nations, officials decided that Canada could ill-afford not to participate for prestige reasons. The UN Chapter 7 intervention was very different from Canada's previous involvement in peacekeeping. No central government existed to invite UN forces into Somalia, and various competing clans lorded over a starving population. UN troops arrived heavily armed and authorized to use necessary force for self-defence and protection of relief shipments. At the time, the background and training of the Canadian Airborne Regiment seemed particularly suited to such an operation. A Canadian joint-force headquarters was established at Mogadishu, and Canadian troops deployed in and around an airfield at Belet Huen. Although the Canadian Airborne Regiment accomplished considerable good in Somalia, misconduct by a few soldiers sullied the entire mission and the reputation of the whole Canadian Forces.

The offences in Somalia were among the most serious crimes a soldier can commit under the laws of war, the Code of Service Discipline, and the Canadian Criminal Code. The ambiguous nature of the mission's rules of engagement and standing orders accentuated disciplinary problems, training deficiencies, and a poor knowledge of military law among Canadian officers and soldiers, who were ill-equipped to deal with the complicated non-combat problems at Belet Huen. On 4 March 1993, Canadian soldiers killed a fleeing Somali who had attempted to infiltrate into the compound to steal food. A military doctor who examined the body subsequently told the press that the man might have been shot in the head as he lay wounded on the ground. The Department of National Defence downplayed the event, but worse was yet to come. Late on the night of 16 March, Master Corporal Clayton Matchee and Private Kyle Brown, two soldiers from the Canadian Airborne Regiment's 2nd Commando, tortured and beat to death Shidane Abukar Arone, a young Somali man caught earlier inside the compound.[84] The media quickly learned about the event after Matchee unsuccessfully tried to commit suicide while under detention. On the basis of the findings of a military police investigation team sent from Ottawa to Belet Huen on 23 March, military authorities laid charges against those involved in the shooting incident and Arone's death. As news of the atrocities reached home, the Canadian public was appalled at the conduct of Canadian soldiers in Somalia. A full investigation was demanded.

The Department of National Defence hoped to avoid more negative publicity surrounding the incidents in Somalia because the minister of national defence, Kim Campbell, was the favourite for the Conservative Party's impending re-election bid. On 28 April 1993, the chief of the defence staff, Admiral John Anderson, established a board of inquiry to examine the leadership, discipline, operations, actions, and procedures of the Canadian Airborne Regiment Battle Group in Somalia.[85] The board comprised senior military officers and a civilian academic with close ties to the Department of National Defence: Major General T.F. de Faye, Brigadier General C.J. Addy, Brigadier General J.C.A. Emond, and Professor Harriet Critchley from the University of Calgary. A JAG officer, Lieutenant Colonel Kenneth Watkin, was appointed as legal advisor. Working to a tight deadline, the board of inquiry delivered a number of specific recommendations in regard to discipline, rules of engagement, racism, and training.[86] Although a number of disciplinary problems were found to have existed in the Canadian Airborne Regiment before its deployment, the board of inquiry concluded that the misbehaviour in Somalia was the exception rather than the rule. In keeping with the Charter, ongoing military police investigations and impending trials prevented the board of inquiry from delving into the cases of particular individuals. These matters were left to judicial prosecution.

Although the civil Criminal Code took precedence over the charged soldiers once in Canada, the Canadian Forces proceeded with trial by military courts martial. In 1994, separate courts martial tried members of the Canadian Airborne Regiment for their participation or lack of intervention in Arone's beating death. Torture and murder charges against Matchee were stayed indefinitely because he was declared mentally incompetent to stand trial. In a transparent attempt to placate public opinion, the Canadian Forces scrutinized the events behind the murder and punished the main culprits through the military justice system within a year of the ill-fated incident. A court martial convicted Private Brown, the other soldier most directly implicated in the 16 March incident, on a reduced charge of manslaughter and imposed a sentence of five years' imprisonment and dismissal with disgrace from the Canadian Forces; Brown was subsequently released on parole after serving little more than a year in a military prison and a federal penitentiary. In a subsequent book with a well-known journalist, Brown portrayed himself as a scapegoat of a military establishment that was determined to shift blame for the events in Somalia away from senior officers and National Defence Headquarters.[87] Whether the allegation had some basis or not, Brown's unrepentant tone and reluctance to accept the consequences of his actions mirrored the general mood of insolence pervading the Canadian Airborne Regiment. A horrible crime was committed by Canadian soldiers in Somalia, and no one felt responsible, even after trials and convictions before military courts.

New details about disciplinary problems in the Canadian Airborne Regiment and allegations of indiscretions in the highest echelons of the Canadian Forces eventually forced Jean Chrétien's Liberal government to go further. In early 1995, the minister of national defence, David Collenette, disbanded the Canadian Airborne Regiment after the media uncovered embarrassing videos of ritualist hazing of new recruits. Although service authorities decried the blatant political move, Collenette made the right decision because the bad behaviour of airborne troops was no longer tolerable from a military perspective. Flouting all attempts at discipline or responsibility for what happened in Somalia, the Canadian Airborne Regiment impaired the operational effectiveness of the whole Armed Forces by turning public opinion against the Canadian military. To the general public, the military formation was inexorably linked with misconduct, torture, and murder. Traditions could be bad as well as good, and disbanding the Canadian Airborne Regiment seemed a small sacrifice to save the good reputation of the Canadian Forces. On 20 March 1995, Collenette appointed a three-member public commission of inquiry, to examine the predeployment, in-theatre, and postdeployment activities of Canadian Forces in Somalia. In Parliament, the prime minister and minister of national defence repeatedly deferred questions about the "Somalia affair," as it was dubbed by the press, until completion of the commission of inquiry's work. The Department of National Defence established a special liaison team of military lawyers from the JAG office to work with the commissioners. As the first public inquiry relating to discipline and military law in the Canadian Armed Forces since the Mainguy Commission in 1949, the Somalia inquiry represented an independent review by commissioners with full judicial powers to call witnesses and examine documents.

Despite a good beginning, relations between the commission of inquiry and the Department of National Defence deteriorated almost to the point of open confrontation. The reasons were simple. The commission of inquiry believed that defence officials were not entirely honest and forthcoming, and the Department of National Defence gradually lost confidence in the commissioners' ability to deal with matters impartially.[88] As the two sides drifted further and further apart, recriminations and accusations increased. Gilles Létourneau, the commission of inquiry's chairperson, interpreted the commission's terms of reference so broadly that the commission could not finish within the original time limit and budget. The commission of inquiry asked for and received two extensions from the minister of national defence. From the start, Létourneau wanted to cover everything in a highly legal manner. By granting standing to counsel representing certain individuals, he allowed lawyers to hijack the proceedings. Questions asked by the commissioners and attending counsel often disclosed an inexcusable ignorance of military affairs and the reasons for the existence of the Armed Forces. When some senior officers felt uncomfortable, Létourneau and his colleagues accused them of deceit and contempt. The commissioners declared that military officials were hiding key documents and then complained about the excessive number provided by the Department of National Defence. The commission of inquiry became sidetracked from understanding what went wrong in Somalia by getting drawn into irrelevant details and matters of legal process.

Collenette showed a great deal of patience, even as the commission of inquiry dragged on month after month and the Canadian Forces faced regular chastisement from the media. But after Collenette was forced to resign in October 1996 over a conflict of interest issue, a new minister of national defence with less tolerance, Doug Young, arrived on the scene. With a reputation as a no-nonsense individual and a hatchet-man from his time at the Department of Transport, Young turned down Létourneau's request for a third extension and ordered the commission of inquiry to issue a final report by 30 June 1997. During several televised press conferences, the three commissioners shamelessly blamed the Department of National Defence rather than themselves for the inability to complete a full investigation. After more than two years of work, it was hard to say how much more time the commission of inquiry actually needed. Before the deadline arrived, Young lost his seat in the June 1997 federal election, just as Frederick Borden had done eighty-six years before. Although Young's political defeat probably gave Létourneau and his colleagues immense satisfaction, the minister of national defence was the victim of a grassroots revolt against the Liberal government's cut-backs to unemployment benefits in the Maritime provinces rather than being punished for his decision to curtail the Somalia inquiry. Arthur Eggleton, a former mayor of Toronto and Liberal cabinet minister, took over the defence portfolio in Young's place.

Pending completion of the commission of inquiry's final report, Young had asked two groups of outside experts to complete studies on various related matters pertaining to the Canadian Forces. The first group, which included three prominent Canadian military historians – Desmond Morton, Jack Granatstein, and David Bercuson – examined issues of morale, leadership, training, accountability, and combat capability; the second was a special advisory group on military justice and military police investigations with former chief justice Brian Dickson as chairperson and Lieutenant General Charles H. Belize and J.W. Bud Bird as members. The eighty-year-old Dickson had lost his right leg as a major in the Royal Canadian Artillery during the Second World War and had retired from the Supreme Court of Canada in 1990 after a long and distinguished legal career. In the first report on 25 March 1997, Dickson's special advisory group recommended setting down the JAG's responsibilities in the National Defence Act; publishing the JAG's annual report; appointing an independent director of prosecutions responsible to the JAG; restricting punishment handed down by summary trial to a maximum of thirty days' detention; the right to consult counsel before electing court martial; better training and education in military law for all commanding, delegated, and assisting officers; removing the death penalty from the scale of punishments; and creating an independent office of complaint and system supervision.[89] Without fanfare and under budget, Dickson's special advisory group made serviceable and meaningful suggestions for improvements to the military justice system in far less time than the Somalia inquiry. The JAG's influence was conspicuous in a number of the recommendations, and Dickson naively accepted the military's explanations at face value without independent research. This shortcoming was even more evident in Dickson's second report on the quasi-judicial role of the minister of national defence in the administration of military justice and his or her relationship with the JAG.[90] The special advisory group relied largely on personal interviews because records that related to the way the minister had exercised quasi-judicial roles in the past were said to be unavailable. Consequently, Dickson and his colleagues made some recommendations on the basis of incomplete and perhaps unreliable information.

Although the report of Dickson's special advisory group pre-empted the conclusion of the higher-profile public inquiry, the report submitted by Létourneau and his fellow commissioners to Eggleton at the end of June – and published almost immediately for sale and circulation – attracted greater attention. The large, glossy five-volume document reflected the lack of structure and clear sense of purpose that had characterized the commission of inquiry since its inception.[91] Relatively straightforward events were covered in minute detail, and simple subjects were made complex. A chapter devoted to military justice made several recommendations, including a restructured system with three classes of conduct; improvements to the military police; right to elect trial by civil court for any charge with a sentence over five years' imprisonment; appointment of an inspector general with duties related to military justice; more training in the law of war by dedicated staffs; and dissolution of the JAG office in favour of creation of two separate offices, a chief military judge and a director general of military legal services. The Somalia inquiry's report concluded: "The office of the JAG is another unfortunate vestige of the past. The very title, Judge Advocate General, highlights the inherent conflict of interest – that between judge and advocate – and the lack of independence within the present military justice system ... Abolishing the office of the JAG would go beyond a cosmetic name change and would have profound significance for the rule of law and the integrity of the military justice system."[92]

Despite the JAG office's long tradition and proven track record in maintaining discipline with the Canadian Armed Forces during war and peace, the commissioners furnished little background material to support the recommendation. In reality, Canadian military law's difficulties stemmed primarily from complacency and neglect rather than structural defects and lack of independence. The JAG was part of the problem, but wholesale reorganization was unwarranted. The motivation behind this recommendation and others was certainly suspect; resentment toward truncation of the Somalia inquiry's activities turned the five-volume report into a vehicle to lash back at the Liberal government and Department of National Defence. Almost daily coverage in the media and on television increased the profile of military law in Canada, but in the end, the commission of inquiry provided a poor return on the millions of public dollars and thousands of hours spent on its proceedings.

Given the poisoned atmosphere that accompanied the shutting down of the Somalia inquiry and vocal condemnation in the media from the commissioners, the Department of National Defence was under extreme pressure to act quickly upon the recommendations. Ignoring the report ran the risk of alienating public opinion, even though the commissioners created an adversarial relationship toward the military where none should have existed. On 14 October 1997, Eggleton issued a detailed response to the Somalia inquiry's final report, accepting 132 out of 160 recommendations.[93] Part II of Eggleton's response specifically dealt with military justice issues. Defence officials expressed willingness to learn from criticism and to implement major improvements in line with the Somalia inquiry's suggestions, but where Dickson's recommendations diverged from those of the commission's, Eggleton preferred Dickson's. In other words, the Department of National Defence used its hand-picked special advisory group on military justice and police investigation services to minimize the full impact of the Somalia inquiry's conclusions. Defence officials proposed, besides a number of procedural changes and suggestions concerning legal training, reforms to the summary trial process, organization of the chief military trial judge as a separate office, independent grievance and complaints boards, and retention of the JAG with more delineated responsibilities. Basically, the Department of National Defence took advantage of differences between the two independent investigations into the military justice system to justify the recommendations it wanted to accept and those it did not. Proposed changes to Canadian military law were skewed in favour of the military viewpoint. A monitoring committee of eight individuals was established to oversee the progress of the Canadian Forces in carrying out the announced reforms from the Somalia inquiry's report over the next two years, and the minister of national defence inaugurated steps to amend and modernize the existing National Defence Act.

These amendments, introduced by Eggleton in a bill before Parliament on 4 December 1997, were the most comprehensive changes to defence legislation in Canada since the National Defence Act was introduced in 1950. In substance, the changes clarified the roles and responsibilities of various authorities in the military justice system, including the minister of national defence and the JAG; clearly defined investigative, prosecutorial, defence and judicial functions; reformed summary trials; strengthened supervision and review by forming new grievance and complaints bodies; and eliminated the death penalty from the list of punishments.[94] Henceforth, the JAG was required to submit an annual report, which was to be tabled in Parliament, on the administration of military justice in the Canadian Forces. And Eggleton promised a major review of the National Defence Act, five years after the amendments came into force. Although some amendments unnecessarily entrenched military prerogatives, the general direction of the proposed changes moved toward more integrity and fairness in the application of Canadian military law as a distinct system of justice. During the bill's second reading in the House of Commons on 19 March 1998, defence critics from the opposition parties made clear that they believed it did not go far enough in terms of improved accountability and substantive changes to the military justice system in Canada. One parliamentary member described the proposed legislation as "a series of half measures."[95] Still, the fateful events at Belet Huen during the Somalia deployment started a process that resulted in separate examinations into the operation of military justice and definite amendments to the National Defence Act. The entire episode fit neatly into the reactive and haphazard development of military law in Canada.

Conclusion: Beyond Somalia

The incidents in Somalia and subsequent high-profile cases involving misbehaviour and misconduct in the Canadian Forces transformed Canadian military law from a relatively ignored field of justice into an object of intense public scrutiny. The Department of National Defence proved sensitive to concerns about the perceived need for more fairness in the application of military law. In one much publicized case, Lieutenant Commander Dean Marshaw, a submarine commander accused of physical harassment and abuse of authority, was not retried by court martial after the Court Martial Appeal Court struck down his previous conviction.[1] Even though the overall number of courts martial in recent years was actually lower than at any time in the previous two decades, military authorities laboured against public perception that impropriety within the Canadian Forces was endemic. Sensational disclosures about alleged sexual harassment and abuse of women in the Canadian Armed Forces created new doubts about the effectiveness of military justice and its ability to deal with offenders adequately.

Senior officers and officials within the Department of National Defence adopted a strong and unequivocal stance toward alleged criminal offences against female members of the Canadian Forces. By 1998, almost 6,800 women served in the Canadian Forces, more than four times the number in 1971 when the Department of National Defence decided to expand opportunities and recruitment following recommendations from a royal commission on the status of women.[2] More military occupations progressively opened up to women under the Canadian Human Rights Act and the Charter of Rights and Freedoms until the landmark 1989 Human Rights Tribunal decision finally lifted restrictions on employment of females in combat roles. Except for duty on submarines, women became eligible for all occupations and trades, underwent the same selection criteria and training as men, and followed a standard career progression. An advisory board on women in the Canadian Forces, renamed the Minister's Advisory Board on Gender Integration in the Canadian Forces in June

1993, studied and oversaw the phased assimilation of women, to be completed by the target year of 1999.[3] Members of the Canadian Forces received training on gender issues; harassment advisors worked in military units from 1995 onward; and the Canadian Forces National Investigation Service, an independent military police formation responsible for investigating complaints, was created in September 1997.

Nonetheless, when the national news magazine *Maclean's,* in its 25 May and 1 June 1998 issues, reported twenty-six unresolved cases relating to rape, assault, and sexual harassment in the Canadian Forces, defence officials were forced to review implementation of existing policies. In a highly personal public letter, General Maurice Baril, the chief of defence staff, issued a reminder to all officers and other ranks:

> We are not in the business of hurting, abusing, or exploiting people under our protection or in our custody. We are most definitely not in the business of hurting, abusing, or taking advantage of our own, especially our most vulnerable members and those with subordinate status or less power ... I will not allow the Canadian Forces to become a refuge or a training ground for thugs and brutes. Misconduct shall not be ignored. Apathy is unacceptable. Everyone in a leadership or supervisory position has been given certain responsibilities for others and the necessary lawful authority to enforce the Code of Service Discipline. We must relearn the Code and use the authority we have been given.[4]

The statement was tantamount to an admission that proper knowledge of military law in the Canadian Forces was lacking. Baril encouraged military personnel to use the toll-free telephone number that was established by the Department of National Defence to handle complaints of sexual harassment and assault. Furthermore, on 9 June 1998, Eggleton appointed André Marin, formerly director of the Special Investigations Unit in Ontario's Ministry of the Attorney General, as the first ombudsman for the Canadian Forces.[5] In dealing with grievances and complaints, Marin was independent of the military chain of command and reported directly to the minister of national defence even though his exact authority was not clearly set out in any legislation. The Canadian Forces National Investigation Service laid charges under the Criminal Code of Canada in several cases involving alleged sexual assaults. Trial of such offences generally took place before civil courts rather than courts martial, unless the act was committed outside Canada or pertained to some particular breach of military discipline.

In spite of the Department of National Defence's strong commitment to gender equality in the Canadian Forces, many women still confronted a climate of prejudice and discrimination in a male-dominated military hierarchy. Old habits died hard, and some males, even among the most senior ranks, treated women soldiers at best with a sense of outdated paternalism and at worst with downright disrespect. The forms of discrimination were often subtle rather than open. These ranged from inappropriate comments or touching to promises of promotion or advancement in return for sexual favours. Women were generally left to deal with situations themselves or told to report alleged misbehaviour to superior officers. The military justice system became involved only when the threshold of physical coercion, on which a criminal charge could be based, was crossed. Commanding officers usually preferred to ignore the problem altogether or settled the matter quietly within the unit, unless a pattern of misconduct emerged as more incidents occurred or other female victims came forward. In the end, some women chose to leave the Canadian Forces rather than endure continued inappropriate behaviour and abuse until military law went into operation.[6] Concerns about retention and recruitment of women prompted the Department of National Defence to run advertisements on cable television that were targeted at a female audience. But promises of excitement and adventure could not overcome the feeling that the Armed Forces was an uninviting environment for women, arising not from the nature of military service but the sexist attitudes of male colleagues. While complaint to an independent ombudsman was now an option, entrenched attitudes toward women meant incidents of sexual harassment and abuse continued to arise.[7] Resort to the sanctions of military or civil law was the manifestation of an institution with serious unresolved problems with ethics, training, and professionalism. An amendment to the National Defence Act giving military authorities discretion to try sexual assault in Canada by court martial rather than, as previously, by a civil court hardly inspired confidence in the military to handle such cases with sufficient concern for women.[8] If the disciplinary problems confronting the Canadian Forces were ranked, the mistreatment of prisoners in Somalia would be highest, cases of sexual harassment and abuse would be somewhere in the middle, and the normal run of military offences would be at the low end.

Soldiers in the Canadian Forces, both men and women alike, as well as the public at large need to have faith in the fair and proper working of military justice. To this end, the separate investigations into the military justice system in recent years made many broad recommendations pertaining to legal activities in Canada's Armed Forces. The view prevailed that major changes were required to Canadian military law and the legal structure that administers its application. Improvements within the existing structure are certainly needed, but a drastic reorganization of the military justice system deserves serious consideration before implementation. Although the Canadian Forces has every reason to be ashamed of its conduct in Somalia, change for the sake of change is potentially detrimental to the effectiveness of Canadian military law in the field during active operations.

The negative publicity surrounding the Somalia affair, the subsequent commission of inquiry, and ongoing disclosures of misbehaviour in the Canadian Forces have made some change inevitable. Previous royal commissions and commissions of inquiry in Great Britain and Canada acknowledged public concerns about military law and identified key areas in need of reform. The process of the Somalia inquiry was deeply flawed in many respects, and military officials became convenient targets for condemnation. Certain persons in the field and at National Defence Headquarters made bad decisions, but military officials never tried to hide the whole truth about events in Somalia from the Canadian people, as the inquiry implied in its final report. Canadian military authorities realize better than anyone else that something went seriously wrong in Somalia. The Canadian Armed Forces now live with the stigma of torture and murder, crimes that the public usually associates with the armed forces of less enlightened countries in other parts of the world.

A small number of soldiers reminded Canadians that no armed forces are immune to brutal misbehaviour during active operations. During a press conference in May 1993 to announce the laying of charges in Shidane Arone's murder, the JAG, Brigadier General Pierre Boutet, told the media that the Somalia disaster was the first time Canadian soldiers had committed these types of crimes on peacekeeping or related operations.[9] The statement was less than truthful. The Canadian Armed Forces were no strangers to misconduct. Long before the Somalia affair, Canadian soldiers committed questionable acts against civilians and prisoners of war during the Boer War and the Korean War. The ignorance of history by the JAG, whose business one would assume is to know about these things, places the JAG office at a distinct disadvantage in explaining the relevance of Canadian military law and the legal institutions that support it. Charting a course for the future development of the military justice system is hard when the past is unknown or misunderstood.

A major overhaul of defence legislation in Canada appears long overdue. Historically, efforts in this direction have taken place every forty to fifty years: in 1868, 1904, and 1950. In spite of limited amendments before the Somalia affair, the National Defence Act remained largely unchanged from the time it was introduced by Brooke Claxton five decades ago to the more substantial amendments introduced at the end of 1997 in response to the Somalia inquiry's report. The Canadian Armed Forces and Canadian society have changed considerably since the National Defence Act was originally drafted. Back then, the National Defence Act harmonized the disciplinary systems of three distinct services in the context of the Cold War; now, it applies to a smaller, unified Armed Forces deployed in a variety of general purpose roles and peacekeeping. Single QR&O were issued in 1968 and most recently in 1994.[10] Certain provisions require review to fit new circumstances and legislation such as the Charter. The extensive powers of summary punishment available to commanding officers still constitute a particular area of concern.[11] As in the past, the initiative for drafting new defence legislation in Canada must come from the minister of national defence in response to practical needs, demanded economy, and a perceived need for reform. Eggleton's amendments are no more than a prelude to what will have to be fresh defence legislation.

Previous experience has shown that an entirely new National Defence Act represents a major project and would entail months and even years of work by dedicated staffs and committees of the Department of National Defence. The time to start is now. The content of military law requires input from service authorities, the JAG, and Parliament at various stages. Eggleton or the minister of national defence of the day will have to convince the prime minister and the cabinet that new legislation is important, decide when timing is opportune, and show sufficient resolve and commitment to see the long process through to the end. A new National Defence Act perhaps represents the best way to indicate intention of serious reform and restore public confidence in the Canadian Forces. In the meantime, small modifications and greater emphasis on certain legal activities are possible to enhance the effectiveness of existing military law without fundamentally altering its character.

The post of JAG should be opened to a prominent civilian lawyer, selected by the governor-in-council. The original National Defence Act stipulated only that the person appointed to the position should be a qualified lawyer of ten years' standing. In practice, the JAG in Canada has always been a military officer. On advice from the JAG, Dickson's special advisory group suggested amending the National Defence Act to restrict the appointment to a commissioned officer with experience in military legal duties.[12] The new amendment, however, is restrictive and unnecessary. The argument that the JAG should be a military person because a military officer has always held the position rests on a weak foundation. Ignoring the advice of his Militia Council and prevailing British practice, Frederick Borden selected a militia officer rather than a civilian lawyer as the first JAG for personal reasons. Although temporarily in uniform, Oliver Biggar was at heart a civilian lawyer. Members of the JAG office subsequently filled the position for reasons of convenience, expertise in a highly specialized field of law, and promotional advancement within the military's legal office. The latest string of JAGs spent most of their careers in the military rather than in the larger legal profession in Canada. On 14 April 1998, Jerry Pitzul was appointed JAG, in spite of ineffectual prosecutions in the Westray mine disaster while he was director of Nova Scotia's public prosecution service.[13] Pitzul, who had been a long-time member of the JAG office until his retirement from the Canadian Forces in 1995, was reinstated with the military rank of brigadier general. The minister of national defence missed a rare opportunity to appoint an obviously civilian JAG with extensive military experience. After Boutet's less than stellar performance during the Somalia affair, Pitzul, as a military JAG, will have to work hard to restore public confidence in military law.

The appointment of a civilian lawyer would not preclude a military lawyer from becoming a JAG in the future. Indeed, the JAG should be placed on the same footing as comparable positions in National Defence Headquarters, where civilians and military officers are interchangeable. Other armed forces have civilian JAGs or director generals of law: the British JAG has been a civilian lawyer for a long time, and the Admiralty's judge advocate of the Fleet was previously a civil solicitor kept on retainer. In Australia, the JAG is selected from judges of the federal court or state supreme court.[14] No valid reason exists why Canada cannot have a civilian as JAG. If the arrangement proved unsatisfactory, a qualified military lawyer could again assume the post. The Somalia inquiry's proposed restructuring of legal organizations into separate branches, on the other hand, introduces an unwelcome degree of complexity with no guarantee of greater efficiency or real independence from the larger military institution. Once implemented, such restructuring might well ruin rather than improve Canada's military justice system, leading to greater public calls for reform. While the perception of independence is important, the Court Martial Appeal Court and Supreme Court of Canada provide adequate judicial review over courts martial. The appointment of qualified civilian lawyers to the post of JAG might better suit the purposes of the Canadian Forces without irretrievably destroying a system that works well most of the time. Most important, the option of having a military or civilian JAG maintains flexibility for unforeseen situations in peace and war.

To give civilian lawyers more opportunities to gain experience in military law, positions in the JAG office should be open to both civilian and military lawyers. General Charles Foulkes suggested partial civilianization of the JAG office in 1949. The same reasons hold true today because certain fields of law, such as claims, human rights, legislation, property, and international law, would be better served by civilian lawyers. Canada's military lawyers have become far too specialized; they are lawyers in uniform rather than soldiers with legal training. To alleviate limited career prospects and promotional stagnation, military lawyers should gain better opportunities to fill staff and operational positions outside the JAG office. The Canadian Forces could then take better advantage of their legal training and increase the coverage of military law. Over the past twenty years, the Department of National Defence has incurred considerable expense on military lawyers through subsidized education plans and in-house training. The resources of the JAG office represent an investment that should not be squandered, as the Somalia inquiry proposed.[15] Military lawyers make important contributions in the Canadian Forces. The introduction of civilian lawyers would not materially change the nature of the work and would allow military lawyers to concentrate on instruction, discipline, and military justice. Partial civilianization augments rather than replaces the talent already existing in the JAG office. The result would be a leaner and more efficient organization.

The operational demands of the Armed Forces and the circumstances of given situations will determine the right mixture of civilian and military lawyers. For example, in times of war or conflict, a higher proportion of military lawyers might be needed, whereas during peacetime, civilian lawyers might be in the majority. Use of civilian lawyers facilitates potentially lower overall staff levels and greater flexibility because, unlike military lawyers, they do not depend on a military career path. With a staff of some eighty military lawyers, the current JAG office handles roughly the same number of courts martial as Orde and his tiny staff did in the interwar period. Yet implementation of the recommendations by the Somalia inquiry and the Dickson special advisory group will increase, not reduce, the number of military lawyers.

The Canadian Forces could certainly function with fewer legal officers. Large numbers of military lawyers represent an expensive luxury for a small peacetime armed forces with a limited defence budget. The Canadian Forces have undertaken significant reductions in support of the federal government's fight against the national deficit and debt.[16] Why has not a corresponding decrease taken place in the JAG's personnel levels and establishment? Many legal activities could be performed by civilian lawyers from the public service commission or farmed out to other government departments, thus allowing military lawyers to focus mostly on military justice duties. The JAG would reserve the right to appoint lawyers, civilian or military, to any directorate in the JAG office to gain necessary experience and expertise in specialized fields. Overspecialization, especially in international law, has had a detrimental effect on the balance of legal activities within the JAG office. The presence of civilian lawyers in positions requiring a great deal of specialization would allow the remaining military lawyers to be generalists. In a projected regular force of 60,000 full-time military personnel and an overall defence budget of only $9 billion, the level of work justifies a decrease in the present JAG establishment by at least a third.[17] Canadian military lawyers have used public concerns about the military justice system to maintain the status quo and ignore the fiscal realities facing the Department of National Defence. Remarkably, the JAG's plans for the development of the legal branch in the immediate future assume constant or increased funding for growth in the bureaucracy.[18]

Whatever changes in structure and form are eventually made to the administration of military justice, better instruction in military law must receive high priority. As a start, the Department of National Defence should appoint a professor of law at the Royal Military College of Canada. In the past, military law was an important part of the curriculum. Military officers taught the subject on a formal basis from the late nineteenth century until it was gradually phased out during the early 1960s. Unlike the US service academies, the Royal Military College of Canada provides almost no instruction in military law beyond a half hour lecture on the Geneva Conventions. The appointed professor of law should be a military or civilian lawyer from the JAG office, rotated every two or three years. An ideal candidate would possess a master's of law degree from a recognized university as well as practical experience in the field and at National Defence Headquarters. At present, several military lawyers are qualified to fill the position. The prestige associated with a professorship and better possibilities for later employment at a law school after release from the Canadian Forces would make the position attractive to most candidates. Furthermore, such a professorship could alleviate promotional stagnation within the JAG office by providing another avenue for career advancement. The position would prepare promising lawyers for higher responsibility at the DJAG or JAG level. As in the past, the academic duties of the professor of law should include instructing officer cadets, preparing lectures and syndicate questions for the staff college, attending legal conferences, and compiling study guides on current military and civil legal literature.

The Canadian Forces currently lacks a comprehensive manual on Canadian military law. Before enactment of the National Defence Act in 1950, the Canadian Armed Forces predominantly used British handbooks and manuals. The British *Manual of Military Law,* issued in various editions from 1884 onward, was the standard reference source on military law. Why has no equivalent Canadian official manual been prepared since the Second World War? The sources of Canadian military law remain scattered in various legislative statutes, regulations, and administrative orders. Officers and other ranks require a single reference guide to explain the background, purpose, and content of military law in a simple and concise manner. Written in legalese, the present QR&O are too complicated for most service personnel to understand without additional assistance. In conjunction with the Department of Justice and interested experts, the JAG should prepare a manual of Canadian military law, similar to manuals used by armed forces in other countries.

Besides relevant information on the administration of military justice, the manual must include, at the very least, the history of Canadian military law, notes on evidence, rules of procedure at courts martial and summary courts, the National Defence Act, the Canadian Bill of Rights, the Charter of Rights and Freedoms, a comprehensive explanation of the relationship of the soldier to civil society, and extracts from relevant civil codes. Additional handbooks or pamphlets could simplify or amplify particular topics. The JAG has already made a start in this direction with a short bilingual guide on the election to be tried by summary trial or court martial for accused and assisting officers, which was published at the end of 1997.[19] Older manuals also require periodic amendment and revision to reflect changes to the law, the Armed Forces, and Canadian society. Lieutenant Colonel Kenneth Watkin, a good choice as the director of law/training and a JAG officer with a promising future, hopes as much as possible "to integrate both discipline and Law of Armed Conflict training into the CF mainstream."[20] Past experience has shown that official books encourage military officers and legal experts to write and publish on a private basis. The paucity of publications on Canadian military law today stands in stark contrast to the number available fifty or a hundred years ago. A manual of Canadian military law and associated publications would provide the foundation for study and instruction in military law for all officers and other ranks in the Canadian Forces.

Due to the absence of official publications and training manuals, general knowledge of military law within the Canadian Armed Forces has decreased over time. Although this lack of attention was typical for a peacetime Armed Forces, structural defects and poor emphasis in Canada's military training and educational system aggravated existing deficiencies. Officers need to receive instruction early in their careers and thereafter constant reinforcement throughout their careers to achieve proficiency in the intricacies of military law. As presently structured, the existing officer professional development system lacks quality assurance, regular review, and adequate resources.[21] Officers received outdated information about military law in a small number of short, intensive periods. The small volume of peacetime legal work does not provide sufficient opportunities for practical everyday application of military law. Implementing Lieutenant Colonel Watkin's proposed improvements to training and legal education will take time and consistent attention. There is no quick fix.

Military law remains an important subject, which many officers and other ranks will need to be familiar with, either as participants or as administrators, at some point during their careers in the Canadian Forces. A simple solution would be to include observers, particularly those likely by rank to be involved in future legal proceedings, to attend courts martial held in the Canadian Forces. It must be widely understood that military justice takes place in an open court, not behind closed doors. Military lawyers represent a resource aid rather than a substitute for a sound grounding in military law among all officers, on whose shoulders the responsibility for military justice and interpretation of rules of engagement will fall during operations.[22] War and peacekeeping conditions demand quick, informed, and decisive action by individuals on the spot to preserve discipline and maximum fighting efficiency, particularly when a military lawyer may not always be available to give advice on a given situation or legal matter. A good working knowledge of military law among all officers remains the best means for service personnel to recognize and avoid injustice, serious improprieties, and breaches of Canada's Code of Service Discipline. In Somalia, knowledge about military law was clearly wanting. Under an effective military justice system, soldiers know that illegal acts and misbehaviour have consequences and that superior authorities act judiciously and appropriately in the circumstances.

To meet present and future operational commitments, the JAG's reserve component requires expansion and improved training. The Department of National Defence's 1994 white paper called for integration of the regular and reserve forces to the fullest extent possible.[23] The reserves provide a large and accessible talent pool for the Canadian Forces. Every effort should be made to encourage practising lawyers to join the JAG's reserve. These lawyers possess knowledge, experience, and contacts that the Armed Forces could never attempt to develop or emulate itself. Upon joining the military, lawyers are exposed to a wide range of unique legal problems outside their normal activities or particular fields of expertise. Employing reservist lawyers for trial work and on regular courts martial would allow legal officers from the JAG office to devote more attention to instruction and training. Financial benefits might also accrue because in contrast to permanent staff, reservist lawyers would be paid by the Canadian Forces only when they are needed. In the event of war or large scale operational commitments, the existence of a sizable JAG reserve facilitates rapid expansion of military legal staffs with little requirement for additional training or qualification. During both world wars, civilian lawyers in uniform performed the bulk of work connected with courts martial and the prosecution of war crimes. Furthermore, the JAG reserve provides a convenient way to strengthen ties between the Canadian Forces and the legal profession in Canada.

For many decades, military law has been marginalized from the mainstream Canadian legal community. The limited number of books dealing with Canadian military law that are on the shelves of law schools reflects a sad state of affairs. Most legal educators and practitioners view military law as a quaint field of law out of step with developments in the modern world rather than a subject for serious study. In spite of its active involvement during the Second World War, the Canadian Bar Association has no equivalent to the American Bar Association's standing committee on armed forces law.[24] Even with the active efforts of JAG members at learned conferences and seminars, the Canadian Forces has met with little success in overcoming military law's presumed inferiority. The in-house character of the JAG office reinforces an added sense of isolation and separateness. After graduating from law schools, military lawyers learn, work, and function almost entirely within the military environment.

The Department of National Defence should sponsor courses at a reputable university law school to bring military law to a wider audience, influence aspiring lawyers to join the regular force or JAG reserve, and promote interest among an impressionable group, some of whom are destined for important positions in private and public life. Courses should augment the JAG's own educational activities as much as possible; but a military law program or chair at an established Canadian university is preferable to the creation of a separate JAG school. Military or civilian lawyers who intend to pursue graduate degrees could attend a formal military law program in Canada rather than in foreign countries. Canadian military law would only benefit from the critical academic scrutiny of a combination of military and civilian students in a classroom. Sponsorship of military law courses should take place on a trial basis at a selected law school and, if successful, be placed on a more permanent footing. In terms of investment, the financial commitment should be kept as reasonable as possible, with perhaps some sort of cost-sharing agreement with the selected university. The Department of National Defence already has an established network of military and strategic studies centres at universities across the country.

Readily available information on Canadian military law is hard to find outside the JAG office. Although lawyers and judges make frequent use of decisions in serialized Court Martial Appeal Court cases and reports from the Supreme Court of Canada, court martial proceedings are not in the public domain. In contrast to the US armed services, the Canadian Forces does not publish summaries of military trials with particular relevance to service and civil law, the equivalent of civilian case law. Since 1974, the JAG library has retained copies of court martial proceedings for the reference of military lawyers at National Defence Headquarters; this resource base is remote to lawyers outside the National Capital Region and requires permission for use. Consequently, Canadian judges and lawyers often refer to US precedents shelved in law school and law firm libraries rather than to more applicable Canadian cases. A glaring need exists for wider public circulation of decisions from Canadian military courts and for general information on military law. American military lawyers have been pioneers in the use of electronic and computer technology for legal research, training, and preparation of cases; informing the public about their activities is important for the armed forces and the nation.[25] At the very least, Canada's JAG office should have a Web page on the Internet with a brief history of Canadian military law, its annual report to the minister and Parliament, and a description of its current activities.

In terms of publicizing their work, Canadian military lawyers lag behind counterparts in other countries, especially the United States. Whereas each of the three US armed services produce legal journals at regular intervals, the *Canadian Forces JAG Journal,* the Canadian military's legal periodical, has not appeared for several years. In the United States, the National Institute of Military Justice, a private organization established in 1991 to increase the profile of military law in that country, publishes a monthly newsletter, conducts seminars and training for civilian and military personnel, and educates the public through the news media. One of its founders commented: "It is unhealthy, in a democratic society, for the military criminal justice system to exist as unknown territory to the civilian bench and bar."[26] Is a comparable institution to the National Institute of Military Justice needed in Canada? Besides obvious benefits for advanced instruction in military law, better accessibility and coverage would improve the quality and administration of Canadian military justice.

As the Canadian Forces examine the lessons from Somalia, the history of Canadian military law must be kept in perspective. Defence legislation, military legal institutions, and instruction in military law evolved in a pragmatic and haphazard fashion in Canada. It is not a story of steady progress and advancement. Paradoxically, Canadian officers and other ranks in today's Armed Forces probably know less about military law than their predecessors did a century ago. Formal training and instruction are inferior, published manuals and pamphlets are almost non-existent, and military lawyers are overspecialized and ghettoized within the JAG office.[27] The JAG and the assistant deputy minister (personnel) share most of the responsibility for the poor state of military law within the Canadian Forces. Lack of attention and compromises for the sake of false economy allowed serious deficiencies in the general knowledge of military law to develop over a long period of time. It is time for some changes, but the radical restructuring advocated by the Somalia inquiry is unnecessary. The Supreme Court of Canada has recognized the legitimacy of a separate military justice system in Canada. Legislative changes, through amendments to the existing National Defence Act and a new defence statute sometime in the future, are only a partial solution. More improvements in organization and training are required to assure that military law is widely known and properly practised throughout the Canadian Forces. Civilian lawyers in the JAG office, a manual of Canadian military law, and additional legal training seem reasonable to avoid another public disgrace like the incidents in Somalia. Can the Canadian Armed Forces afford to ignore military law any longer?

Appendix 1: Judge Advocate Generals in Canada

1911-8	Major General Henry Smith
1918-20	Lieutenant Colonel Oliver Mowat Biggar
1920-50	Brigadier Reginald John Orde
1950-69	Brigadier William J. Lawson
1969-72	Brigadier General Harold A. McLearn
1972-6	Brigadier General James M. Simpson
1976-82	Major General John Patterson Wolfe
1982-6	Brigadier General Frank Karwandy
1986-90	Brigadier General Robert L. Martin
1990-3	Commodore Peter R. Partner
1993-8	Brigadier General Pierre G. Boutet
1998-	Brigadier General Jerry S.T. Pitzul

Appendix 2: Courts Martial in the Canadian Armed Forces under the National Defence Act

Table 1

Year	Number	Size of regular force	Courts martial per thousand personnel
1950	249	47,185	5.28
1951	427	68,427	6.24
1952	204	95,394	2.14
1953	142	104,427	1.36
1954	150	112,529	1.33
1955	71	118,077	0.60
1956	61	116,678	0.52
1957	54	117,092	0.46
1958	80	119,038	0.67
1959	49	120,412	0.41
1960	47	119,597	0.39
1961	51	120,055	0.42
1962	55	126,474	0.43
1963	43	123,694	0.35
1964	28	120,781	0.23
1965	31	114,164	0.27
1966	22	107,467	0.20
1967	28	105,721	0.26
1968	34	101,676	0.33
1969	62	98,340	0.63
1970	78	93,353	0.84
1971	68	89,563	0.76
1972	58	84,933	0.68
1973	64	82,402	0.78
1974	75	81,822	0.92
1975	118	79,817	1.48
1976	99	79,738	1.24
1977	90	78,800	1.14
1978	128	78,778	1.62

1979	111	78,445	1.42
1980	126	80,166	1.57
1981	157	81,747	1.92
1982	157	82,091	1.91
1983	169	82,000	2.06
1984	152	83,630	1.82
1985	105	83,910	1.25
1986	124	86,036	1.44
1987	121	85,750	1.41
1988	95	87,393	1.09
1989	97	88,331	1.10
1990	74	87,976	0.84
1991	72	87,319	0.82
1992	59	84,792	0.70
1993	65	78,376	0.83
1994	45	75,949	0.59
1995	37	72,079	0.51
1996	33	61,336	0.54
1997	41	60,320	0.68
1998	35	60,000	0.58

Sources: JAG Court Martial Statistics; DND *Annual Reports; Estimates, Part III, National Defence.*

Notes

Introduction: Military Law in Canada

1 Bernard Starkman, "Canadian Military Law: The Citizen as Soldier," *Canadian Bar Review* 43 (1965): 421.

2 National Army Museum (hereafter NAM), Brigadier Humphry Bullock, 6012/266/8, Captain H. Bullock, "The Development of British Military Law," 8 May 1927, 2-6.

3 Barbara Donagan, "Codes and Conduct during the English Civil War," *Past and Present* 116 (1988): 83-7.

4 Parliamentary Counsel's Office (hereafter PCO), *Military Law 1878-9,* Sir Henry Thring, Parliamentary Counsel, "Memorandum on Military Law," 24 May 1878.

5 R.A. McDonald, "The Trail of Discipline: The Historical Roots of Canadian Military Law," *Canadian Forces JAG Journal* 1 (1985): 14.

6 Office of the Adjutant General of the Militia of Lower Canada, *Rules and Regulations for the Formations, Field-Exercise, and Movements of the Militia of Lower Canada* (Quebec: J. Neilson, 1804).

7 Desmond Morton, *A Military History of Canada* (Edmonton: Hurtig Publishers, 1985), 87.

Chapter 1: Modest Beginnings

1 J.R. Dinwiddy, "The Early Nineteenth-Century Campaign against Flogging in the Army," *English Historical Review* 97 (1982): 308-31.

2 "Report from His Majesty's Commissioners for Inquiring into the System of Military Punishments in the Army," *Parliamentary Papers* 22 (1836).

3 Public Record Office (hereafter PRO), WO 93/15, J.R. Mowbray to Sir J.P. Pakington, 17 January 1868.

4 PRO, WO 32/6248, minute by Charles M. Clode, 21 December 1868; PCO, *Military Law 1878-9,* "Memorandum on Corporal Punishment," 23 June 1879.

5 "Second Report of the Commissioners appointed to inquire into the Constitution and Practice of Courts-Martial in the Army and the Present System of Punishment for Military Offences," *Parliamentary Papers* 12 (1868-9): 15-151.

6 PRO, WO 32/6248, D. Robinson to W. Galton, 1 January 1869.

7 PRO, WO 123/182, "Memorandum upon the Military Code under which Her Majesty's Forces are to be Governed," 11 December 1869.

8 "Report from the Select Committee on Mutiny and Marine Acts," *Parliamentary Papers* 10 (1878): 255-9.

9 *The Army Act, 1881, and certain other statutes relating to the Army, together with Rules of Procedure 1881, and Rules for Summary Punishment,* 2nd ed. (London: H.M. Stationery Office, 1882).

10 PRO, WO 123/182, "Memorandum on the Duties of the Judge Advocate General," 13 May 1873.

11 PRO, WO 32/8735, Charles M. Clode, "The Administration of Military Law," 15 August 1879; Gerry R. Rubin, "Parliament, Prerogative, and Military Law: Who Had Legal Authority over the Army in the Later Nineteenth Century," *Journal of Legal History* 18 (April 1997): 50-2.
12 Ibid., Garnet Wolseley to under secretary of state for war, 2 November 1883. The judge advocate general sometimes sought Wolseley's advice on appointments and other legal matters. Hove Central Library (hereafter HCL), Field Marshal Garnet Joseph Wolseley, Reel 5, Sir Francis Jeune to Field Marshal Garnet Wolseley, 22 April 1896.
13 PRO, WO 82/20, JAG office day book, 14 January 1881.
14 Thomas Frederick Simmons, *Remarks on the Constitution and Practice of Courts Martial,* 2nd ed. (London, UK: F. Pinkney, 1835); Charles J. Napier, *Remarks on Military Law and the Punishment of Flogging* (London, UK: J. and W. Boone, 1837); George C. D'Aguilar, *Observations on the Practice and Forms of District, Regimental, and Detachment Courts Martial* (Dublin: M.H. Gill, 1866).
15 Charles M. Clode, *The Administration of Justice under Military and Martial Law* (London, UK: John Murray, 1872), iv.
16 PRO, WO 32/8735, "Report of Military Committee on the Mutiny Act and Articles of War," 7 June 1877.
17 PRO, WO 147/18, Colonel Robert Carey, *Military Law and Discipline* (London, UK: H.M. Stationery Office, 1877).
18 Thring remarked: "The preparation of the text book and rules has been a work of very great labour to the Parliamentary Counsel Office, and during the past twelve months has occupied no small part of the leisure time of the Parliamentary counsel and his assistant. The Parliamentary counsel trusts that the work will be of advantage to the army." PCO, *Army Rules of Procedure 1880-81,* memorandum, "Army Discipline and Regulation Act, 1879," 16 August 1880.
19 PRO, WO 82/20, JAG office day book, 19 July 1883.
20 War Office, *Manual of Military Law 1884* (London, UK: H.M. Stationery Office, 1884).
21 Peter Burroughs, "Tackling Army Desertion in British North America," *Canadian Historical Review* 61 (1980): 36-7.
22 PCO, *Military Law 1878-9,* "Memorandum Explanatory of the Army Discipline and Regulation Act, 1879," 16 July 1879.
23 *Sessional Papers,* no. 8, 5 (1872): 35.
24 *Statutes of Canada,* 1868, 32 Vict., c. 40; Ernest J. Chambers, *The Canadian Militia: A History of the Origin and Development of the Force* (Montreal: L.M. Fresco, 1910), 87-8.
25 *Sessional Papers,* no. 10, 2 (1869): 18-9.
26 National Archives of Canada (hereafter NAC), RG 9 II B1, vol. 6, file 7-1578 1870, Privy Council Order, 4 March 1870. *Regulations and Orders for the Active Militia, the Schools of Military Instruction, and the Reserve Militia (in the cases therein mentioned), of the Dominion of Canada* (Ottawa: George Desbarats, Queen's Printer, 1870).
27 *Sessional Papers,* no. 7, 4 (1871): 12-3.
28 PRO, WO 123/182, George Cartier, "Memorandum as to the Rank of Major-General in the Canadian Militia," 24 January 1872.
29 Gwyn Harries-Jenkins, "The Development of Professionalism in the Victorian Army," *Armed Forces and Society* 1 (1975): 479-80; Stephen John Harris, *Canadian Brass: The Making of a Professional Army 1860-1939* (Toronto: University of Toronto Press, 1988).
30 NAM, General Sir Henry Murray, 7406-36-32, lecture, 9 December 1857.
31 G.R. Rubin, "The Legal Education of British Army Officers, 1860-1923," *Journal of Legal History* 15 (1994): 226-7.
32 *Sessional Papers,* no. 8, 3 (1870): 19.
33 NAC, RG 9 II B2, vol. 46, adjutant general to minister of militia and defence, 14 November 1870.
34 T.C. Scoble, *The Canadian Volunteer's Hand Book for Field Service* (Toronto: Henry Rowsell, 1868), 61-85.
35 A.B. Tulloch, *Elementary Lectures on Military Law* (London, UK: W. Mitchell and Co., 1872), preface.

36 Charles Gorham, *A Text Book of Military Law as Applicable to Persons Subject to the Army Discipline Act to Which Is Added Military Law as Applicable to Persons Subject to the Indian Articles of War,* 3rd ed. (Calcutta: Brown and Co., 1880).
37 C.P. Stacey, *Canada and the British Army 1846-1871: A Study in the Practice of Responsible Government* (Toronto: University of Toronto Press, 1963), 253-5.
38 Thomas Bland Strange, *Gunner Jingo's Jubilee* (1896; reprint, Edmonton: University of Alberta Press, 1988).
39 Liddell Hart Centre for Military Archives (hereafter LHC), Brigadier General Sir James Edward Edmonds, I/1/2a, "General Regulations for the Government of the Royal Military Academy at Woolwich," April 1879.
40 Owen Arnold Cooke, "Organization and Training in the Central Canadian Militia 1866-1885" (M.A. thesis, Queen's University, 1974), 49.
41 *Sessional Papers,* no. 6, 8 (1875): 84-6.
42 *Sessional Papers,* no. 7, 10 (1877): 200; *The Manual for the Militia Artillery of Canada* (Quebec: Gunnery School Press, 1878).
43 Glenbow Museum and Archives (hereafter GMA), Joseph Victor Bégin, M75, box 1, file 7, active militia first class "short course" certificate, 27 January 1883.
44 Richard Arthur Preston, *Canada's RMC: A History of the Royal Military College of Canada* (Toronto: University of Toronto Press, 1969), 18.
45 Henry Charles Fletcher, *Report on the Military Academy at West Point, U.S.,* 1874.
46 *Sessional Papers,* no. 8, 11 (1878): 252.
47 *Sessional Papers,* no. 8, 13 (1880): 402-3.
48 Garnet Joseph Wolseley, *The Soldier's Pocket-Book for Field Service,* 2nd ed. (London, UK, and New York: Macmillan and Co., 1871); HCL, Wolseley, Reel 2, G.L. Craik no. 2, Macmillan and Co. Publishers to Lord Wolseley, 14 July 1885.
49 *Sessional Papers,* no. 9, 14 (1880/81): 361.
50 Walter James, *1,260 Questions in Topography, Tactics, Military Law, Fortification, Military Administration, Drill; Chiefly Those Set at the Various Examinations Held during the Past Seven Years at the Royal Military College, Sandhurst, and for the Admission of Militia Officers to the Army* (London, UK: Harrison, Queen's Printer, 1881), 39-51.
51 "New Books," *Canadian Military Review* 1 (1 September 1880): 115; Douglas F. Jones, *Notes on Military Law for the Use of the Cadets of the Royal Military College of Canada* (Ottawa: Maclean, Roger, and Co., 1880).
52 Douglas F. Jones, *Textbook of Military Law: For the Use of the Gentlemen Cadets of the Royal Military College of Canada* (Kingston, ON: Daily News Steam Printing House, 1882).
53 *Sessional Papers,* no. 9, 15 (1882): 241.
54 *Sessional Papers,* no. 13, 22 (1889): 210.
55 *Sessional Papers,* no. 13, 24 (1891): 156.
56 *Sessional Papers,* no. 7, 10 (1877): 2-3.
57 NAC, RG 9 II B1, vol. 9, file 137-750 1878, examination papers, "Second Class Examination on the Articles of War, Militia Regulations, and the Militia Act," 16 May 1878.
58 NAC, RG 9 II K7, vol. 3, file "RMC Exam Papers 1879," first class certificate examinations, "Questions on Articles of War," 15 April 1879.
59 *Sessional Papers,* no. 8, 17 (1884): 46.
60 NAC, RG 9 II K7, vol. 3, file "RMC Exam Papers 1879," memorandum by the deputy adjutant general, "Suggestions Respecting Examination for Certificates of Qualification at the New Infantry Schools of Instruction," 18 July 1883.
61 NAM, W. Capel, 6609/143/1, "Examination for Promotion: Captains: Military Law," July 1884.
62 Joseph Ernest de Montarville Taschereau, *Code militaire* (Quebec: A. Coté, 1884); William D. Otter, *The Guide: A Manual for the Canadian Militia (Infantry), embracing the Interior Economy, Duties, Discipline, Dress, Books and Correspondence of a Regiment in Barracks, Camp, or Headquarters,* 2nd ed. (Toronto: Copp Clark, 1885), 115-31.
63 House of Commons, *Debates* 2 (1885): 1306.
64 "The Diary of Lieut. J.A.V. Preston, 1885," *Saskatchewan History* 8 (1955): 107.
65 GMA, Robert Kellock Allan, M12, file 2, diary, 22 April 1885.

66 NAC, Charles Arkoll Boulton, MG 29 E3, file 1, Plate 209, order of the day, 6 July 1885.
67 *Sessional Papers,* no. 6, 19 (1886): 14.
68 House of Commons, *Debates* 2 (1885): 2169.
69 GMA, Allan, M12, file 2, diary, 29 April 1885.
70 British Columbia Archives (hereafter BCA), Lieutenant Colonel William Dillon Otter, O/B/Ot8, brigade order, 3 June 1885.
71 Walter Hildebrandt, "Ending the Resistance: The Northwest Campaign of 1885 and the Fall of Batoche," *Journal of the West* 32 (1993): 41.
72 G.F.G. Stanley, "Gabriel Dumont's Account of the North West Rebellion 1885," *Canadian Historical Review* 30 (1949): 266; Private Charles Capp, a soldier who participated in the final assault, gave a different version of events. R.H. Roy, "With the Midland Battalion to Batoche," *Saskatchewan History* 32 (spring 1979): 59.
73 GMA, Staff Sergeant Frederick Marshall Kitchener, M635, diary, 14 May 1885.
74 James Pennington Macpherson, *A Catechism on Military Law as applicable to the Militia of Canada* (Montreal: John Lovell and Son, 1886), 5-6.
75 John Boughey, *The Elements of Military Administration and Military Law, with Synopsis of Army Act, and a Form of Proceedings for a Regimental Court Martial, etc.,* 12th ed. (Yorktown, Surrey, UK: William Webb, 1890).
76 PRO, WO 32/6281, Field Marshal His Royal Highness the Duke of Cambridge to general officers commanding abroad, 12 May 1887.
77 *Sessional Papers,* no. 11, 23 (1890): 172.
78 *Sessional Papers,* no. 19, 25 (1892): 1.
79 NAC, RG 9 II B2, vol. 6, "Return of Courts Martial between 1 Oct and 31 Oct 1892."
80 City of Vancouver Archives (hereafter CVA), 6th Regiment Duke of Connaught's Own Rifles, add. mss. 48, vol. 1, file 4, Lieutenant Colonel E.G. Prior to Captain T.O. Townley, 30 May 1894.
81 H.M. Mowat, "The Law and the Soldier," *Selected Papers from the Transactions of the Canadian Military Institute* 9 (1897-9): 43-4.
82 Desmond Morton, "Bayonets in the Streets: The Canadian Experience of Aid of the Civil Power 1867-1990," *Canadian Defence Quarterly* 20 (spring 1990): 31.
83 Henry Smith, "Military Aid of the Civil Power," *Selected Papers from the Transactions of the Canadian Military Institute* 10 (1900): 88.
84 Roy MacLaren, *Canadians on the Nile 1882-1898* (Vancouver: University of British Columbia Press, 1978), 127-8.
85 PRO, WO 147/33, H. Brackenbury, "Deficiencies of Troops – Imperial and Local – in our Colonial Garrisons," 8 May 1888.
86 PRO, WO 82/22, JAG office day book, 6 September 1889.
87 PCO, *Army 1881-2,* Sir Henry Thring, "Volunteers," 12 May 1881.
88 PRO, WO 82/21, JAG office day book, 14 April 1885.
89 PRO, WO 82/22, JAG office day book, 22 January 1889.
90 PRO, WO 82/23, JAG office day book, 9 November 1894.
91 PCO, *Miscellaneous 1895,* memorandum, "Discipline in Mixed Bodies of Regular and Colonial Forces."
92 PRO, WO 82/23, JAG office day book, 14 December 1894.
93 Richard A. Preston, *Canada and "Imperial Defense,"* (Toronto: University of Toronto Press, 1967), 241-2.
94 PRO, WO 82/21, JAG office day book, 3 June 1887.
95 PRO, WO 32/8247, Ralph Thompson, for secretary of state for war, to under secretary of state for the colonies, 28 April 1892.
96 *Sessional Papers,* no. 19, 32 (1898): 23.
97 PRO, WO 82/24, JAG office day book, 3 April 1897.
98 Ibid., 2 July 1898.
99 PRO, ADM 1/8904, Colonial Defence Committee, memorandum "Canada: Defence of Dominion," 31 March 1896.
100 *Sessional Papers,* no. 19, 33 (1899): 25. Warren Perry, "Military Reforms of General Sir Edward Hutton in New South Wales: 1893-96," *Australian Quarterly* 28 (1956): 65-75.

101 LHC, Major John Frederick Maurice, 2/2/45, Field Marshal Garnet Wolseley to Queen Victoria, 8 March 1899.

Chapter 2: In Defence of Empire

1 *Sessional Papers,* no. 20, 34 (1900): 37-8; Desmond Morton, "Canada's First Expeditionary Force: The Canadian Contingent in South Africa, 1899-1900," *Canadian Defence Quarterly* 15 (winter 1985/86): 41.
2 Provincial Archives of Manitoba (hereafter PAM), Boer War (Lord Strathcona's Horse), MG 6 F1, militia order no. 26, 1 February 1900.
3 PRO, WO 108/359, *Conditions of Service of South African and Overseas Contingents Employed in the South African War 1899-1902,* (London, UK: H.M. Stationery Office, Harrison and Sons, 1904), 91-9.
4 GMA, Charles A. Clark, M223, diary, 5 June 1900.
5 Ibid., Private John S. Robson, M7908, Trooper George Alexander Bowers' diary, 26 August 1900.
6 PRO, WO 108/184, "Notes by Colonel J.M. Grierson, RA, on Return from South Africa."
7 Robert Higginbotham, "Case Studies in the Law of Land Warfare," *Military Review* 63 (January 1983): 62.
8 LHC, Maurice, 3/1/2/40, Maurice to wife, 7 July 1900. Under the 1864 Geneva Convention, wounded officers and soldiers released by the Boers could not bear arms for the duration of the conflict unless duly exchanged. LHC, General Sir Ian Hamilton, 24/7/3/11, South African Field Force, circular memorandum no. 6, 1 February 1900.
9 GMA, Corporal Ivor Edward Cecil Rice-Jones, M1037, diary, 30 August 1900. Among the nine were soldiers captured on 1 July, the first day of fighting for the Strathcona's Horse in South Africa. *Sessional Papers,* no. 35a, 35 (1901): 163.
10 CVA, Canadian Contingent (South Africa), add. mss. 49, file 1, Private Sumner O'Brien, "A" Company RCR, South African Field Force to officers and soldiers, Duke of Connaught Rifles, Vancouver, 5 October 1900; GMA, Rice-Jones, M1037, diary, 4 September 1900.
11 PRO, WO 108/260, Major General W.F. Kelly, deputy adjutant general Pretoria, "Report on Adjutant-General's Department – Rendered to the Field Marshal Commanding-in-Chief, by the Deputy Adjutant-General," 14 July 1900, 2.
12 NAM, Lance Corporal R. Moore and Private Williams, 8110-7, scrap book, army orders South African Field Force, 23 June 1900; Desmond Morton, "Colonel Otter and the First Canadian Contingent in South Africa, 1899-1900," in *Policy by Other Means: Essays in Honour of C.P. Stacey,* ed. Michael Cross and Robert Bothwell (Toronto: Clarke, Irwin and Co., 1972), 119.
13 NAM, Moore and Williams, 81110-7, scrap book, army order no. 255, 31 December 1900.
14 GMA, Clark, M223, diary, 3 November 1900.
15 Carman Miller, *Painting the Map Red: Canada and the South African War, 1899-1902* (Montreal and Kingston: McGill-Queen's University Press, 1993), 324.
16 GMA, Robson, M7908, Trooper George Alexander Bowers's diary, 12 October 1900.
17 PRO, 30/57/20, Field Marshal Lord Roberts to Earl Kitchener, 13 July 1901.
18 PRO, WO 108/110, South African Field Force, army order no. 480, 14 January 1902.
19 Ibid., army order no. 487, 27 January 1902.
20 George Witton, *Scapegoats of Empire,* (Melbourne: D.W. Paterson, 1907); Barry Bridges, "Lord Kitchener and the Morant-Handcock Executions," *Journal of the Royal Australian Historical Society* 73 (June 1987): 24-40; Kit Denton, *The Breaker* (New York: Pocket Books, 1981).
21 PRO, WO 32/8730, Kitchener to adjutant general, War Office, 6 November 1901.
22 Ibid., F.H. Jeune to adjutant general, War Office, 24 January 1902; PRO 30/57/22, Broderick to Kitchener, 3 May 1902.
23 PRO, WO 108/110, South African Field Force, army order no. 520, 27 March 1902.
24 PRO, 30/57/22, Kitchener to Broderick, 25 January 1901.
25 Ibid., 6 April 1902.
26 Ibid., 23 March 1902.
27 Ibid., Broderick to Kitchener, 22 February 1902.

28 LHC, Hamilton, 13/1/1-7, *Minutes of Evidence taken before the Royal Commission on the War in South Africa* (London, UK: H.M. Stationery Office, 1903); Jay Charles Stone, "The Boer War and Its Effects on British Military Reform" (Ph.D. diss., City University of New York, 1985).
29 PRO, WO 32/4513, E.W.D. Ward, War Office, "Memorandum on the Report of Committee on Punishments on Active Service," 16 February 1904.
30 PCO, *Army 1905-07,* Sir F. Liddell, parliamentary counsel, "Minute of a Conference held at the War Office between Colonel Robb, Colonel Lake, Mr. Brade, and Myself," 1904.
31 PRO, WO 32/8699, director of personnel services to adjutant general, 19 February 1906.
32 PRO, WO 32/8700, "Report of the Committee on Military Punishments, and the Method of Recording Them," 8 June 1906.
33 *Sessional Papers,* no. 35, 37 (1903): 34; W.E. Hodgins, "Law Applicable to the Militia of Canada," *Canadian Law Times* 21 (1901): 176; John G. Armstrong, "The Dundonald Affair," *Canadian Defence Quarterly* 11 (autumn 1981): 39-45.
34 House of Commons, *Debates* 1 (1904): 205-8.
35 *Statutes of Canada,* 1904, 4 Edw. 7, c. 23.
36 CVA, Major John Reynolds Tite, add. mss. 50, vol. 8, "Regulations and Orders for the Militia of Canada, 1904," 29 October 1904; *Sessional Papers,* no. 35, 39 (1905): 49.
37 *Sessional Papers,* no. 35, 39 (1905): 52. Major W.H. Ames, "The Military Education of Officers of the Auxiliary Forces," *Selected Papers from the Transactions of the Canadian Military Institute* 13 (1903): 62.
38 NAC, RG 9 II A2, vol. 24, minutes of Militia Council, 18 April 1905.
39 PRO, ADM 1/8904, Colonial Defence Committee, "Canada: Command and Efficiency of Militia," 28 July 1903. *Sessional Papers,* no. 35, 38 (1904): 42.
40 The entrance examination to the staff college was difficult and required a great deal of preparation and reading, even for officers on active service. LHC, Maurice, 3/1/2/13, Maurice to wife, 29 July 1900.
41 NAC, RG 9 II A2, vol. 28, minutes of Militia Council, 4 November 1909; *Sessional Papers,* no. 33, 45 (1911): 9; War Office, General Staff, *Staff Manual: War (Provisional) 1912,* 28 October 1912.
42 LHC, Edmonds, I/2A/1a, War Office, *Regulations Respecting the Staff College* (London, UK: Harrison and Sons, H.M. Stationery Office, 1894), 16-7; PRO, WO 82/24, JAG office day book, 20 July 1895.
43 T.E. Holland, *The Laws and Customs of War on Land, as Defined by the Hague Convention of 1899* (London, UK: Harrison and Sons, 1904), ix.
44 LHC, Edmonds, I/2B/7a, notes on staff college course, "Military Law, etc.," 1907.
45 LHC, Brigadier Sir Bernard Edward Fergusson, file 3, Colonel Pemberton, "Lectures on Military Law," 1909.
46 LHC, Edmonds, 4/7/1-34, lecture by Colonel J.E. Edmonds to eastern command intelligence and reconnaissance class at Lewes, "The Laws and Usages of War," July 1910.
47 J.E. Edmonds and L. Oppenheim, *Land Warfare: An Exposition of the Laws and Usages of War on Land, for the Guidance of Officers of His Majesty's Army* (London, UK: Harrison and Sons, H.M. Stationery Office, 1912); LHC, Edmonds, V/5/6B, "Statement with regard to the publications on the subject of the Customs of War on Land."
48 NAC, RG 9 II A2, vol. 25, minutes of Militia Council, 9 November 1906.
49 PRO, WO 32/9102, Major General Percy Lake to adjutant general, War Office, 1 May 1907; NAC, RG 9 II A2, vol. 26, minutes of Militia Council, 11 June 1907.
50 PRO, WO 32/9102, F.W. Borden to Bertram Cox, Colonial Office, 10 May 1907.
51 Ibid., memorandum by F.F. Liddell, parliamentary counsel, 8 January 1908.
52 PRO, WO 32/9103, J.R. Chancellor, secretary, Colonial Defence Committee, memorandum no. 402M, "Colonial Military Law: Application of Army Act to Colonial Troops when Employed on Active Service with Imperial Troops," 16 July 1908.
53 PRO, WO 32/9104, Frederick Borden to governor general, 10 March 1909.
54 NAC, RG 24, Reel C-5055, file C-871, Lieutenant Colonel Henry Smith to adjutant general, Department of Militia and Defence, 18 March 1909.
55 PRO, WO 32/9104, Major General Percy Lake to Frederick Borden, "The Army Act as Applicable to the Militia," 17 November 1908.

56 PRO, WO 32/9482, R.H. Brade, War Office, to under secretary of state, Colonial Office, 8 September 1909.
57 PRO, WO 32/9105, minute by F.F. Liddell, parliamentary counsel, 14 February 1910.
58 NAC, RG 9 II A2, vol. 24, minutes of Militia Council, 31 January 1905.
59 Ibid., 14 February 1905.
60 PRO, WO 123/182, R.H. Brade to secretary of state for war, "The Judge Advocate General," May 1906. The relationship between the judge advocate general and the adjutant general remained virtually unchanged under the new arrangement. PRO, WO 32/8740, J.S. Ewart to JAG, 2 September 1911.
61 NAM, Bullock, 6012/266/5, "Judge Advocates General in India," 15 June 1948; O.P. Sharma, *Military Law in India,* 2nd ed. (Bombay: N.M. Tripathi Private, 1990), 22-4.
62 NAC, RG 9 II A2, vol. 24, minutes of Militia Council, 2 May 1905.
63 NAC, RG 24, vol. 6646, file 7, memorandum by Lieutenant Colonel Henry Smith, 1909.
64 NAC, RG 9 II A2, vol. 28, minutes of Militia Council, 23 December 1909.
65 NAC, RG 9 II A2, vol. 29, minutes of Militia Council, 12 September 1910; Militia general order no. 166, 24 October 1911.
66 *Sessional Papers,* no. 35a, 45 (1911): 29.
67 LHC, Hamilton, 13/1/14/23, "Report by the Inspector-General of the Overseas Forces on the Military Institutions of Canada," 1913, 23.
68 Ibid., 4.
69 LHC, Hamilton, 38/5/10/2/2, General Ian Hamilton to General John French, 15 June 1913.
70 Royal Westminster Regiment, case 2, file 58D-12-6, Private S. Dailey, Sergeant's certificate of military instruction, 6th Regiment Duke of Connaught's Own Rifles Headquarters, Vancouver, 13 March 1909.
71 Militia general order no. 185, 1 December 1911; W.E. Hodgins, "Military Law," *Canadian Law Times* 30 (1910): 487-9.
72 Sisson C. Pratt, *The Military Law Examiner, Containing the Questions Set at Examinations in Military Law up to July, 1911, together with the Answers to Them and References to the Official Books,* 8th ed. (London, UK: Gale and Polden, 1911); J. Atkinson, *Guide for Officers and Non-Commissioned Officers of the Territorial Force,* 2nd ed. (London, UK: Gale and Polden, 1911).
73 NAC, RG 24, vol. 19,054, file 1451-90/M4, "History of the McGill Contingent Canadian Officers Training Corps (148th Bn CEF)"; NAC, RG 9 II A2, vol. 31, minutes of Militia Council, 4 April 1912.
74 CVA, 11th Regiment Irish Fusiliers of Canada, add. mss. 51, Lieutenant T.B. Harston, "C Company Parades," 3 February 1914.
75 PRO, 30/57/56, Duke of Connaught to Field Marshal Kitchener, 12 September 1914.
76 CVA, 6th Regiment Duke of Connaught's Own Rifles, add. mss. 48, vol. 2, file 4, adjutant general to Lieutenant Colonel J.H.D. Hulme, officer commanding, 6th Regiment Duke of Connaught's Own Rifles, 6 August 1914.
77 Robert Dennistoun, "Canadian Military Law Overseas," *Canada Law Journal* 56 (February 1920): 44-5.
78 Desmond Morton, *A Peculiar Kind of Politics: Canada's Overseas Ministry in the First World War* (Toronto: University of Toronto Press, 1982), 87.
79 Donald M.A.R. Vince, "Development in the Legal Status of the Canadian Military Forces, 1914-19, as Related to Dominion Status," *Canadian Journal of Economics and Political Science* 20 (1954): 364-8.
80 *Report of the Ministry of Overseas Military Forces of Canada,* (London, UK: Ministry, Overseas Military Forces of Canada, 1918), 37.
81 BCA, Major George Griffiths Aitken, add. mss. 1913, box 3, file 5, lecture notes, "Military Law," 15 November 1915; PAM, Captain Clarence Montague Boswell, MG 14 C4, box 19, Lieutenant Clarence Boswell, 90th Battalion, CEF, course notes, "Military Law," February 1916.
82 NAC, RG 9 III B1 series 2, vol. 645, file D-18-2/3, Major J.N.H. D'Aeth, DAAG and QMG, Shorncliffe Command, to Major Maurice Alexander, 29 February 1916.

83 Francis D. Grierson, *The A.B.C. of Military Law: A Concise Guide for the use of Officers, N.C.O.'s and Men* (London, UK: T. Fisher Unwin, 1916); A.P. Birchall, *Rapid Training of a Company for War,* 2nd ed. (London, Aldershot, and Portsmouth, UK: Gale and Polden, 1915), 3-6; DHist, file 78/44, A Military Lawyer, *Military Law in Tables with Notes* (London: Hugh Ress, 1917); General Staff, Canadian Headquarters, Great Britain, *Training in Canadian Reserve Battalions* (London, UK: Harrison and Sons, 1917), 9-11.
84 NAC, RG 9 III B1 series 1, vol. 395, file C-71-1, Canadian Headquarters Brighton, "Notes for Presidents of Courts Martial," 5 December 1916; War Office, *Circular Memorandum on Courts-Martial for the Use of Convening and Staff Officers, and of Officers Giving Instruction on This Subject* (London, UK: Adjutant General's Branch, Stationery Services, 1916); E.W. Pope, *The Canadian Officer's Guide to the Study of Military Law,* (London, UK: Methuen and Co., 1916); Sisson C. Pratt, *Military Law: Its Procedure and Practice,* 19th ed. (London, UK: Kegan Paul, Trench, Trübner and Co., 1915).
85 NAC, RG 9 III B1 series 2, vol. 624, file C-248-2, Major J.N.H. D'Aeth, Shorncliffe Command, to Canadian Headquarters, 21 August 1917.
86 PAM, Dennistoun, MG 14 B24, box 1, file 2, diary, 19 February 1917.
87 R.M. Dennistoun, *Notes on Military Law* (Winnipeg: Ladies' Home Workers' Association of the 53rd Overseas Battalion, 1916); R.M. Dennistoun, *Notes on District Courts Martial,* 2nd ed. (London, UK: Hugh Rees, 1917).
88 NAC, RG 24, vol. 6644, file 7, adjutant general, Canadian Headquarters, "General Instructions to Local Canadian Commands Regarding Courts Martial," 29 September 1917.
89 NAC, RG 9 III A1, vol. 92, file 10-12-28, deputy minister, Overseas Ministry to adjutant general, Canadians, "Legal Aid to Officers and Soldiers," 8 March 1917.
90 War Office, *Manual of Military Law 1914* (London, UK: H.M. Stationery Office, 1914), 631-6. Princess Patricia's Canadian Light Infantry Regiment, file 30 (13)-8, Lieutenant Colonel G.H. Fowke, circular memorandum, "Field General Courts Martial," 14 April 1918.
91 Princess Patricia's Canadian Light Infantry Regiment, file 30 (6)-3, register of courts martial, March 1915 to January 1919.
92 Princess Patricia's Canadian Light Infantry Regiment, file 30 (13)-8, Major General A.F. Sillem, 3rd army circular memorandum no. 43, "Court Martial Officers," 8 August 1917.
93 NAC, RG 9 III B1 series 3, vol. 919, file C-73-3, Lieutenant Colonel P.J. Montague, AA and QMG, 2nd Canadian Division to sub-commands, 26 April 1918; PAM, Major General Percival John Montague, MG 14 B40, box 2, "2nd Canadian Division: Field General Court-Martial Cases 1918."
94 Anthony Babington, *For the Sake of Example* (London, UK: Leo Cooper, 1983); Julian Putkowski and Julian Sykes, *Shot at Dawn,* (Barnsley, South Yorkshire, UK: Wharncliffe Publishing, 1989).
95 Imperial War Museum (hereafter IWM), misc. 79, item 1216, nominal rolls of Canadian officers and other ranks tried by general court martial and field general court martial. See also PRO, WO 93/43-45; Desmond Morton, "The Supreme Penalty: Canadian Deaths by Firing Squad in the First World War," *Queen's Quarterly* 79 (autumn 1972): 345-52.
96 Calgary Highlanders Regiment, 51 (63)-1, Company Quarter Master Sergeant William Alexander, "Casualty Form: Active Service." Records relating to the field general courts martial and executions are on microfilm reel C-5053 at the National Archives of Canada.
97 CVA, Lieutenant Colonel John Weightman Warden, add. mss. 58, vol. 4, file 2, notation in notebook no. 2.
98 PRO, WO 32/5484, Field Marshal Sir Douglas Haig to secretary, War Office, 23 June 1918.
99 NAC, RG 9 III A1, vol. 40, file 8-2-23, J.D. Ousten to Major General J.W. Carson, 29 August 1916.
100 Militia general order no. 18, 1 March 1916. For the purposes of discipline, CEF members who returned to Canada automatically fell under the authority of district officers commanding. CVA, Military District No. 11, add. mss. 52, file 1, district orders, 25 September 1917.
101 W.B. Wood, *The Complete Guide to Military Lectures: For Candidates for Lieutenants', Captains' and Field Officers' Certificates* (Winnipeg: Military News Agency, 1916), 2.
102 GMA, Major John Andrew Birney, M3972, file 1, biography, 4 June 1965.

103 Royal Westminster Regiment, case 9, file 58B-1-23, 104th Regiment Westminster Fusiliers, "Register of Deserters," 1916.
104 Militia general order, no. 61, 23 June 1916.
105 NAC, RG 24, vol. 6643, file 5, Major General Henry Smith, JAG, to assistant adjutant general, "Letter of Deputy Minister of Justice Re – Enlistment of Minors," 21 August 1916.
106 *Statutes of Canada,* 1917, 7-8 Geo. 5, c. 19; NAC, RG 24, vol. 6644, file 9, memorandum, "Military Service Act 1917," 18 September 1922; *Military Service Act, 1917: Manual for the information and guidance of tribunals in the consideration and review of claims for exemptions* (Ottawa: Military Service Council, 1918).
107 NAC, RG 24, vol. 6645, file 11, JAG branch *Annual Report,* 23 August 1920.
108 Canadian Expeditionary Force (hereafter CEF), part II, supplement to routine order no. 173, 8 February 1918.
109 Ibid., part I, routine order no. 327, 16 March 1918.
110 *Statutes of Canada,* 1909-10, 9-10 Edw. 7, c.43; *Le Bill de la Marine,* 1910; Gilbert Norman Tucker, *The Naval Service of Canada,* vol. 1 (Ottawa: King's Printer, 1952), 140.
111 A.T. Carter, *The Admiralty Statutes,* vol. 1 (London, UK: Eyre and Spottiswoode, King's Printer, 1905), 8-35.
112 DHist, file 81/520/1540-12, naval historical section, Ottawa, "Legislative History of the Office of the Chief of the Naval Staff of Canada, 1910-1928, with Some Discussion of the Control of the Royal Canadian Navy by the Government of Canada," 6 February 1958.
113 PRO, ADM 1/8384/190, order-in-council, 16 July 1914.
114 PRO, ADM 116/3154, "Report of Committee on Naval Discipline 1912," 8 July 1912.
115 PRO, ADM 1/8397/360, staff minute by H. Eastwood for secretary of Admiralty, 14 October 1914.
116 PCO, *Army, Navy, Air Force and Munitions 1914-1918,* minutes of a meeting in the second sea lord's room, 5 July 1915.
117 PRO, ADM 1/8479/22, staff minute by Charles J. Adams, 13 February 1917.
118 PRO, ADM 1/8505/261, director of Naval Service of Canada to secretary of Admiralty, 22 November 1917.
119 DHist, file 81/520/1540-1, dispatch from Naval Service of Canada to Admiralty, 4 December 1917.
120 PRO, ADM 1/8498/202, Admiralty to under secretary of state, Colonial Office, 15 December 1917.
121 *Statutes of Canada,* 1918, 8-9 Geo. 5, c. 34. The RCN's courts martial registers for officers and other ranks started recording cases around this date. DHist, file 82/401, vols. 2 and 4.
122 PRO, ADM 1/8498/202, order-in-council, 28 June 1920.
123 PRO, ADM 1/8556, memorandum by R.B.D. Acland, judge advocate of the Fleet, 12 April 1919.
124 NAC, Biggar, MG 30 E85, vol. 2, file 7, Biggar to wife, 8 December 1918.
125 IWM, Munro, AMM/23, Munro to parents, 27 November 1918. The air force maintained its own court martial system at this time. NAM, Lieutenant Colonel A.W.C. McFall, 8407-20-20, Brigadier General A.L. Goaman, commanding south-western area RAF to Colonel A.W.C. McFall, 12 April 1919.
126 Julian Putkowski, *The Kinmel Park Camp Riots 1919* (Clwyd: Flintshire Historical Society, 1989). PAM, Dennistoun, MG 14 B24, box 1, file 3, diary, 7 March 1919.
127 IWM, misc. 58, item 849, list of soldiers tried by courts martial after the Kinmel Park camp riot.
128 IWM, misc. 155, item 24, Captain George Black to Sir Robert Borden, 21 June 1919.
129 PAM, Dennistoun, MG 14 B24, box 1, file 2, diary, 13 June 1918.
130 NAC, Biggar, MG 30 E85, vol. 2, file 7, Biggar to wife, 19 November 1918; PAM, Dennistoun, MG 14 B24, box 1, file 2, diary, 7 December 1918.
131 NAC, Biggar, MG 30 E85, vol. 2, file 9, M.P.A. Hankey to Sir Robert Borden, 29 March 1919.
132 PAM, Dennistoun, MG 14 B24, box 1, file 3, diary, 29 July 1919.
133 Ibid., 8 August 1919.
134 PRO, WO 32/5475, O.A.R. Murray to Sir Charles Darling, 1 April 1919.

135 "Report of the Committee Constituted by the Army Council to Enquire into the Law and Rules of Procedure Regulating Military Courts-Martial," *Parliamentary Papers,* 10 (1919): 165.
136 PRO, WO 32/5478, Brigadier General A.H.C. James to deputy adjutant general, "Notes on the Report of the Committee on Courts-Martial Procedure," 4 September 1919.
137 War Office, *Circular Memorandum on Courts-Martial for Use on Active Service* (London, UK: Adjutant General's Branch, General Headquarters, 1918).
138 PRO, WO 32/5478, Field Marshal Douglas Haig to secretary, War Office, 20 November 1919.
139 PRO, WO 32/5477, Field Marshal Douglas Haig to secretary, War Office, 19 August 1919.
140 PRO, WO 32/5478, Felix Cassel to Sir H.J. Creedy, 27 February 1920.
141 PRO, WO 32/3949, Felix Cassel to Winston Churchill, secretary of state for war, 14 June 1920.
142 Ibid., "Report of the Legal Officer and Education Committee," 14 June 1920; Percy H. Winfield, "Courts-Martial from the Lawyer's Point of View," *Law Quarterly Review* 34 (1918): 147-50.
143 PRO, WO 32/3949, adjutant general to secretary of state for war, 20 October 1921.
144 CEF, part II, supplement to routine order no. 1815, 21 March 1919.
145 NAC, Biggar, MG 30 E85, vol. 2, file 9, Colonel Oliver Biggar to Captain R.J. Orde, 28 March 1919.
146 NAC, RG 24, vol. 6644, file 7, Major R.J. Orde to general officer commanding, Military District 1, "Method of Exercising Clemency in Cases of Men Convicted by Courts Martial," 7 October 1919.
147 NAC, RG 24, vol. 6642, file 3, Major Reginald Orde to minister of militia and defence, "Remission of Sentences," 12 December 1918.
148 NAC, RG 24, vol. 6645, file 11, JAG branch *Annual Report,* 23 August 1920. The amnesty excluded soldiers convicted by British civil courts and imprisoned in Great Britain because the British Home Office possessed final authority in disposition of these cases. NAC, RG 24, vol. 6643, file 5, memorandum for the minister of militia and defence, 15 September 1919.
149 CEF, routine order no. 2280, 21 November 1919.
150 Ibid., supplement to routine order no. 2393, 19 February 1920.
151 NAC, RG 24, vol. 3192, Air Board Committee meeting, 19 August 1921; NAC, Biggar, MG 30 E85, vol. 3.

Chapter 3: Coming of Age

1 DHist, file 000.9 (D78), DND army public relations, "Brigadier Reginald John Orde," 23 February 1945.
2 *Sessional Papers,* no. 36, 58 (1922): 29.
3 NAC, RG 24, vol. 6643, file 5, JAG to adjutant general, 27 December 1920.
4 NAC, RG 24, vol. 6644, file 7, Major General E.C. Ashton, adjutant general to general officers commanding, Military Districts, "District Courts Martial," 24 April 1920.
5 *Sessional Papers,* no. 17, 59 (1923): 37-8.
6 GMA, Lieutenant Colonel Louis Oluf Svendsen, M5771, box 1, file 5, "Militia Staff Course, 1922-23, 'A' Staff Duties (5), Military Law"; BCA, Aitken, add. mss. 1913, box 2, file 7, "Militia Staff Course, 1922-23, 'A' Staff Duties (5), Military Law"; *Sessional Papers,* no. 17, 60 (1924): 6.
7 *Statutes of Canada,* 1922, 12-13 Geo. 5, c. 34.
8 *Sessional Papers,* no. 17, 60 (1924): 65.
9 NAC, RG 24, vol. 6643, file 4, minister of national defence to governor-in-council, 9 January 1924.
10 *Statutes of Canada,* 1919, 9-10 Geo. 5, c. 11.
11 NAC, RG 24, vol. 3192, minutes of Air Board Committee meeting, 23 September 1920.
12 NAC, RG 24, vol. 6645, file 11, Lieutenant Colonel Reginald Orde to chief of general staff, 24 October 1922.
13 NAC, RG 24, vol. 17,804, file 828-21/1, Wing Commander W.G. Barker to chief of general staff, 31 January 1924.

14 Ibid., JAG to chief of staff, 18 May 1923.
15 Ibid., Wing Commander W.G. Barker to deputy minister, 27 February 1924.
16 *King's Regulations and Orders for the Royal Canadian Air Force 1924* (Ottawa: F.A. Acland, King's Printer, 1924).
17 NAC, RG 24, vol. 17,804, file 828-21/1, Major General J.H. MacBrien, "King's Regulations and Orders for the Royal Canadian Air Force – 1924," 22 March 1924.
18 PRO, ADM 1/8583/45, staff minute by H. Eastwood, 5 February 1920.
19 NAC, RG 24, vol. 6645, file 10, naval secretary to deputy minister, 4 February 1922.
20 PRO, ADM 1/8583/45, director of Naval Service of Canada to secretary of Admiralty, 10 February 1920.
21 Ibid., Admiralty to under secretary of state, Colonial Office, 25 March 1920.
22 Ibid., Admiralty to director of Naval Service of Canada, 28 November 1921. The minister of the Naval Service of Canada had already issued a warrant to the commander-in-chief North America and West Indies station, authorizing him to convene courts martial for the trial of Canadian officers. DHist, file 81/520/1540-1, Captain Walter Hose, director of Naval Service of Canada to commander-in-chief North America and West Indies, 7 June 1921.
23 DHist, file 81/520/1540-1, secretary of Admiralty to director of Naval Service of Canada, 11 April 1922.
24 Ibid., secretary of Admiralty to director of Naval Service of Canada, 22 April 1922.
25 NAC, RG 24, vol. 6645, file 10, order-in-council to minister of naval service, 24 November 1922; NAC, RG 24, vol. 6643, file 5, Colonel Reginald Orde to Paymaster Captain E.S. Measham, deputy judge advocate of the Fleet, 25 September 1929.
26 NAC, RG 24, vol. 6647, file 10, JAG to director of naval service, 11 December 1925.
27 PRO, ADM 116/2175, NL 3186/1922, "Admiralty Memorandum on Naval Court Martial Procedure."
28 PRO, ADM 1/8619/22, staff minute by H. Eastwood for head of naval law branch, 31 January 1922.
29 DHist, file 81/520/1540-1, JAG to deputy minister, 23 February 1923.
30 Esquimalt Naval and Military Museum (hereafter ENMM), Commander John Christopher Fawcett, fonds 37, file 3, "Examination for the Rank of Paymaster Lieutenant-Commander," July 1925.
31 E.W. Bush, *How to Become a Naval Officer (Special Entry)* (London, UK: Gieves, 1929), 21-4.
32 NAC, RG 24, vol. 6642, file 2, JAG to adjutant general, 21 February 1924; Richard O'Sullivan, *Military Law and the Supremacy of the Civil Courts,* (London, UK: Stevens and Sons, 1921), 12.
33 E.J. Simon, "Correspondence Courses for the Canadian Militia," *Canadian Defence Quarterly* 1 (1923-4): 46.
34 NAC, RG 24, vol. 6644, file 7, Major General A. Panet, adjutant general to district officers commanding, "Amendments by Army (Annual) Act 1922," 2 January 1924.
35 CVA, Brigadier Sherwood Lett, add. mss. 361, vol. 3, file 3, militia staff course lecture notes, "Military Law."
36 T.V. Anderson, "Qualifying for Promotion in the Permanent Force," *Canadian Defence Quarterly* 2 (1924-5): 328.
37 Department of National Defence (hereafter DND), *Annual Report,* 1925, 83.
38 DND, *Annual Report,* 1926, 89; *The King's Regulations and Orders for the Canadian Militia 1926* (Ottawa: F.A. Acland, King's Printer, 1926); *Regulations and Instructions for the Clothing of the Non-Permanent Active Militia 1926* (Ottawa: F.A. Acland, King's Printer, 1927); NAC, RG 24, vol. 6646, file 7, Colonel Reginald Orde to Major General J.H. Elmsley, district officer commanding, Military District 3, 14 September 1926.
39 NAC, RG 24, vol. 6643, file 4, "Notes for Officers Proceeding to Staff College."
40 NAC, RG 24, vol. 6645, file 10, Colonel Reginald Orde to deputy minister, 7 September 1926. Felix Cassel had earlier insisted that the Treasury continue to perform legal work for the War Office. PRO, WO 32/3950, "Report of a Conference held at 3:30 p.m. in Room 354, 18th September, 1922, to consider details in connection with the formation of a Military Department in the Office of the Judge Advocate General," 15 September 1922.

41 PRO, WO 32/3953, "Memorandum as to the Office of Judge Advocate General and the Functions and Duties Attaching Thereto," 17 September 1934; NAC, RG 24, vol. 6644, file 8, "Military Department, Judge Advocate General's Office Lectures 1926-27."
42 NAC, RG 24, vol. 6645, file 10, Colonel Reginald Orde to deputy minister, "Instruction in Military Law," 10 September 1926.
43 Ibid., Colonel Reginald Orde to adjutant general, "Instruction in Military Law," 7 October 1926.
44 NAC, RG 24, vol. 6645, file 10, Colonel Reginald Orde to deputy minister, 23 November 1926.
45 NAC, RG 24, vol. 6642, file 3, Major General H.A. Panet, adjutant general to all district officers commanding, "Revised Rules of Procedure," 6 December 1926; Royal Westminster Regiment, case 17, file 58D-11-53, Military District 11 to all heads of departments, services, and units, "Revised Rules of Procedure," 15 December 1926.
46 H.T. Cock, "Thoughts on Discipline and Co-operation," *Journal of the Alberta Military Institute* 7 (1926): 74.
47 DND, *Annual Report,* 1927, 79. NAC, RG 24, vol. 6644, file 8, "Programme – Court Martial Demonstration," 7 December 1926.
48 NAC, RG 24, vol. 6642, file 3, JAG to adjutant general, "Courts Martial," 13 September 1927.
49 NAC, RG 24, vol. 6644, file 8, lecture notes, Petawawa, "Military Law," August 1927.
50 J.W.A. Wallace, "Training of N.C.O.'s of the Permanent Active Militia in Peacetime," *Canadian Defence Quarterly* 3 (1925-6): 474; T.J. Edwards, *The Non-Commissioned Officers' Guide to Promotion in the Infantry* (Aldershot, UK: Gale and Polden, 1927), 3-21.
51 NAC, RG 24, vol 6644, file 8, "Questions on the Administration of Discipline and Military Law," April 1923-October 1928. War Office, *Examination of Officers for Promotion: Regular Army, Royal Marines, Indian Army, Supplementary Reserve and Territorial Army – (Voluntary Subjects), Papers Set in October, 1926 with Remarks by Examiners* (London, UK: H.M. Stationery Office, 1926), 7-10, 35-7.
52 H. Meredith Logan, "Some Courts-Martial of the Past," *Canadian Defence Quarterly* 5 (1927-8): 69. A naval officer wrote a similar article on naval mutinies. C. Radcliffe, "Some Naval Mutinies," *Canadian Defence Quarterly* 7 (1929-30): 208-13.
53 DND, *Annual Report,* 1928, 85.
54 NAC, RG 24, vol. 6645, file 11, Colonel R.J. Orde to adjutant general, 5 May 1928.
55 NAC, RG 24, vol. 6644, file 8, "Notes on Military Law."
56 W.A. Griesbach, "Military Study," *Canadian Defence Quarterly* 7 (1929-30): 23. Griesbach, a member of the Senate, had expounded his six branches of military study in earlier addresses before the Alberta Military Institute at Calgary on 14 September 1920 and the Edmonton Military Institute on 28 September 1920. W.A. Griesbach, "Some Tactical Situations during the Last Months of the Great War," *Journal of the Alberta Military Institute* 1 (1920): 31.
57 DND, *Annual Report,* 1929, 83.
58 NAC, RG 24, vol. 6645, file 10, Colonel Reginald Orde to assistant deputy minister, "Junior Departmental Solicitor, Colonel J.S. Rankin," 17 August 1929.
59 NAC, RG 24, vol. 6644, file 8, Colonel Reginald Orde to adjutant general, 3 July 1929.
60 War Office, *Manual of Military Law 1929* (London, UK: H.M. Stationery Office, 1929); War Office, *Notes for the Guidance of Staff and Other Officers Concerned in the Preparation of a Case for Trial by Court-Martial, the Convening of the Court, the Trial, and the Confirmation of the Proceedings* (London, UK: Harrison and Sons, King's Printer, 1929).
61 H.M. Logan, "The New Manual of Military Law," *Canadian Defence Quarterly* 7 (1929-30): 104.
62 NAC, RG 24, vol. 6644, file 8, H.M.L., "Notes on Military Law Syllabi."
63 Ibid., précis no. 1, "Notes on Military Law."
64 A.C. Garner, "Impressions of the Militia Staff Course Western Canada, 1928-1929," *Canadian Defence Quarterly* 7 (1929-30): 377-9; BCA, Lieutenant Colonel Charles Edward Connolly, add. mss. 1260, militia staff course précis no. 40, "Staff Duties (17), Military Law," February 1931; *Memorandum for Camps of Instruction Canadian Militia 1930,* Part II: Administration (Ottawa: F.A. Acland, King's Printer, 1930).

65 NAC, RG 24, vol. 6644, file 8, Colonel H.E. Boak for chief of general staff to district officers commanding, "Instruction in Military Law," 5 November 1930; DND, *Annual Report,* 1930, 81.
66 Ibid., first paper, "Military Law for Permanent Force Officers 1930-31," November 1930.
67 Robert James Wilkins and Walter Sydney Chaney, *Handbook of Military Law* (London, UK: William Clowes and Sons, 1930), iii.
68 Royal Westminster Regiment, case 21, file 58D-11-85, Major R.O.G. Morton, "Training Memorandum Military District No. 11, 1931-32," 1 October 1931.
69 R.J. Orde, "The Statute of Westminster: Notes on the Application of the Statute and Complementary Legislation to the Armed Forces of Canada," *Canadian Defence Quarterly* 11 (1933-4): 214-5.
70 NAC, RG 24, Reel C-5075, file HQC 5030, deputy minister of national defence to high commissioner for Canada in London, 23 December 1930.
71 NAC, RG 24, vol. 6643, file 5, DJAG, "Memorandum on Dominion Forces Bill," 24 August 1931.
72 NAC, RG 24, vol. 6644, file 7, Colonel Reginald Orde to deputy minister, "Departmental Legislation for Parliamentary Session 1932," 21 December 1931.
73 NAC, RG 24, vol. 6643, file 5, JAG to John E. Read, legal advisor to Department of External Affairs, "Dominion Forces Bill," 14 April 1932.
74 *Statutes of Canada,* 1932-3, 23-4 Geo. 5, c. 21. Orde prepared the draft bill. DND, *Annual Report,* 1933, 74.
75 NAC, RG 24, vol. 6644, file 7, Colonel Reginald Orde to deputy minister, 29 September 1933.
76 Ibid., 24 February 1936.
77 Royal Westminster Regiment, case 21, file 58B-1-31, K.C. Macgonou, staff course notes, "Discipline," 1932.
78 D.E. Cameron, "Aid to the Civil Power," *Journal of the Alberta Military Institute* 13 (1932): 62.
79 Princess Patricia's Canadian Light Infantry Regiment, file 50 (6)-2, list of students who attended provisional schools in Military District 11, January 1933-December 1937.
80 Calgary Highlanders Regiment, 71 (1)-2 box 2, file 9, Donald G. MacLauchlan, notebook.
81 R. Townshend-Stephens, *A Practical Digest of Military Law* (London, UK: Sifton Praed and Co., 1933), vii-ix.
82 NAC, RG 24, vol. 6645, file 10, Colonel Reginald Orde to adjutant general, 1 March 1932.
83 Ibid., file 11, Colonel Reginald Orde to deputy minister, "Courts Martial Annual Return," 20 April 1933.
84 NAC, RG 24, vol. 6646, file 7, lecture by Colonel Reginald Orde, "Notes on Application of Statute of Westminster to the Armed Forces of His Majesty," 5 December 1932; W.R.P. Bridger, "Education and the Royal Military College of Canada," *Canadian Defence Quarterly* 8 (1930-1): 450.
85 DHist, file 113.302009 (D74), "Digest of Opinions and Rulings compiled from the records of the Office of the Judge Advocate General at National Defence Headquarters," September 1934.
86 Royal Westminster Regiment, case 24, file 58D-11-101, Major R.O.G. Morton to all commanding officers, "Training of the Active Militia 1934-35," 25 May 1935.
87 DND, *Annual Report,* 1936, 7; NAC, RG 24, vol. 6644, file 8, Colonel Reginald Orde to Director of Military Training and Staff Duties, "Advanced Course N.P.A.M. Officers, 1935-36," 17 October 1935; NAC, RG 24, vol. 6644, file 8, Colonel G.R. Pearkes to district officers commanding, "Course of Instruction: Military Law, Permanent Force Officers," 30 November 1935.
88 War Office, *Notes on Procedure, etc., in Connection with Trials by Court-Martial* (London, UK: H.M. Stationery Office, 1936).
89 DND, *Annual Report,* 1935, 7.
90 NAC, RG 24, vol. 6645, file 11, Colonel Reginald Orde to deputy minister, 24 April 1934.
91 Calgary Highlanders Regiment, 71 (1)-1, file 3, Donald MacLauchlan, militia staff course notes, 2 November-9 December 1936.

92 "Individual Study by Officers," *Canadian Defence Quarterly* 15 (1937-8): 32-3.

93 Royal Westminster Regiment, case 25, file 58D-11-105, Major J.C. Murchie to officers commanding non-permanent active militia units, Military District 11, "Advanced Militia Staff Course 1937-38," 15 September 1937.

94 M. Barry Watson, "The Advanced Militia Staff Course: From the Viewpoint of a N.P.A.M. Officer," *Canadian Defence Quarterly* 16 (1938-9): 68-9. Watson's suggestion was not popular at the time because considerable pressure existed within the non-permanent active militia for shorter qualifying courses. E.W. Sansom, "Current Training Problems, Canadian Militia," *Selected Papers from the Transactions of the Canadian Military Institute* 33 (1937-8): 26-7.

95 PRO, WO 32/15262, Colonel H. Scott Barrett to Henry MacGeagh, 16 June 1938.

96 "Report of the Army and Air Force Courts-Martial Committee 1938," *Parliamentary Papers,* 4 (1939-40): 59. See also PRO, WO 225/9.

97 PRO, WO 32/4552, "Report of the Interdepartmental Courts-Martial Committee 1939 to the Secretaries of State for War and Air," 23 March 1939. See also WO 225/10.

98 PRO, ADM 116/4291, Lord Stanhope to Sir Kingsley Wood, 13 January 1939.

99 PRO, WO 32/4553, Lord Stanhope to Hore-Belisha, "Status of the Judge Advocate General and the Judge Advocate of the Fleet," 4 February 1939.

100 PRO, WO 32/4553, Lord Stanhope to Lord Maugham, 27 March 1939.

101 PRO, WO 32/15263, S.F. Muspratt, India Office, to under secretary of state, War Office, 15 August 1939.

102 PRO, WO 32/4553, H. Eastwood, Admiralty, to G.W. Lambert, War Office, 28 September 1939.

Chapter 4: Total War

1 NAC, RG 24, vol. 6643, file 5, "Committee on Legal and Constitutional Questions Affecting Canadian Forces Serving outside of Canada," 26 October 1939.

2 PRO, AIR 2/4632, H.J.B. Clough, War Office to E.W. Handley, Air Ministry, "Conference held at the War Office on Friday 19th April, 1940, at 11 a.m.," 25 April 1940.

3 NAC, RG 24, vol. 12,771, file 29/VISFORCES/2, "Minutes of a Meeting held on Wednesday 20th March, at 11 a.m. to discuss draft letter on the subject of the Visiting Forces Act in its application to the Canadian Forces in the United Kingdom," 25 March 1940.

4 NAC, RG 24, vol. 6644, file 7, adjutant general's letter no. 35/1939, "Discipline Generally: Canadian Active Service Force," 27 September 1939.

5 Canadian Army, supplement to routine order no. 642, 29 August 1940.

6 NAC, RG 24, vol. 19,207, file 2140-75/4/1, Brigadier Reginald Orde to deputy minister, "HWE – JAG Office," 6 December 1944.

7 NAC, RG 24, vol. 6644, file 7, Brigadier A.S. Nash for Major General B.W. Browne, adjutant general to district officers commanding, "Duties and Responsibilities District A.J.A.G.'s," 25 November 1940.

8 Canadian Army, routine order no. 862, 4 January 1941.

9 Canadian Army, *Handbook on District Courts-Martial 1941 (December)* (Ottawa: Edmond Cloutier, King's Printer, 1941); DHist, file 111.6002 (D1), JAG circular no. 1/1941, 15 January 1941.

10 Canadian Army, supplement to routine order no. 2540, 9 November 1942. Monthly reports from the inspector of courts martial between 1943 and 1947 are on microfilm reel C-5329 at the National Archives of Canada.

11 Canadian Army, supplement to routine order no. 2897, 17 February 1943; Calgary Highlanders Regiment, 71 (2)-1, "Biography of Colonel Norman D. Dingle."

12 GMA, Lieutenant John Stewart Mavor, M6850, scrapbook "Political and Court Cases."

13 Canadian Army, supplement to routine order no. 551, 5 July 1940.

14 DHist, file 111.6 (D1), Brigadier R.J. Orde to director of staff duties, "Incoming N.D.H.Q. Staff Officers Instructional Pamphlet," 6 November 1942.

15 NAC, RG 24, vol. 6645, file 10, Brigadier Reginald Orde to private secretary, DND, 21 April 1941; DND, *Annual Report,* 1941, 9.

16 Canadian Army, supplement to routine order no. 1296, 19 September 1941.

17 PRO, AIR 2/4652, Malcolm Macdonald, British high commissioner Ottawa, to Viscount Cranborne, 19 November 1943.

18 NAC, RG 24, vol. 19,207, file 2140-75/4, Brigadier Reginald Orde to deputy minister (army), "H.W.E. – J.A.G. Branch," 14 August 1943.

19 R.J. Orde, "Some Aspects of Canadian Service Law and of the Office of the Judge Advocate-General in Canada," *Judge Advocate Journal* 1 (December 1944): 11, 18; PRO, WO 81/179, Henry MacGeagh to Frederick Bovenschen, 17 July 1945.

20 NAC, RG 24, vol. 12,763, file 29/AID/1, T.W. Laidlaw, secretary treasurer, Canadian Bar Association, to Colonel W.A.I. Anglin, "War-time Legal Services for Canadian Soldiers," 30 October 1942.

21 Canadian Army, routine order no. 2577, 18 November 1942.

22 NAC, RG 24, vol. 12,763, file 29/AID/1, Brigadier R.J. Orde to senior officer, CMHQ London, "Legal Aid for Personnel of the Canadian Army (Active)," 17 November 1943; DND, *Annual Report,* 1944, 55.

23 Canadian Army, routine order no. 3519, 14 August 1943; Royal Westminster Regiment, case "P," file 58P-4-35, Canadian Military Headquarters Overseas, "Notes for the Guidance of Officers Administering or Rendering Legal Aid," 6 April 1943.

24 NAC, RG 24, vol. 12,763, file 29/AID/1/3, Major J. Rosenblum to VJAG, "Summary of Legal Aid Administered in the Canadian Army Overseas," 12 December 1945.

25 "Syllabus of Refresher Course for Members of the Canadian Military Institute," *Selected Papers from the Transactions of the Canadian Military Institute* 35 (1940-1): 35. Questions on military law and discipline also appeared in the 1940 promotion examinations for officers in the militia. *Examination of Officers Non-Permanent Active Militia for Promotion: Papers Set in August, 1940 with Notes to Solutions* (Ottawa: Edmond Cloutier, King's Printer, 1940).

26 War Office, *Field Service Pocket Book,* pamphlet no. 11 (London, UK: H.M. Stationery Office, 1939), 4-10; Canadian Army, *A General Instructional Background for the Young Soldier 1940,* training pamphlet no. 1 (Ottawa: J.O. Patenaude, King's Printer, 1940), 193-9; Canadian Army, *How to Qualify 1941,* training pamphlet no. 8 (Ottawa: Edmond Cloutier, King's Printer, 1941); War Office, *The Rights of a Soldier When in Arrest Charged with an Offence under the Army Act* (Ottawa: J.O. Patenaude, King's Printer, 1940).

27 P.M.C. Hayman, *Some Elementary Notes on Military Law and Procedure,* 4th ed. (London, UK: Forster Groom and Co., 1943), 12.

28 S.T. Banning, *Military Law,* 21st ed. (Aldershot, UK: Gale and Polden, 1941); H.M. Shurlock, *600 Questions and Answers on Military Law* (Aldershot, UK: Gale and Polden, 1939); H.M. Sherlock, *Army District Court Martial Procedure and Notes on Field General Court Martial* (Aldershot, UK: Gale and Polden, 1941).

29 F.J.O. Coddington, *A Young Officer's Guide to Military Law,* 19th ed. (Aldershot, UK: Gale and Polden, 1943), viii.

30 R.J.S. Langford, *Corporal to Field Officer,* 2nd ed. (Toronto: Copp Clark, 1939), 74-84.

31 Corporal J.W. Mickleborough, lecture notes, February 1944.

32 Burrell M. Singer and R.J.S Langford, *Handbook of Canadian Military Law* (Toronto: Copp Clark, 1941), 21.

33 Canadian Army, *Extracts from Manual of Military Law 1929 Reprinted for Use in the Canadian Army* (Ottawa: Edmond Cloutier, King's Printer, 1941).

34 Clarence Richard Young, *Notes on Elementary Military Law for Canadian Officers* (Toronto: University of Toronto Press, 1939).

35 Brooke Claxton, *Notes on Military Law and Discipline for Canadian Soldiers* (Montreal: McGill University Contingent COTC, 1939), 5.

36 University of Manitoba COTC contingent, *Notes and Excerpts from Official Publications for the Qualification of Officers and Non-Commissioned Officers of the Canadian Army (R),* vol. 2, October 1942, 251-68; University of Toronto COTC contingent, *Lecture Notes for Officer Training Canadian Army (Reserve)* (Toronto: University of Toronto Press, 1943), 81-5.

37 NAC, RG 24, vol. 12,763, Colonel Reginald Orde to Colonel P.J. Montague, 15 November 1939; Canadian Army, supplement to routine order no. 495, 1 June 1940.

38 PAM, Montague, MG 14 B40, box 1, file "Biography," obituary, 13 June 1966.

39 NAC, RG 24, vol. 12,767, file 29/HOSPITALITY/1, Major General P.J. Montague to Roy Robinson, sub-treasurer Inner Temple, 3 April 1944.
40 NAC, RG 24, vol. 12,766, file 29/GEN/1, Major General P.J. Montague to deputy adjutant general; AJAG, "J.A.G. Branch," 31 December 1940.
41 NAC, RG 24, vol. 6644, file 7, Major General H.F.G. Letson to Brigadier Reginald Orde, 17 June 1942.
42 NAC, RG 24, vol. 12,763, file 29/APPT/1, order-in-council, 20 December 1943.
43 PRO, WO 32/10633, Foreign Office to G.W. Lambert, War Office, 23 September 1940.
44 Charles Perry Stacey and Barbara Wilson, *The Half-Million: The Canadians in Britain 1939-1946* (Toronto: University of Toronto Press, 1987), 156-9.
45 NAC, RG 24, vol. 12,771, file 29/SUMMARIES/1, Lieutenant S.G. Parent to AJAG, CMHQ, 28 August 1941.
46 NAC, RG 24, vol. 12,766, file 29/ICORPS/1, "Minutes of Conference held at HQ, 1 Cdn Corps 25 Sep 42 – 1500 hours," 30 September 1942.
47 NAC, RG 24, vol. 12,768, file 29/OFFICE DUTIES/1/1/2, Captain W.B. Bredin to DJAG, CMHQ, "Report on Review Section," 26 January 1943; NAC, RG 24, vol. 12,767, file 29/MILLAW/1, Lieutenant Colonel J.J. Kelly, AJAG 1st Canadian army to HQ 2nd Canadian artillery group, "Lectures on Military Law," 27 January 1943.
48 NAC, RG 24, vol. 12,766, file 29/FORMS/1, Lieutenant Colonel W.H. Parker to Colonel W.A.I. Anglin, 1 November 1943.
49 Metropolitan College, St. Albans, *Military Law,* course 317A, part II studies, 4-7 (Watford, UK: William Brendon and Son, 1942).
50 NAC, RG 24, vol. 12,771, file 29/SUMMARIES/1, Lieutenant Colonel J.J. Kelly, AJAG, CMHQ, "Summaries of Evidence," 22 April 1943.
51 NAC, RG 24, vol. 12,769, file 29/QUASH/1, Lieutenant Colonel T.G. Norris to legal officers, 1st Canadian army, "Courts Martial Review Drill," 11 January 1944.
52 NAC, RG 24, vol. 12,766, file 29, 1CDNARMY/1, Lieutenant Colonel T.G. Norris to DJAG, CMHQ, 16 February 1944.
53 NAC, RG 24, vol. 12,763, file 29/BAOR/1, Colonel T.G. Norris to DJAG, CMHQ, "Functions of DJAG and his Staff," 23 June 1944.
54 PRO, WO 32/11078, Henry MacGeagh to secretary of state for war, 7 July 1944.
55 IWM, W.F. Gow, 76/97-98/1, War Office, "Field General Courts-Martial on Active Service 1944. The Green Book, Revised Edition," 15 March 1944.
56 NAC, RG 24, vol. 12,763, file 29/BAOR/1, Colonel T.G. Norris to DJAG, CMHQ, "Courts-Martial Centre," 11 September 1944.
57 Canadian section General Headquarters 1st echelon, 21st Army Group, *Commanding Officers' Guide to Discipline (Canadian),* 1944; NAC, RG 24, vol. 12,767, file 29/LIBRARY/1, Major W.H. Waugh, DJA, Canadian section 2nd Echelon, HQ 21st Army Group to DJAG, CMHQ, 16 January 1945.
58 Terry Copp and Bill McAndrew, *Battle Exhaustion: Soldiers and Psychiatrists in the Canadian Army, 1939-1945* (Montreal and Kingston: McGill-Queen's University Press, 1990), 106.
59 Robert Tooley, "Appearance or Reality? Variations in Infantry Courts Martial – 1st Canadian Division: 1940-1945," *Canadian Defence Quarterly* 22 (1992): 40. Although records are incomplete, extracts from field general courts martial are in DHist, file 111.6 (D3).
60 LHC, Major General James Scott-Elliot, commander, 56th (London) division, "Battle Absentees," 10 April 1944.
61 NAC, RG 24, vol. 12,767, file 29/MILLAW/1, Major T.G. Norris to DJAG, CMHQ, "Sentences of Death A.C.I. 570 of 1918," 13 April 1943.
62 NAC, RG 24, vol. 12,768, file 29/MILLAW/1/3, Major General P.J. Montague to secretary, DND, Ottawa, "Promulgation of Death Sentence prior to Confirmation," 22 August 1944.
63 DHist, file 1B, Hunter, 94-9; Princess Patricia's Canadian Light Infantry Regiment, file 78 (21)-1; Pat Sullivan, "Still on the Books," *Legion* (May 1985): 14-5. The British implemented thirty-six death sentences in the field during the Second World War. PRO, WO 93/40, "Particulars of Death Sentences Carried out from 1941 to 1953."
64 PRO, AIR 2/5066, Vincent Massey, Canadian high commissioner in London to Anthony

Eden, Dominions Office, 22 April 1940; PRO, AIR 2/4632, Group Captain G.V. Walsh to secretary to Canadian high commissioner in London, "Instruction regarding control and administration R.C.A.F. serving overseas," 19 April 1940.

65 NAC, RG 24, vol. 6646, file 7, Squadron Leader G.A. Ault to secretary, National Defence for Air, "R.C.A.F. court martial – eligibility of R.A.F. Officers to sit on," 17 October 1941. PRO, AIR 2/4774, "Notes of Meetings held on 12th and 15th July, 1941 to Discuss Disciplinary Questions as between R.A.F. and R.C.A.F. Personnel."

66 PRO, AIR 2/4632, Patrick Duff, British high commissioner in Ottawa, to secretary of state for external affairs, 25 September 1942; DHist, file 111.6 (D2), "Historical Development of the Legal Status of the R.C.A.F. out of Canada."

67 C.P. Stacey, *Arms, Men and Governments: The War Policies of Canada 1939-1945* (Ottawa: Queen's Printer, 1970), 305.

68 PRO, WO 32/4553, F.G. Bovenschen, War Office, to Sir John Abraham, Air Ministry, 13 August 1944.

69 PRO, AIR 2/4847, court martial warrant forms distributed to RAF groups and army co-operation command RAF, 25 May 1942.

70 PRO, AIR 2/9845, court martial warrants distributed by air officer commander-in-chief RCAF overseas to air or other officers commanding RAF, 1 June 1944.

71 Air Ministry, *Manual of Air Force Law 1933* (London, UK: H.M. Stationery Office, 1943).

72 Group Captain, *The Air Force Guide* (Toronto: Copp Clark, 1940), 74-82.

73 H.M. Shurlock, *600 Questions and Answers on Air Force Law,* 2nd ed. (Aldershot, UK: Gale and Polden, 1940).

74 NAC, RG 24, vol. 17,805, file 828-21/9, Group Captain H. Edwards to JAG, "Proposed Amendment to KR (Air)," 11 April 1940.

75 PRO, AIR 2/4632, Squadron Leader G. Morrow for chief of the air staff, RCAF, to UK liaison mission in Ottawa, "Report on Action Taken with Respect to Legal Status of RAF Units and Personnel in Canada, Subsequent to Air Training Conference, Ottawa, May 1942," 30 October 1942.

76 NAC, RG 24, vol. 17,806, file 828-21/14, air member personnel to directorates, "Revision of KR (Air)," 9 April 1942.

77 *King's Regulations for the Royal Canadian Air Force 1943,* (Ottawa: Edmond Cloutier, King's Printer, 1943).

78 Royal Canadian Air Force, *Extracts from the Manual of Air Force Law 1944* (Ottawa: Edmond Cloutier, King's Printer, 1944).

79 GMA, Wing Commander T.H. Spear, "Biography."

80 PRO, ADM 1/9475, staff minute by head Commission and Warrant Branch, 19 July 1933.

81 E.R. Mainguy, "Canada's Existing Permanent and Reserve Naval Forces: Their Organization and Training," *Journal of the Alberta Military Institute* 18 (1937): 17.

82 DHist, file 82/401, vols. 2-4, registers of officers and men of the Canadian Naval Service tried by courts martial and disciplinary courts, 1911-52. Presumably, records for additional cases are held at the PRO.

83 Jason Sears, "Discipline in the Royal Navy, 1913-1946," *War and Society* 9 (1991): 41-3.

84 Naval order no. 2549, 6 February 1943.

85 IWM, Commander F. Poole, P190T, World War II Memoirs, 173-5.

86 DHist, file 81/520/1540-1, chief of naval staff to JAG, 26 June 1941.

87 Ibid., E.C. Russell to C.P. Stacey, "Naval Courts Martial," 12 August 1965.

88 Ibid., "Notes on telephone conversation Capt. Hurcomb/Thorgrimsson," 4 August 1965.

89 ENMM, Fawcett, fonds 37, file 2, commanding officer, reserve divisions, "Royal Canadian Naval Volunteer Reserve Lectures for Syllabus of Training, Lecture 8: Naval Law, Articles of War," 15 April 1943.

90 NAC, RG 24 Acc. 83-84/167, vol. 574, file 1700-910/2, director of accountant personnel to chief of naval personnel, "Activities of D.A.P. 1st April – 30 June 1943," 25 June 1943.

91 ENMM, Fawcett, fonds 37, file 3, accountant training school, HMCS *Cornwallis,* "Captain's Office Notes," October 1943.

92 NAC, RG 24 Acc. 83-84/167, vol. 670, file 1900-3/1, minute for DJAG, "Lawyers in Civil Life," 10 August 1943.

93 A.D. Duckworth, *An Introduction to Naval Court Martial Procedure,* 4th ed. (Devonport, UK: Hiorns and Miller, 1948), 11.
94 Naval orders no. 3522, 2 September 1944, and no. 4076, 11 November 1944.
95 Admiralty, *The King's Regulations and Admiralty Instructions for the Government of His Majesty's Naval Service,* 2 vols. (London, UK: H.M. Stationery Office, 1939). The Admiralty's fleet orders are in ADM 182 at the PRO.
96 *Regulations and Instructions for the Royal Canadian Navy,* (Ottawa: J.O. Patenaude, King's Printer, 1940).
97 NAC, RG 24, vol. 6193, "Royal Canadian Naval Reserve Regulations"; Royal Canadian Navy, *Regulations for Royal Canadian Naval Volunteer Reserve 1938* (Ottawa: J.O. Patenaude, King's Printer, 1938).
98 *King's Regulations and Admiralty Instructions for the Government of His Majesty's Naval Service* (Ottawa: King's Printer, 1942).
99 NAC, RG 24 Acc. 83-84/167, vol. 670, file 1900-3/1, secretary, Naval Board, to deputy minister, "Revision of Canadian Naval Regulations," 4 June 1943.
100 *Statutes of Canada,* 1944-5, 8 Geo. 6, c. 23.
101 NAC, RG 24 Acc. 83-84/167, vol. 574, file 1700-910/4, Commander Horace Read to minister of national defence for the Naval Service, 9 March 1945.
102 Royal Canadian Navy, *The King's Regulations for the Government of His Majesty's Canadian Naval Service 1945,* 2 vols. (Ottawa: Edmond Cloutier, King's Printer, 1945).
103 DND, *Annual Report,* 1945, 73.
104 NAC, RG 24, vol. 12,773, file 29/WAR CRIMES/1, letter of authority from Brigadier Beverley Matthews, deputy adjutant general, CMHQ, 5 July 1945; DHist, file 159.95023 (D1), "Report of No. 1 Canadian War Crimes Investigation Unit on Miscellaneous War Crimes against Members of Canadian Armed Forces in the European Theatre of Operations 9 Sept 1939 to 8 May 1945," parts I and II.
105 NAC, RG 24, vol. 12,773, file 29/WAR CRIMES/1, "Minutes of a Meeting held in the Office of the High Commissioner for Canada on Tuesday, 24th April, 1945."
106 PRO, WO 32/12199, "Minutes of Meeting in Attorney-General's Room, Law Courts, on 8th June, 1945, at 10:30 a.m."
107 Patrick Brode, "Bruce Macdonald and the Drafting of Canada's War Crimes Regulations: 1945," *Gazette* 24 (1995): 277; "Canadian Law Concerning Trials of War Criminals by Military Courts," *Law Reports of War Criminals* 1 (1945): 12-130.
108 Patrick Brode, *Casual Slaughters and Accidental Judgments: Canadian War Crimes and Prosecutions, 1944-1948* (Toronto: Osgoode Society, University of Toronto Press, 1997). Canadian officers also participated in the prosecution of Japanese war criminals in Hong Kong and Japan. PRO, WO 32/12201, Eric Machtig, Dominions Office to H.E. Horne, Canada House, London, 7 August 1946; DHist, file 113.3A1013 (D1), "Final Report War Crimes Investigation Section Directorate of Administration Army Headquarters," 30 August 1947.
109 DHist, file 159.95023 (D7), "Record of Proceedings (Revised) of the Trial by Canadian Military Court of S.S. Brigadeführer (Major General) Kurt Meyer held at Aurich, Germany 10-28 December 1945"; B.J.S. Macdonald, *The Trial of Kurt Meyer* (Toronto: Clarke, Irwin and Co., 1954).
110 Chris Vokes and John P. Maclean, *Vokes: My Story* (Ottawa: Gallery Books, 1985), 202-8; Tony Foster, *Meeting of Generals* (Toronto: Methuen, 1986), 488-9.
111 DHist, file 159.95023 (D5), "Record of Proceedings of the Trial by Canadian Military Court of Wilhelm Jung and Johann George Schumacher held at Aurich, Germany, 15-25 March, 1946"; DHist, file 159.95023 (D3), "Record of Proceedings of the Trial by Canadian Military Court of Robert Holzer, Walter Weigel, and Wilhelm Ossenbach held at Aurich, Germany 25th March 1946 to 6th April 1946."
112 PRO, WO 235/1121, petition for pardon from Wilhelm Ossenbach, 24 June 1947; NAC, RG 24, vol. 6646, file 3, Brigadier Reginald Orde to under secretary of state for external affairs, "Petition for Clemency – Johann Neitz," 8 May 1947; PRO, WO 235/602, petition for clemency from Johann Nietz, 24 November 1947.
113 PRO, WO 32/12195, J.A. Walsh, Dominions Office to Major P.C.F. Allen, "Imprisonment

of War Criminals Sentenced by the Canadian Authorities," 4 March 1947; LHC, Major General D.A.L. Wade, file I, "Final Report by the No. 1 War Crimes Review of Sentences Board on European War Criminals Sentenced by British Military Courts under the Authority of the Royal Warrant (Army Order 81 of '45)," August 1949.

114 PRO, WO 235/570, Brigadier Russell of Liverpool to general officer commander-in-chief, BAOR, "Military Court (War Crimes) Trial Le Mesnil Patry," 27 November 1948.

115 DHist, file 76/166, information file on Wilhelm Mohnke.

116 PRO, WO 235/600A, remission board order, "Kurt Meyer," 13 August 1954; James M. Whalen, "The Face of the Enemy: Kurt Meyer: Normandy to Dorchester," *The Beaver* 74 (April/May 1994): 23; Ray Gardner, *Wanted for Murder ... SS Brigadeführer Kurt Meyer* (pamphlet, Vancouver, 1951); Kurt Meyer, *Grenadiers* (Winnipeg: J.J. Fedorowicz, 1994), 228.

117 Jules Deschênes, *Commission of Inquiry on War Criminals Report Part I: Public* (Ottawa: Supply and Services Canada, 1986).

118 A.P.V. Rogers, *Law on the Battlefield* (Manchester, UK: Manchester University Press, 1996), 130-7.

119 Canadian Army, routine order no. 5493, 28 March 1945.

120 R.L. Kellock, *Report on the Halifax Disorders May 7th-8th, 1945* (Ottawa: Edmond Cloutier, King's Printer, 1945), 5; James M. Cameron, *Murray: The Martyred Admiral* (Hantsport, NS: Lancelot Press, 1980).

121 Canadian Army, routine order no. 6173, 1 November 1945.

122 NAC, RG 24, vol. 6646, file 3, Brigadier R.J. Orde to director of personnel, "Discharge Review Board: Courts Martial Cases," 30 December 1946.

123 PRO, WO 32/14979, director of personnel services, "Disposal of Canadian Absentees and Deserters," 31 December 1946. There were still 102 deserters from the Canadian Army Overseas unaccounted for by 1949. NAC, Claxton, MG 32 B5, vol. 105, file "Defence Statistics," memorandum, "Deserters at Large," 31 March 1949.

Chapter 5: Under the National Defence Act

1 DHist, file 111.6013 (D1), "A Précis of the Development of the Office of the Judge Advocate General."

2 DHist, file 112.3M2 (D116), "Extract from Minutes of 352nd Meeting of the Chiefs of Staff Committee – held May 21st 46."

3 DND, *Annual Report,* 1947, 65.

4 NAC, RG 24 C1, vol. 19,207, file C-2140-75/4, Brigadier Reginald Orde to adjutant general, "Office of the Judge Advocate General Establishment," 8 July 1947.

5 NAC, RG 24 C1, vol. 19,207, file C-2140-75/4/1, Brigadier Reginald Orde to chief of general staff, "Office of the JAG," 7 November 1946.

6 Ibid., Major General E.G. Weeks to Brigadier Reginald Orde, 15 March 1949.

7 C. Vokes, "The Army and the Citizen," *Selected Papers from the Transactions of the Canadian Officers Club and Institute* 41 (1946): 35.

8 NAC, Claxton, MG 32 B5, vol. 105, minister of national defence, "Military Training: 1947," 22 January 1947.

9 Royal Westminster Regiment, case 38, file 58D-11-122, Royal Canadian school of infantry, "Senior NCOs Qualifying Course RCIC Reserve Force," November 1948.

10 Calgary Highlanders Regiment, 154 (1)-1, box 1, command contingent plan, "Military Law."

11 Calgary Highlanders Regiment, 91 (4)-1, box 3, file 10, Army Headquarters, director of military training, "Canadian Army Study Papers: Military Law," August 1949.

12 Royal Westminster Regiment, case 39, file 58D-10-30, Canadian Army policy statement no. 54, "Professional Advancement: Reserve Force," 11 November 1949.

13 Calgary Highlanders Regiment, 91 (4)-1, box 2, file 8, "Canadian Army Reserve Force: Qualifying Examination 1949 Second Lieutenant to Lieutenant."

14 NAC, RG 24 C1, vol. 19,207, file C-2140-75/4/1, Brigadier Reginald Orde to chairman, Personnel Members Committee, 26 November 1947.

15 Ibid., Brigadier Reginald Orde to deputy minister, "Establishment: Office of the Judge Advocate General," 19 March 1949.

16 DHist, file 112.3M2 (D120), "Extract from Minutes of 447th Meeting of Chiefs of Staff Committee held 23 May 1949."
17 NAC, RG 24 C1, vol. 19,207, file C-2140-75/4/1, "Extract from Minutes of 41st Meeting of Defence Council held on 17 June 1949."
18 Ibid., Colonel W.J. Lawson, VJAG, to chairman, Personnel Members Committee, "Office of JAG: Proposal to Place on Civilian Basis," 18 October 1949.
19 Ibid., director of army personnel to adjutant general, "Establishment: Office of the JAG," 30 November 1949.
20 David Jay Bercuson, *True Patriot: The Life of Brooke Claxton* (Toronto: University of Toronto Press, 1993), 151-5.
21 DHist, 79/137, P.C. Paterson, "The Defence Administration of Brooke Claxton 1946 to 1954," (M.A. extended essay, Royal Military College of Canada, April 1975), 39.
22 W.J. Lawson, "Canadian Military Law," *Canadian Bar Review* 29 (1951): 248.
23 NAC, RG 24, vol. 6646, file 5, Brigadier Reginald Orde to Brooke Claxton, 1 June 1948. Orde also kept Claxton informed about discussion on the Senate's Banking and Commerce Committee in respect of amendments to the existing Militia Act and National Defence Act. NAC, Claxton, MG 32 B5, vol. 105, file "Defence Statistics," Brigadier R.J. Orde to minister of national defence, "Bills 14 and 19," 14 March 1947.
24 William T. Generous, Jr., *Swords and Scales: The Development of the Uniform Code of Military Justice* (Port Washington, NY: Kennikat Press, 1973), 16-21.
25 Edmund Morgan, "The Background of the Uniform Code of Military Justice," *Vanderbilt Law Review* 6 (1953): 169-85.
26 Generous, *Swords and Scales,* 54-6.
27 United States, *Manual for Courts-Martial United States 1951* (Washington, DC: United States Government Printing Office, 1951).
28 PRO, WO 32/14082, G.W. Lambert to secretary of state for war, "Enquiry into Army Disciplinary System," 22 October 1946.
29 Ibid., John Lang, Admiralty, to Eric Speed, War Office, 21 October 1946.
30 "Report of the Army and Air Force Courts-Martial Committee 1946," *Parliamentary Papers,* 14 (1948-9): 113-21.
31 PRO, WO 32/14083, Erich Machtig, Commonwealth Relations Office, to Eric Speed, War Office, 21 May 1948.
32 PRO, ADM 1/5734, "Report of the Inter-departmental Committee to consider the Recommendations in the Report of the Army and Air Force Courts-Martial Committee, 1946," 28 October 1948.
33 NAC, Claxton, MG 32 B5, vol. 105, file "Defence Organization," Brooke Claxton to A.V. Alexander, 31 July 1947.
34 Peter Archambault, "The Canadian Naval Mutinies of the 1940s and the Imperial Naval Tradition" (M.A. thesis, University of New Brunswick, 1993).
35 Mainguy was a close personal friend of Claxton. He became chief of the naval staff in December 1951. Audette, who had served on various warships in the North Atlantic and Mediterranean during the war, retired from the RCNVR in 1945 as a commander. He was director of various Crown corporations in the postwar period. Brockington, a former chairman of the Canadian Broadcasting Corporation and special wartime assistant to the prime minister, was counsel with the law firm of Gowling, MacTavish, Osborne, and Henderson in Ottawa.
36 L.C. Audette, "The Lower Deck and the Mainguy Report of 1949," in *RCN in Retrospect 1910-1968,* ed. James A. Boutilier (Vancouver: University of British Columbia Press, 1982), 242-3. Ignoring directions to destroy all materials, Audette later donated his notes and copies of testimony before the commission to the National Archives of Canada. NAC, Louis de la Chesnaye Audette, MG 31 E18, vols. 1-4.
37 *Report on Certain "Incidents" Which Occurred on Board H.M.C. Ships ATHABASKAN, CRESCENT and MAGNIFICENT and on Other Matters Concerning the Royal Canadian Navy* (Ottawa: Edmond Cloutier, King's Printer, 1949), 56-7.
38 Naval order no. 30.25/1, 6 November 1949.
39 PRO, ADM 1/5734, Admiral Harold Burrough to secretary of Admiralty, "Naval Court Martial Sentences," 24 March 1947.

40 PRO, ADM 116/5714, "The Lewis Committee Report: Minutes of an Ad Hoc Meeting held in the Lord Chancellor's Office on Thursday, 9th December 1948."
41 PRO, ADM 1/21300, first lord of Admiralty, "Committee on the Naval Court Martial System," 17 January 1949.
42 "First Report of the Committee Appointed to Consider the Administration of Justice under the Naval Discipline Act 1950," *Parliamentary Papers* 17 (1950-3): 554-8.
43 "Second Report of the Committee Appointed to Consider the Administration of Justice under the Naval Discipline Act 1950," *Parliamentary Papers* 17 (1950-3): 586-8.
44 PRO, ADM 1/21984, staff minute by H.D. Samuel, naval law branch, 15 December 1950.
45 PRO, WO 32/14083, Albert Napier to secretary of state for war, "Report of Inter-Departmental Working Party on Comparison of the Major Proposals of the Lewis and Pilcher Committees," 3 July 1950.
46 PRO, ADM 1/22624, Noel Hutton, PCO, to H.D. Samuel, Admiralty, "Naval Discipline Bill," 31 May 1951.
47 PRO, WO 32/14949, "Report from the Select Committee on the Army Act and Air Force Act Together with the Proceedings of the Committee, Minutes of Evidence and Appendices," 20 October 1953.
48 *Journals of Senate of Canada* 91 (second session 1949): 193.
49 House of Commons, *Debates* 2 (second session 1949): 1946-9.
50 House of Commons, *Debates* 2 (1950): 1081.
51 Ibid., 1681-2; NAC, RG 24, vol. 6646, file 5, "The Department of National Defence Act."
52 *Special Committee on Bill No. 133: An Act Respecting National Defence* (Ottawa: Edmond Cloutier, King's Printer, 1950), 9. Claxton was a member of the special committee.
53 House of Commons, *Debates* 3 (1950): 2539.
54 House of Commons, *Debates* 4 (1950): 3317.
55 *Journals of Senate of Canada* 92 (1950): 375; *Statutes of Canada,* 1950, 14 Geo. 6, c. 43.
56 NAC, RG 24 C1, Acc. 83-84/242, vol. 8, file 143-13-6/5, Lieutenant Colonel L.W. Sharpe to deputy adjutant general, "Revision of K.R. (CAN) 1939," 23 January 1947.
57 NAC, RG 24 B2, vol. 9291, file 2-70-169/1, Brigadier T.G. Gibson, vice adjutant general, to secretary, Personnel Members Committee, "National Defence Act – Draft Bill: Rewrite of King's Regulations," 6 December 1948.
58 Ibid., Brigadier Reginald Orde to secretary, Regulations Revision Advisory Committee, 28 July 1949.
59 Ibid., Wing Commander J.H. Hollies to secretary, Regulations Advisory Committee, "Revision of Regulations: Disciplinary Regulations," 10 March 1950.
60 DHist, file 112.3M2 (D113), Major General W.H.S. Macklin, adjutant general, to general officer commanding all commands, "National Defence Act," 16 December 1950.
61 NAC, RG 24 B2, vol. 9291, file 2-70-169/3, minister of national defence to governor-in-council, 28 March 1951.
62 Ibid., file 2-70-169/4, Brigadier William Lawson to deputy minister, "New King's Regulations for Three Services," 25 May 1951. As an alternative, military authorities distributed material for a course of lectures based on the new National Defence Act. 15th Field Artillery Regiment, box 1 "Administration," "Canadian Military Law," 25 June 1951.
63 Herbert Fairlie Wood, *Strange Battleground: The Operations in Korea and Their Effects on the Defence Policy of Canada* (Ottawa: Roger Duhamel, Queen's Printer, 1966), 23-4; Jean Pariseau, "La participation des forces armées canadiennes à la guerre de corée," *Canadian Defence Quarterly* 17 (autumn 1987): 55-60.
64 DHist, file 112.3H1.009 (D27), paper on absence without leave prepared by historical section, Canadian Army Special Force, 1951. C.G. Rennie, "Mobilization for War: Canadian Army Recruiting and the Korean Conflict," *Canadian Defence Quarterly* 15 (summer 1985): 49-50.
65 NAC, RG 24, vol. 18,318, war diary, 2nd battalion, Princess Patricia's Canadian Light Infantry Regiment, 12 March 1951. "The Patricia's in Korea," *Canadian Army Journal* 5 (January 1952): 17.
66 *Court Martial Appeal Reports,* vol. 1 (Ottawa: Edmond Cloutier, Queen's Printer, 1957), 36.
67 Ibid., 15.

68 NAC, RG 24, vol. 18,223, adjutant general's branch war diary, 31 July 1951; "Three Canadians in Korea Facing Murder Charge," *Toronto Star,* 2 August 1951, 1.
69 JAG, court martial ledger "Korea"; Princess Patricia's Canadian Light Infantry Regiment, file 16 (39)-4, "Sentence Pat to Life: See Murder Charge Cut for Korea Pats," 29 August 1951.
70 Blank was released from his term of life imprisonment on 8 July 1952. Davis's sentence of eighteen months imprisonment was set aside on 7 March 1952, and Gibson's two years less a day was set aside on 22 July 1952. JAG, court martial charge cards.
71 NAC, RG 24, vol. 19,207, file 2140-75/4, JAG to adjutant general, "Legal Services for Overseas Forces," 23 May 1951.
72 DND, *Annual Report,* 1952, 25.
73 DHist, file 410B25.019 (D14), program for visit of Brooke Claxton; Peter Inglis, "Canadians in Korea: Their Real Gripe," *Saturday Night* 67, 9 February 1952, 10, 17.
74 NAC, RG 24, vol. 19,367, file 2140-1923/0, memorandum from Colonel W.M.W. Shaw, DJAG to director of organization, "A Standing Court Martial Establishment," 16 December 1952.
75 JAG, court martial ledger "Korea." In contrast, the British held 1,103 courts martial in Korea between 25 June 1950 and 27 July 1953. PRO, WO 93/59, registrar, JAG office to adjutant general, "Korea," 15 January 1954.
76 These remissions were in addition to those already exercised by confirming authorities, which the JAG felt did not go far enough. NAC, RG 24, vol. 6646, file 3, Colonel W.J. Lawson, VJAG, to adjutant general, "Remission of Sentences," 8 February 1950.
77 G.I.A.D. Draper, "The Exercise of Criminal Jurisdiction under the NATO Status of Forces Agreement, 1951," *Transactions of the Grotius Society* 44 (1958): 10.
78 NAC, RG 24, vol. 6646, file 1, F.P. Varcoe, Department of Attorney General of Canada, to Colonel W.M.W. Shaw, JAG office, "Employment of Lawyers outside of Canada," 26 February 1953.
79 *Court Martial Appeal Reports,* vol. 1, 243-7; DHist, file 112.1 (D100), headquarters, 1st Canadian Infantry Brigade Group, to Army headquarters for director of administration and JAG, 30 December 1953. Canadian military authorities commuted Mitchell's sentence to life imprisonment. This case appears to be the last death sentence handed down by a court martial in the Canadian Armed Forces. JAG, appeal register no. 180.
80 NAC, RG 24 Acc. 83-84/167, vol. 308, file 1540-24, Brigadier W.J. Lawson to secretary, Personnel Members Committee, "Proposed New Legislation Affecting the Canadian Forces," 24 August 1955.
81 Michele A. Pineau, "Civilians under Military Justice: A Canadian Study," *McGill Law Journal* 25 (1979): 6.
82 NAC, RG 24, vol. 19,369, file S-240-1936-0, Colonel W.M.W. Shaw to War Establishments Committee, "Detachment Judge Advocate General: No. 1 and No. 2 Administrative Echelons," 18 December 1958.
83 J.H. Hollies, "Courts Martial in the Canadian Forces," *Criminal Law Quarterly* 2 (1959-60): 75.
84 NAC, RG 24 B2, vol. 9261, file 200-68-4/2, H.J. Jackson to JAG, "Entry of Appeals," 3 March 1952.
85 NAC, RG 24 B2, vol. 9291, file 2-70-169/3, Brigadier J.W. Bishop to secretary, Personnel Members Committee, "Principal Inter-Service Differences: vol. II," 1 February 1951.
86 J.H. Hollies, "Canadian Military Law," *Military Law Review* 13 (1961): 73.
87 NAC, RG 24, vol. 19,367, file 2140-19123/0, F.R. Miller, deputy minister to Defence Council, "Administration of Canadian Military Law," 28 February 1957.
88 James B. Jacobs, "Legal Change within the United States Armed Forces since World War II," *Armed Forces and Society* 4 (1978): 394.
89 NAC, RG 24 Acc. 83-84/167, vol. 621, file 1834-102/3, chief of naval personnel to chief of naval staff, "Amendments to Queen's Regulations," 31 December 1958; *Statutes of Canada,* 1960, 8-9 Eliz. 2, c. 44; John W. Mason, "Basic Freedoms in the Canadian Armed Forces" (M.A. thesis, Carleton University, 1972), 12.
90 W.H.S. Macklin, "Military Law," *Canadian Army Journal* 8 (January 1954): 31-2.

91 Canadian Army, *Canadian Army Manual of Unit Administration and Discipline 1957* (Ottawa: Army Headquarters, 1957); Royal Canadian Navy, *Manual of Rank Requirements,* BRCN 3047, 15 November 1961; Royal Canadian Air Force, *Notes for the Guidance of Officers,* RCAF pamphlet 4, January 1964.
92 War Office, *Manual of Military Law Part I 1956* (London, UK: H.M. Stationery Office, 1956). This was particularly true for the third part, which covered the law of war on land. Prepared by Sir Hersch Lauterpacht, this loose-leaf volume was substantially based on chapter 14 in earlier editions of the *Manual of Military Law,* and updated to take into account significant changes to international law since the Second World War and the Korean War. War Office, *The Law of War on Land being Part III of the Manual of Military Law* (London, UK: H.M. Stationery Office, 1958).
93 *Canadian Armed Forces Manual of Training: Conduct after Capture 1960* (Ottawa: Department of National Defence Headquarters, 1960).
94 Canadian Army, *Catalogue of Training Publications and Training Aids (1964)* (Ottawa: Canadian Forces Headquarters, May 1965).
95 JAG monthly letter no. 53, 10 September 1957.
96 J. Alfred Crowe, "Droit militaire canadien," *Thémis* 9 (1958-9): 81-8.
97 Directorate of postings and careers, air force headquarters, "Officers' Qualifying Examinations," *The Roundel* 6 (October 1954): 3-4.
98 Royal Westminster Regiment, case 42, file 58D-11-298, Lieutenant E.O. Roberts, examination workbook for qualification examination: lieutenant to captain, "Military Law," 1959.
99 JAG, Flight Lieutenant C.R.J. Skatfeld, "Lectures on Military Law," January 1955.
100 Calgary Highlanders Regiment, 91 (48)-1, *Question Papers of the Militia Staff Course Part 1 Examination for 1959* (Ottawa: Queen's Printer, 1959), 73.
101 GMA, Department of National Defence (23rd Militia Group), M2371, box 7, file 51, "Young Soldiers Training – 1958: Detailed Syllabus," 10.
102 Calgary Highlanders Regiment, 154 (2)-1, Canadian Army Examining Board, *Comments on the Canadian Army (Regular) Qualification Examination Lieutenant to Captain Part 1 December 1961 and March 1962* (Ottawa: Army Headquarters, 1962), 75.
103 Richard A. Preston, *To Serve Canada: A History of the Royal Military College since the Second World War* (Ottawa: University of Ottawa Press, 1991), 55.
104 Keith L. Sellen, "The United States Military Academy Law Department – Yesterday and Today: Purpose – Challenge – Reward," *Federal Bar News and Journal* 37 (1990): 236. A separate department of law with service officers as professors had existed at West Point since 1874. Charles W. West, "The Department of Law at the United States Military Academy," *Judge Advocate Journal* 1 (December 1944): 34.
105 NAC, RG 24 Acc. 83-84/167, vol. 621, file 1834-102/3, Captain L.L. Atwood, director of naval training, to secretary, ISCJT, "Publications for CANSERVCOLS: QR Navy, Army, Air," 21 January 1958.
106 Robert E. Joseph, "The Need for Including a Course on Military Justice in the Law School Curriculum," *Journal of Legal Education* 7 (1954): 83; Walter B. Raushenbush, "Military Law Courses Can Serve Scholarly Objectives," *Journal of Legal Education* 16 (1963): 195.
107 John Jay Douglass, "Military Law: Stepchild of Legal Education," *Journal of Legal Education* 26 (1974): 475-6.
108 JAG monthly letter no. 36, 5 March 1956.
109 NAC, RG 24 Acc. 83-84/167, vol. 574, file 1700-910/5, Commodore (S) R.A. Wright, "RCN Supply Branch: August, 1955," 12 August 1955.
110 DHist, file 181.009 (D30), "Judge Advocate General."
111 NAC, RG 24, vol. 19,207, file 2140-75/4, Group Captain H.A. McLearn, DJAG, to secretary, rank structure committee, "JAG Establishment," 4 August 1960.
112 JAG monthly letter no. 89, 10 January 1961.
113 JAG monthly letter no. 44, 3 December 1956.
114 JAG monthly letter no. 82, 27 May 1960.
115 DHist, file 72/202, A.B. Wyland, "Canadian Military Assistance to Developing Countries," 10.

116 G.D. Hunt, "Recollections of the Canadian Armed Forces Training Team in Ghana, 1961-1968," *Canadian Defence Quarterly* 18 (spring 1989): 47.
117 Bruce McDougall, "Be All You Can Be," *Canadian Lawyer* 15 (May 1991): 28.
118 Greg Donaghy, "The Rise and Fall of Canadian Military Assistance in the Developing World, 1952-1971," *Canadian Military History* 4 (spring 1995): 83.
119 G.W.L. Nicholson, "The Canadian Militia's Introduction to Civil-Defence Training," in *Policy by Other Means,* 228.
120 Calgary Highlanders Regiment, 154 (6), box 2, Lieutenant Colonel F.H. Clarke, "The Calgary Highlanders Training Plan 1961-1962."
121 Calgary Highlanders Regiment, 91 (4)-1, box 2, file 8, 19th Medium Artillery Regiment, "Canadian Army (Militia) Field Officers Course: Part 1 Section 1 Study Course," April 1963.
122 Canadian Army, *Manual of Individual Training Standards, M.I.T.S. (1964)* (Ottawa: Army Headquarters, 1964), chapter 21, serial 2113.6.
123 Canada, *White Paper on Defence* (Ottawa: Queen's Printer, March 1964).
124 *Statutes of Canada,* 1966-7, 14-15-16 Eliz., 2, c. 96; Paul Hellyer, *Address on the Canadian Forces Reorganization Act, on moving second reading of Bill C-243 in the House of Commons,* 7 December 1966, 5.
125 Jean Victor Allard (with Serge Bernier), *The Memoirs of General Jean V. Allard* (Vancouver: UBC Press, 1988), 246-55.
126 *Queen's Regulations and Orders for the Canadian Forces,* 3 vols. (Ottawa: Roger Duhamel, Queen's Printer, 1967-8).
127 15th Field Artillery Regiment, box 1 "Administration," 988-202-3, "General Military Training: Military Law," June 1968.
128 Paul Hellyer, *Damn the Torpedoes: My Fight to Unify Canada's Armed Forces* (Toronto: McClelland and Stewart, 1990), 212.

Chapter 6: A Gradual Slide

1 Gerald Porter, *In Retreat: The Canadian Forces in the Trudeau Years* (Ottawa: Deneau and Greenberg, 1978), 10.
2 Canada, *Defence in the Seventies* (Ottawa: Information Canada, 1971).
3 Douglas L. Bland, *Chiefs of Defence: Government and the Unified Command of the Canadian Armed Forces* (Toronto: Canadian Institute of Strategic Studies, 1995), 161-2. Drawing authority from the Interpretation Act, the Financial Administration Act, and the Public Service Employment Act, the deputy minister was officially "responsible for ensuring all policy direction emanating from the Government is reflected in the administration of the Department and in military plans and operations." DND, *Defence 1975* (Ottawa: Information Canada, 1976), 16.
4 W. Harriet Critchley, "Changes in Canada's Organization for Defense, 1963-1983," in *Reorganizing America's Defense: Leadership in War and Peace,* ed. Robert J. Art, Vincent Davis, and Samuel P. Huntington (Washington, DC: Pergamon-Brassey's, 1985), 147.
5 R.B. Byers, "Structural Change and the Policy Process in the Department of National Defence: Military Perceptions," *Canadian Public Administration* 16 (1973): 220-42.
6 John M. Gates, "The 'New' Military Professionalism," *Armed Forces and Society* 11 (1985): 434.
7 R.A. McDonald, "The Legal Branch Law Firm of the Canadian Forces," *Canadian Forces JAG Journal* 2 (1987): 3.
8 J.M. Simpson, "Making Humanitarian Law Applicable to Non-International Armed Conflicts," *Canadian Defence Quarterly* 1 (1971): 22-8.
9 JAG monthly letter, no. 153, November 1966.
10 H.G. Oliver, "Canadian Military Law," *Chitty's Law Journal* 23 (1975): 109-19.
11 JAG monthly letter, no. 179, 9 February 1970.
12 JAG monthly letter, 13 July 1973; James B. Fay, "Canadian Military Criminal Law: An Examination of Military Justice," *Chitty's Law Journal* 23 (1975): 120.
13 JAG, Treasury Board to DND, "Subsidization: Legal and Academic Training, Officers – Canadian Forces (Regular)," 23 August 1973.
14 DND, *Defence 1973* (Ottawa: Information Canada, 1974), 84.

15 JAG monthly letter, no. 1/75, 25 April 1975; DND, *Defence 1975,* (Ottawa: Information Canada, 1976), 77.
16 JAG, B.A. Marsh and D.S. Cotterill, "Impact of a Three Tier Career Plan on the Legal Officer Classification: MOC 67 Manpower Modelling Analysis," 1979.
17 Lynne Hough, "No Life Like It," *Canadian Lawyer* 6 (October 1982): 12.
18 J.P. Wolfe, "Changes in the Law of Armed Conflict," *Canadian Defence Quarterly* 8 (1978): 16-21, 48; J.P. Wolfe, "War and Military Operations," in *Canadian Perspectives on International Law and Organization,* ed. R. St. J. Macdonald (Toronto: University of Toronto Press, 1974), 620-44.
19 Charles A. Cotton, Rodney K. Crook, and Frank C. Pinch, "Canada's Professional Military: The Limits of Civilianization," *Armed Forces and Society* 4 (1978): 380.
20 *Basic Officer Training: Military Knowledge Manual,* CFP 195, 15 September 1972.
21 DHist, file 91/86, "FMC Professional Development Training (PDT) Programme: Military Law Study Guide," 31 May 1974.
22 DND, *Defence 1977* (Ottawa: Supply and Services Canada, 1978), 80.
23 JAG, "Minutes of a Meeting of the OPDP 4 Planning Committee held in the JAG Conference Room at 10:00 hours, Monday 25 Mar. 96," 3 April 1996.
24 Mobile Command, *Reserve Commanders' Conference 26 February 1971,* FMC 1180-22, 10 March 1972, 10.
25 DND, *Defence 1977,* 101; D.H. Brown, "The Militia Individual Training and Career Profile," *Canadian Defence Quarterly* 8 (winter 1978-9): 56-61.
26 H.G. Needham, "Militia Individual Training and Career Progression (MITCP): The Time Has Come for a Reappraisal," *Canadian Defence Quarterly* 10 (winter 1980/81): 27.
27 *General Military Training,* vol. 4, *Unit Guide to the Geneva Conventions,* CFP 318 (4), 15 June 1973; *Manual on the Geneva Conventions of August 12, 1949,* CFP 122, 31 August 1973.
28 DND, *Defence 1979* (Ottawa: Supply and Services Canada, 1980), 54-5.
29 R.B. Byers and C.S. Gray, eds., *Canadian Military Professionalism: The Search for Identity* (Toronto: Canadian Institute for International Affairs, 1973).
30 Samuel P. Huntington, *The Soldier and the State* (New York: Vintage Books, 1957); Morris Janowitz, *The Professional Soldier,* (New York: Free Press, 1960); John W. Hackett, *The Profession of Arms* (London, UK: Times Publishing Co., 1962).
31 R.B. Byers, "The Canadian Military and the Use of Force: End of an Era?" *International Journal* 30 (1975): 289-90.
32 K. George Wolf, "The Military Profession in Canada: A Matter of Opinion," *Command and Staff Review* (June 1975).
33 *Report of the Officer Development Board,* 3 vols. (Ottawa: National Defence Headquarters, March 1969).
34 Bernd A. Goetze, *Military Professionalism: The Canadian Officer Corps,* National Security Series No. 3/76 (Kingston: Centre for International Relations, Queen's University, 1976).
35 J.C. Eggenberger, "Toward a General Model of Military Leadership for the Canadian Armed Forces," departmental manuscript 79-1, (Kingston: Department of Military Leadership and Management, Royal Military College of Canada, May 1979).
36 David F. Pelly, "Military Education in Canada: Does It Produce the Kind of Professional Needed Today?" *Canadian Defence Quarterly* 10 (summer 1980): 30.
37 *Task Force on Review of Unification of the Canadian Forces: Final Report,* 15 March 1980, 62-80.
38 *Review Group on the Report of the Task Force on Unification of the Canadian Forces: Report,* 31 August 1980, 49.
39 Ibid., 20-1; DND, *Defence 1980* (Ottawa: Supply and Services Canada, 1981), 111.
40 C.A. Cotton, "A Canadian Military Ethos," *Canadian Defence Quarterly* 12 (winter 1982-3): 11.
41 C.A. Cotton, "The Divided Army: Role Orientations among Canada's Peacetime Soldiers" (Ph.D. diss., Carleton University, 1980), 297-9.
42 "*R. v. MacKay,*" *Supreme Court Reports* 2 (1980): 370-411; Marc Gold, "Canadian Bill of Rights – Fair Hearing – Equality before the Law – National Defence Act – Court-Martial Jurisdiction," *Canadian Bar Review* 60 (1982): 137-51.

43 Andrew D. Heard, "Military Law and the Charter of Rights," *Dalhousie Law Journal* 11 (1987-8): 535.
44 Michel Rossignol, *National Defence Act: Reform of the Military Justice System,* 96-1E (Ottawa: Research Branch, Library of Parliament, 22 January 1997), 6-7.
45 S.B. Flemming, "Civilianization Theory and Martial Discipline in the Canadian Forces in the Post-Korean War Period," Staff Note 2/89, Operational Research and Analysis Establishment, Directorate of Social and Economic Analysis, Ottawa, April 1989, 24.
46 David J. Corry, "Military Law under the Charter," *Osgoode Hall Law Journal* 24 (1986): 100-4.
47 Ronald D. Lunau, "Military Tribunals under the Charter," *National Journal of Constitutional Law* 2 (1992): 206-8.
48 Michael Doi, "The Judicial Independence of Canadian Forces General Courts Martial: An Analysis of the Supreme Court of Canada Judgment in R. v. Généreux," *Dalhousie Law Journal* 16 (1993): 246-52.
49 *"R.* v. *Généreux," Supreme Court Reports* 1 (1992): 259-338.
50 Janet Walker, "A Farewell Salute to the Military Nexus Doctrine," *National Journal of Constitutional Law* 2 (1993): 371; Janet Walker, "Military Justice: From Oxymoron to Aspiration," *Osgoode Hall Law Journal* 32 (1994): 32.
51 JAG, "Department of National Defence/Canadian Forces: Office of the Judge Advocate General Business Plan 1996-2000," 30 November 1995, 5-6.
52 R.G. Rousseau, "La Discipline et sens de l'humaine," *Canadian Defence Quarterly* 14 (1984): 33.
53 DND, *Defence 1983* (Ottawa: Supply and Services Canada, 1984), 80-1.
54 Auditor General, *1990 Report,* Chapter 22, "Department of National Defence – Human Resources Management Training and Education," 429.
55 R.E. Park, "Overview of the Social/Behavioural Science Evaluation of the 1979-1985 Canadian Forces Trial Employment of Service Women in Non-Traditional Environments and Roles," Research Report 86-2, Canadian Forces Personnel Applied Research Unit, Willowdale, ON, May 1986; Lewis W. MacKenzie, "The Canadian Forces Evaluation of Mixed-Gender Combat Units," *Canadian Defence Quarterly* 17 (Winter 1987-8): 26.
56 House of Commons, *Equality for All: Report of the Parliamentary Committee on Equality Rights* (Ottawa: Queen's Printer, October 1985), 57.
57 Ronald Arthur McDonald, "Equality Issues in the Canadian Forces under the Canadian Charter of Rights and Freedoms: A Study of the Effect of the Canadian Charter of Rights and Freedoms on Certain Policies of the Canadian Forces" (LLM thesis, Queen's University, 1986), 2.
58 Ellen Symons, "Under Fire: Canadian Women in Combat," *Canadian Journal of Women and Law* 4 (1991): 499-501. The human rights tribunal superseded the planned CREW trials and made employment of females in combat-related occupations alongside male soldiers a matter of policy. C.D. Lamerson, "The Evolution of a Mixed-Gender Canadian Forces," Canadian Forces Personnel Applied Research Unit, Willowdale, ON, 26 October 1989, 3.
59 Eric T. Reynolds, "Ethical Competence and the Profession of Arms: A Contemporary Challenge to Military Institutions," *Canadian Defence Quarterly* 23 (December 1993): 35.
60 Paul D. Manson, "Officer Professional Development: Foundation for the Future," *Canadian Defence Quarterly* 17 (summer 1987): 20.
61 *Officer Corps Study: Phase One,* 14 June 1989, 6-2.
62 Richard Evraire, "General and Senior Officer Professional Development in the Canadian Forces," *Canadian Defence Quarterly* 20 (winter 1990): 33.
63 Margo J. Mayo, "Computer Assisted Learning in the Canadian Forces: Training the Trainers" (M.Sc. thesis, University of Calgary, 1990), 123-4.
64 W.J. Fenrick, "The Law of Armed Conflict: The Cushie Weapons Treaty," *Canadian Defence Quarterly* 11 (1981): 25-30.
65 L.C. Green, *Essays on the Modern Law of War* (Dobbs Ferry, NY: Transnational Publishers, 1985).
66 JAG, *You and the Law of War,* 1981.

67 W.J. Fenrick, "Canadian Forces Law of Armed Conflict Manual," second draft, 1984, I. At Wolfe's suggestion, Green had prepared most of the original draft during a period of employment in Ottawa. JAG, Office of the JAG, "Report on the Law of Armed Conflict Survey: The Development of a Training Strategy," May 1998, 7-9.

68 Michael Bothe, ed., *National Implementation of International Humanitarian Law: Proceedings of an International Colloquium Held at Bad Hamburg, June 17-19, 1988* (Dordrecht, Boston, and London: Martinus Nijhoff, 1990), 209. The law of armed conflict manual was not revised and translated until late 1998, more than a decade after its original revision. JAG, Lieutenant Colonel K.W. Watkin to OPDP Det. Comd.; DLaw/T2, "Translation of Law of Armed Conflict Material for OPDP 4," 14 May 1998.

69 Bruce T. Smith, "Uncle Sam's Newest Recruits: A Look at Three JAG Schools, Their Curricula, and Continuing Education Programs," *Federal Lawyer* 42 (September 1995): 22-6.

70 By special arrangement, Canadian legal officers could take selected basic and graduate courses offered by the US Army's JAG school through correspondence. JAG newsletter, no. 2/89, February 1989.

71 Rudolph C. Barnes, Jr., *Military Legitimacy: Might and Right in the New Millennium* (London, UK, and Portland, US: Frank Cass, 1996), 174-5.

72 Auditor General, *1992 Report,* Chapter 18, "National Defence: The Canadian Reserves," 25.

73 DND, *Challenge and Commitment: A Defence Policy for Canada,* (Ottawa: Supply and Services Canada, 1987), 65-7.

74 DND, *Defence 1988* (Ottawa: Supply and Services Canada, 1989), 24.

75 Senate, *Report of the Special Committee of the Senate on National Defence: Canada's Land Forces* (Ottawa: Supply and Services Canada, October 1989), 52.

76 DND, *Defence 90* (Ottawa: Supply and Services Canada, 1991), 12.

77 Sean M. Maloney, "'Missed Opportunity': Operation Broadsword, 4 Brigade and the Gulf War, 1990-1991," *Canadian Military History* 4 (spring 1995): 37-46.

78 W.J. Fenrick, "International Legal Aspects of Canadian Forces Experience in the Recent Gulf Conflict," *Canadian Council on International Law* (1991): 13.

79 Françoise J. Hampson, "Means and Methods of Warfare in the Conflict in the Gulf," in *The Gulf War 1990-91 in International and English Law,* ed. Peter Rowe (London, UK, and New York: Routledge, 1993), 89-110.

80 Auditor General, *1994 Report,* Chapter 24, "National Defence-Management Systems," 54.

81 W.J. Fenrick, "The United Nations Commission of Experts on War Crimes in the Territory of the Former Yugoslavia, A Personal Assessment," *Canadian Council on International Law* 23 (1994): 49.

82 Kim Carter, "Proof beyond a Reasonable Doubt? Collecting Evidence for the International Criminal Tribunal for the Former Yugoslavia," *Canadian Yearbook of International Law* 32 (1993): 250-62.

83 Randy Ray, "Law in the Trenches," *National* 4 (March 1995): 18.

84 David Jay Bercuson, *Significant Incident: Canada's Army, the Airborne, and the Murder in Somalia* (Toronto: McClelland and Stewart, 1996), 10-3.

85 *Board of Inquiry Canadian Airborne Regiment Battle Group: Phase I Report,* vol. 11, 3236-55.

86 Ibid., vol. 12; Bruce Wallace, "Too Few Good Men," *Maclean's* 106 (13 September 1993): 16-7.

87 Peter Worthington and Kyle Brown, *Scapegoat: How the Army Betrayed Kyle Brown* (Toronto: Seal Books, 1997).

88 Peter Desbarats, *Somalia Cover-Up: A Commissioner's Journal* (Toronto: McClelland and Stewart, 1997).

89 *Report of the Special Advisory Group on Military Justice and Military Police Investigation Services,* 25 March 1997, 68-73.

90 *Special Advisory Group on Military Justice and Military Police Investigation Services: Report on the Quasi-Judicial Role of the Minister of National Defence,* 10 October 1997. This report was actually delivered to the minister of national defence on 25 July 1997.

91 *Dishonoured Legacy: Report of the Commission of Inquiry into the Deployment of Canadian Forces to Somalia,* 5 vols. (Ottawa: Canadian Government Publishing, 1997).

92 *Dishonoured Legacy,* vol. 5, 1306.
93 DND, *A Commitment to Change: Report on the Recommendations of the Somalia Commission of Inquiry,* 14 October 1997.
94 House of Commons, *Bill C-25: An Act to Amend the National Defence Act and to Make Consequential Amendments to Other Acts,* 4 December 1997.
95 House of Commons, *Debates* (19 March 1998), 5139.

Conclusion: Beyond Somalia

1 DND, press release NR-97.054, "Defence Minister Decides No Marshaw Retrial," 14 October 1997.
2 DND, press release BG-98-002, "Women in the Canadian Forces," February 1998.
3 DND, *National Defence 1994-95 Estimates, Part III: Expenditure Plan* (Ottawa: Minister of Supply and Services Canada, 1994), 86.
4 DND, press release, "Sexual Harassment, Sexual Misconduct, and General Military Discipline in the Canadian Forces," 9 June 1998.
5 DND, press release NR-98.040, "Defence Minister Announces First Ombudsman," 9 June 1998; House of Commons, *Debates* (10 June 1998), 7944.
6 House of Commons, *Debates* (10 June 1998), 7950-1. The director of law/training, sensitive to sexual harassment allegations, prepared a study unit in the OPDP that "focuses on the legal and ethical responsibilities of CF members with respect to sexual violence and acquaints the member with the longstanding regulations and policies regarding sexual offences." JAG, Lieutenant Colonel K.W. Watkin to OPDP 4 Training Coordinator, "OPDP 4 – Sexual Offences/Sexual Harassment Submission," 12 August 1998.
7 Jane O'Hara, "Of Rape and Justice: Has Anything Really Changed in the Canadian Forces?" *Maclean's* 111 (14 December 1998): 16-22.
8 DND, *Amendments to the National Defence Act: Background and Amendment Highlights,* December 1997, 11.
9 "Four Canadians Charged in Death of Somali Civilian," *Vancouver Sun,* 20 May 1993, 1.
10 DND, *The Queen's Regulations and Orders for the Canadian Forces,* 4 vols. (Ottawa: Queen's Printer, 1994).
11 Kenneth W. Watkin, "Canadian Military Justice: Summary Proceedings and the Charter" (LLM thesis, Queen's University, 1990), 3; Martin Friedland, *Controlling Misconduct in the Military* (Ottawa: Commission of Inquiry into the Deployment of Canadian Forces to Somalia, 1997), 92-4.
12 *Report of the Special Advisory Group on Military Justice and Military Police Investigation Services,* 21-2.
13 DND, press release NR-98.012, "Appointment of the New Judge Advocate General," 12 March 1998; House of Commons, *Debates* (19 March 1998), 5123-4.
14 James W. O'Reilly and Patrick Healy, *Independence in the Prosecution of Offences in the Canadian Forces* (Ottawa: Commission of Inquiry into the Deployment of Canadian Forces to Somalia, 1997), 85-6.
15 Ira Lewis, "Public Service 2000 and Cultural Change in the Department of National Defence," *Canadian Public Administration* 37 (1994): 263.
16 DND, *National Defence 1995-96 Estimates, Part III: Expenditure Plan* (Ottawa: Minister of Supply and Services Canada, 1995), 27.
17 DND, *National Defence 1998-99 Estimates, Part III: Report on Plans and Priorities* (Ottawa: Minister of Public Works and Government Services Canada, 1998), 44.
18 JAG, "Department of National Defence/Canadian Forces: Office of the Judge Advocate General Business Plan 1998-2002," 24 November 1997, 11-2.
19 DND, *The Election to Be Tried by Summary Trial or Court Martial: Guide for Accused and Assisting Officers (Bilingual),* A-L-G-050-000/AF-001, 30 November 1997.
20 JAG, Lieutenant Colonel K.W. Watkin to DJAG/operations, "Staffing of DLAW/T," 20 August 1998.
21 *Final Report of the Officer Development Review Board,* vol. 1, 15 September 1995, 37-8.
22 Mark S. Martins, "Rules of Engagement for Land Forces: A Matter of Training, not Lawyering," *Military Law Review* 143 (1994): 9-10.

23 *Special Commission on the Restructuring of the Reserves: Report* (Ottawa: Department of National Defence, 1995), 10.
24 David A. Schlueter, "Military Justice for the 1990's: A Legal System Looking for Respect," *Military Law Review* 133 (1991): 28.
25 Dulaney L. O'Roark, Jr., "Transformational Leadership: Teaching the JAG Elephant to Dance," *Military Law Review* 146 (1994): 230-2.
26 Eugene R. Fiddell, "The National Institute of Military Justice: A Status Report," *Naval Institute Proceedings,* 124 (August 1998): 77.
27 JAG, Office of the JAG, "Report on the Discipline Survey: The Development of a Training and Education Strategy," 1998, 7-13.

Bibliography

Primary Sources

Archives

National Archives of Canada, Ottawa

RG 9	Department of Militia and Defence
RG 24	Department of National Defence
MG 29 E3	Charles Arkoll Boulton
MG 29 E45	Private Murray Matheson
MG 30 E51	Major General Willoughby Garnons Gwatkin
MG 30 E85	Lieutenant Colonel Oliver Mowat Biggar
MG 32 B5	Brooke Claxton
MG 30 E166	Lord Strathcona's Horse in South Africa
MG 31 E18	Louis de la Chesnaye Audette

Directorate of History, Department of National Defence Headquarters, Ottawa

Lieutenant Colonel T.M. Hunter, "Some Aspects of Disciplinary Policy in the Canadian Services, 1914-1946."

Files and historical reports

Judge Advocate General's Office, Department of National Defence Headquarters, Ottawa

Chief judge advocate's reviews of courts martial, 1952-66

Courts martial statistics, 1951-98

Courts martial ledgers and "dead" cards

Flight Lieutenant C.R.J. Skatfeld, lectures on military law, January 1955

JAG business plans, 1995-7

JAG monthly letters, 1951-78

JAG military letters, 1975-82

JAG newsletters, 1987-97

OPDP 4 materials

Provincial Archives of Manitoba, Winnipeg

M 6 F1	Boer War (Lord Strathcona's Horse)
MG 12 B1	Lieutenant Governor Alexander Morris
MG 14 B24	Colonel Robert Maxwell Dennistoun
MG 14 B40	Major General Percival John Montague
MG 14 C4	Captain Clarence Montague Boswell

Glenbow Museum and Archives, Calgary

Private Robert Kellock Allan

Major Frederick Augustus Bagley
Superintendent Joseph Victor Bégin, RCMP
Major John Andrew Birney
Charles A. Clarke
Captain Kenneth Cameron Hurt
Department of National Defence (23rd Militia Group)
Staff Sergeant Frederick Marshall Kitchener
Lord Strathcona's Horse
Lieutenant John Stewart Mavor
Brigadier John Wright Proctor
Corporal Ivor Edward Cecil Rice-Jones
Private John S. Robson
Wing Commander T.H. Spear, RCAF
Lieutenant Colonel Louis Oluf Svendsen
Field Marshal Sir Garnet Joseph Wolseley

Museum of the Regiments, Calgary
Calgary Highlanders Museum and Archives
Company Quarter Master Sergeant William Alexander
Major Mark R. Bell
Colonel Norman D. Dingle
Calgary Highlanders Regiment
Major Ernest Bitcon Hetherington
Lieutenant Colonel Donald George MacLauchlan
Corporal Floyd O. Rourke

Princess Patricia's Canadian Light Infantry Regimental Archives
Princess Patricia's Canadian Light Infantry Regiment

City of Vancouver Archives, Vancouver
Canadian contingents (South Africa)
6th Regiment Duke of Connaught's Own Rifles
11th Regiment Irish Fusiliers of Canada
Colonel John Edwards Leckie
Brigadier Sherwood Lett
Military District 11 (1917)
Company Quarter Master Sergeant Nathaniel Rolph
Major John Reynolds Tite
Lieutenant Colonel John Wightman Warden

Museum of the 15th Field Artillery Regiment, Vancouver
Lieutenant Colonel Robert Theodore DuMoulin
15th Field Artillery Regiment

Museum of the Royal Westminster Regiment, New Westminster
Royal Westminster Regiment

British Columbia Archives and Records Service, Victoria
Major George Griffiths Aitken
Lieutenant Colonel Charles Edward Connolly
Lieutenant Colonel Charles Frederick Houghton
Lieutenant Colonel William Dillon Otter

CFB Esquimalt Naval and Military Museum, Esquimalt
Commander John Christopher Fawcett, RCN

Public Record Office, Kew

ADM 1	Admiralty and secretariat files
ADM 116	Admiralty and secretariat cases
AIR 2	Air Ministry general files
PRO 30/57	Field Marshal Lord Kitchener papers
WO 32	War Office general files
WO 82	JAG's office day books
WO 93	JAG's office miscellaneous files
WO 108	South African War papers
WO 123	army circulars, memoranda, orders, and regulations
WO 147	Field Marshal Garnet Joseph Wolseley papers
WO 225	army and air force courts martial committee reports, minutes, and submissions
WO 235	JAG's office war crimes papers
WO 311	JAG's office war crimes papers

Parliamentary Counsel's Office, Whitehall
Bound office volumes:
Military Law 1878-9
Army Rules of Procedure 1880-1
Army 1881-2
Militia and Reserves 1881-2
Miscellaneous 1895 volume 2
Miscellaneous 1897 volume 11
Army 1905-7
Army, Navy, Air Force, and Munitions 1914-8

Imperial War Museum, Lambeth North
W.F. Gow
Private A.M. Munro
Commander F. Poole, RCNR
Admiral of the Fleet Sir Algernon Willis, RN
Miscellaneous files

National Army Museum, Chelsea
Brigadier Humphry Bullock
W. Capel
Lieutenant Colonel Henry Hay
Major General Patrick MacDougall
Lieutenant Colonel A.W.C. McFall
Lance Corporal R. Moore and Private Williams (Boer War Scrapbook)
General Sir Henry Murray
Field Marshal Garnet Joseph Wolseley

Liddell Hart Centre for Military Archives, King's College, University of London
Brigadier General Sir James Edward Edmonds
Brigadier Sir Bernard Edward Fergusson
General Sir Ian Hamilton
Major John Frederick Maurice
Brigadier Edmund James Paton-Walsh
General Sir Henry Crichton Sclater
Major General James Scott-Elliot
Major General Douglas Ashton Lofft Wade

Hove Central Public Library, Sussex
Field Marshal Garnet Joseph Wolseley

Private Papers
Corporal J.W. Mickleborough

Published Documents, Regulations, Handbooks, and Manuals

Adjutant. *A Catechism of Military Law. Being questions and answers on the Army Discipline Act, 1879.* London: W. Clowes and Sons, 1879.

Adye, Stephen Payne. *A Treatise on Courts Martial. To Which Is Added, an Essay on Military Punishments and Awards,* 3rd ed. London: John Murray, 1785.

Alcock, J.H. *Hints and Don'ts for Defending Officers.* Aldershot, UK: Gale and Polden, 1943.

Atkinson, J. *Guide for Officers and Non-Commissioned Officers of the Territorial Force (with Specimen Examination Papers).* 2nd ed. London: Gale and Polden, 1911.

Baker, Harold Trevor. *The Territorial Force: A Manual of Its Law, Organization and Administration.* London: John Murray, 1909.

Banning, Stephen Thomas. *Military Law Made Easy – Subject "C" for the Promotion Examinations. With appendices of the examination papers, fully answered with references to the official books.* London: Gale and Polden, 1901. This book, part of Gale and Polden's military series, appeared in 25 editions between 1901 and 1946.

–. *The Soldier's Pocket Manual of Useful Information.* London: Gale and Polden, 1903.

Birchall, A.P. *Rapid Training of a Company for War,* 2nd ed. London, Aldershot, and Portsmouth, UK: Gale and Polden, 1915.

Boughey, John. *The Elements of Military Administration and Military Law, with Synopsis of Army Act, 1881, and a Form of Proceedings for a Regimental Court Martial,* 12th ed. Yorktown, Surrey, UK: William Webb, 1890.

Burn, Walter Adam, and William Thomas Raymond. *A Manual of the Law Regulating the Volunteer Forces Including the Volunteer Acts 1863 and 1869, and the Other Acts Relating to Volunteers.* London: Stevens and Sons, 1882.

Bush, E.W. *How to Become a Naval Officer (Special Entry).* London: Gieves, 1929.

Canada. *An Act to Amend an Act Respecting the Volunteer Militia Force.* Ottawa: M. Cameron, 1866.

–. *Dishonoured Legacy: The Lessons of the Somalia Affair, Report of the Commission of Inquiry into the Deployment of Canadian Forces to Somalia.* 5 vols. and Executive Summary. Ottawa: Canadian Government Publishing, 1997.

–. *Military Service Act 1917: Manual for the information and guidance of tribunals in the consideration and review of claims for exemption.* Ottawa: Military Service Council, 1918.

–. *Report of the Commissioners Appointed to Report a Plan for the Better Organization of the Department of Adjutant General of Militia, and the Best Means of Reorganizing the Militia of This Province, and to Prepare a Bill Thereon.* Quebec: S. Derbishire and G. Desbarats, 1862.

–. *Statutes of Canada,* 1868-1996.

Canada. Army. *Canadian Army Catalogue of Training Publications and Training Aids (1964).* Ottawa: Canadian Forces Headquarters, May 1965.

–. *Canadian Army Manual of Individual Training Standards M.I.T.S. (1964).* Ottawa: Army Headquarters, 1964.

–. *Canadian Army Manual of Unit Administration and Discipline.* Ottawa: Army Headquarters, 1956.

–. *Canadian Army Manual of Unit Administration and Discipline.* Ottawa: Army Headquarters, 1957.

–. *Canadian Army Manual for the Canadian Officers Training Corps 1962.* Ottawa: Army Headquarters, 1962.

–. *Canadian Army Orders,* 1952-66.

–. *Canadian Provost Corps: Specifications and Syllabus Militia Service Policeman Group 1 Course Blocks 1 and 2,* March 1963.

–. *Extracts from Manual of Military Law 1929: Reprinted for Use in the Canadian Army.* Ottawa: Edmond Cloutier, King's Printer, 1941.

–. *Extracts from Manual of Military Law 1929: Reprinted for Use in the Canadian Army.* Ottawa: Edmond Cloutier, King's Printer, 1943.

–. *Financial Instructions and Allowances for the Canadian Expeditionary Force 1916.* Ottawa: Government Printing Bureau, 1916.
–. *Financial Regulations and Instructions for the Canadian Active Service Force (Canada).* Ottawa: J.O. Patenaude, King's Printer, 1939.
–. *Financial Regulations and Instructions for the Canadian Active Service Force (Canada).* Ottawa: Edmond Cloutier, King's Printer, 1942.
–. *Financial Regulations and Instructions for the Canadian Active Service Force (Canada).* Ottawa: Edmond Cloutier, King's Printer, 1944.
–. *Financial Regulations and Instructions for the Canadian Active Service Force (Overseas).* Ottawa: Edmond Cloutier, King's Printer, 1945.
–. *A General Instructional Background for the Young Soldier 1940.* Ottawa: J.O. Patenaude, King's Printer, 1940.
–. *A General Instructional Background for the Young Soldier 1942.* Ottawa: Edmond Cloutier, King's Printer, 1942.
–. *Handbook on District Courts Martial 1941 (December).* Ottawa: Edmond Cloutier, King's Printer, 1941.
–. *How to Qualify for Promotion and Staff Courses. Officers: Canadian Army (Regular).* Ottawa: Roger Duhamel, Queen's Printer, 1965.
–. *Instructions for the Canadian Officers' Training Corps 1936.* Ottawa: J.O. Patenaude, King's Printer, 1936.
–. *Instructions for University Contingents of the Canadian Officers' Training Corps 1948.* Ottawa: Edmond Cloutier, King's Printer, 1948.
–. *The King's Regulations and Orders for the Canadian Army 1939.* Ottawa: Edmond Cloutier, King's Printer, 1947.
–. *Notes on Procedure, etc., in Connection with Trials by Court Martial 1936.* Ottawa: J.O. Patenaude, King's Printer, 1939.
–. *Orders and Instructions for Officers Commanding Trains and Details Proceeding by Train.* Ottawa: Edmond Cloutier, Queen's Printer, 1952.
–. *Pay and Allowance Regulations for the Canadian Army 1946.* Ottawa: Edmond Cloutier, King's Printer, 1946.
–. *Principles and Methods of Instruction (1963),* CAMT 2-38. Ottawa: Canadian Forces Headquarters, 1963.
–. *Principles and Organization of Training 1944,* Training Pamphlet No. 3. Ottawa: Edmond Cloutier, King's Printer, 1944.
–. *Provost Duties 1957,* CAMT 10-1. Ottawa: Edmond Cloutier, Queen's Printer, 1957.
–. *The Queen's Regulations and Orders for the Canadian Army,* 3 vols. Ottawa: Edmond Cloutier, Queen's Printer, 1952.
–. *Routine Orders,* 1939-46.
–. *Royal Canadian Army Cadets Training Programme 1943.* Ottawa: Edmond Cloutier, King's Printer, 1943.
–. *Successful Instruction 1951.* Ottawa: Edmond Cloutier, King's Printer, 1951.
Canada. Auditor General. *Reports of the Auditor General to the House of Commons,* 1989-April 1998.
Canada. Canadian Army Overseas. *Canadian Army Overseas System of Providing and Maintaining Personnel for the Canadian Army Overseas, Part III: Canadian Unit Guide to Documentation in a Theatre of War,* Revised May 1944.
Canada. Canadian Expeditionary Force. *Routine Orders,* Parts I and II, 1918-20.
–. *Training in Canadian Reserve Battalions,* London: Harrison and Sons, 1917.
Canada. Court Martial Appeal Court. *Court Martial Appeal Reports,* vol. 1. Ottawa: Court Martial Appeal Board, 1957; vol. 2, Ottawa: Roger Duhamel, Queen's Printer, 1966; vol. 3, Ottawa: Queen's Printer, 1973; vol. 4, Ottawa: Minister of Supply and Services Canada, 1991; vol. 5, Part I, Ottawa: Minister of Supply and Services Canada, 1992.
Canada. Department of Militia and Defence. *The Department of Militia and Defence under the Honourable Sir Adolphe P. Caron, K.C.M.G., and the Military Force of Canada.* Ottawa: MacLean, Roger and Co., 1887.

–. *General Regulations Royal Military College of Canada Kingston, Ont.* Ottawa: MacLean, Roger and Co., 1882.
–. *General Regulations Royal Military College of Canada Kingston, Ont.* Ottawa: MacLean, Roger and Co., 1883.
–. *General Regulations Royal Military College of Canada Kingston, Ont.* Ottawa: MacLean, Roger and Co., 1888.
–. *The King's Regulations and Orders for the Militia of Canada 1904.* Ottawa: Government Printing Bureau, 1904.
–. *The King's Regulations and Orders for the Canadian Militia 1910.* Ottawa: Government Printing Bureau, 1910.
–. *The King's Regulations and Orders for the Canadian Militia 1917.* Ottawa: Government Printing Bureau, 1917.
–. *The Manual for the Militia Artillery of Canada.* Quebec: Gunnery School Press, 1875.
–. *Memorandum for Camps of Instruction 1923.* Ottawa: F.A. Acland, King's Printer, 1923.
–. *Memorandum for Camps of Instruction 1928.* Ottawa: F.A. Acland, King's Printer, 1928.
–. *Memorandum for Camps of Instruction 1930.* Ottawa: F.A. Acland, King's Printer, 1930.
–. *Pay and Allowance Regulations 1912.* Ottawa: Government Printing Bureau, 1912.
–. *Regulations and Orders for the Militia of the Dominion of Canada, 1st September 1887.* Ottawa: Brown Chamberlin, Queen's Printer, 1887.
–. *Regulations and Orders for the Militia of the Dominion of Canada.* Ottawa: MacLean, Roger and Co., 1870.
–. *Regulations for the Royal Military College of Canada, Kingston, Ont. Amended to January, 1914.* Ottawa: Government Printing Bureau, 1916.
–. *Regulations Respecting the Volunteer Militia.* Ottawa: G.E. Desbarats, 1866.
–. *Revised Instructions for Dealing with Deserters and Absentees without Leave.* Ottawa: Government Printing Bureau, 1917.
–. *Royal Military College of Canada: Syllabus of the Course of Instruction,* September 1882.
–. *Royal Military College of Canada: Syllabus of the Course of Instruction,* September 1883.
Canada. Department of National Defence. *Amendments to the National Defence Act: Background and Amendment Highlights,* December 1997.
–. *Annual Reports.* Ottawa: King's/Queen's Printer, 1923-56, 1971-90.
–. *Basic Officer Training, Military Knowledge Manual,* CFP 195, 15 September 1972.
–. *Board of Inquiry Canadian Airborne Regiment Battle Group: Phase I Report,* 1993.
–. *Canadian Defence Policy 1992,* April 1992.
–. *Challenge and Commitment: A Defence Policy for Canada.* Ottawa: Supply and Services Canada, 1987.
–. *A Commitment to Change: Report on the Recommendations of the Somalia Commission of Inquiry,* October 1997.
–. *The Company Sergeant Major,* 24 January 1985.
–. *Conduct after Capture.* Ottawa: Department of National Defence Headquarters, 1960.
–. *The Election to Be Tried by Summary Trial or Court Martial: Guide for Accused and Assisting Officers (Bilingual),* A-L-G-050-000/AF-001, 30 November 1997.
–. *Estimates, Part III, National Defence.* Ottawa: Supply and Services Canada, 1991-7.
–. *Final Report of the Officer Development Review Board,* vol. 1, 15 September 1995.
–. *How to Qualify: Instructions on the Qualification of Officers and Other Ranks for Promotion: Non-Permanent Active Militia 1938.* Ottawa: J.O. Patenaude, King's Printer, 1938.
–. *The King's Regulations and Orders for the Canadian Militia 1926.* Ottawa: F.A. Acland, King's Printer, 1926.
–. *Leadership for the Professional Officer,* CFP 131 (2). Ottawa: Canadian Forces Headquarters, October 1966.
–. *Manual on the Geneva Conventions of August 12, 1949,* CFP 122, 31 August 1973.
–. *Minister's Monitoring Committee on Change in the Department of National Defence and the Canadian Forces: Interim Report – 1998,* 5 November 1998.
–. *The National Defence Act.* Ottawa: Edmond Cloutier, King's Printer, 1951.
–. *National Defence, 1998-99: Report on Plans and Priorities.* Ottawa: Public Works and Government Services Canada, 1998.

–. *Notes on Administration of Discipline.* Ottawa: J.O. Patenaude, King's Printer, 1939.
–. *Notes on Courts of Inquiry 1942.* Ottawa: Edmond Cloutier, King's Printer, 1942.
–. *Officer Corps Study: Phase I Report, Development of a Framework of Principles.* Ottawa: Directorate of Personnel Development Studies, 1989.
–. *Pay and Allowance Regulations for the Permanent and Non-Permanent Active Militia 1927.* Ottawa: F.A. Acland, King's Printer, 1927.
–. *Pay and Allowance Regulations for the Permanent and Non-Permanent Active Militia 1937.* Ottawa: Edmond Cloutier, King's Printer, 1942.
–. *The Queen's Regulations and Orders for the Canadian Forces,* 3 vols. Ottawa: Roger Duhamel, Queen's Printer, 1967-8.
–. *The Queen's Regulations and Orders for the Canadian Forces,* 4 vols. Ottawa: Queen's Printer, 1994.
–. *The Queen's Regulations and Orders for the Canadian Services Colleges.* Ottawa: Roger Duhamel, Queen's Printer, 1961.
–. *Report of the Officer Development Board,* 3 vols. Ottawa: Department of National Defence Headquarters, March 1969.
–. *Report on the Quasi-Judicial Role of the Minister of National Defence: Special Advisory Group on Military Justice and Military Police Investigation Services,* 10 October 1997.
–. *Report of the Special Advisory Group on Military Justice and Military Police Investigation Services,* 25 March 1997.
–. *Review Group on the Report of the Task Force on Unification of the Canadian Forces: Report,* 31 August 1980.
–. *Special Commission on the Restructuring of the Reserves: Report.* Ottawa: Public Works and Government Services Canada, 1995.
–. *Task Force on Review of Unification of the Canadian Forces: Final Report,* 15 March 1980.
–. *Unit Guide to the Geneva Conventions,* CFP 318 (4), 15 June 1973.
–. *White Paper on Defence.* Ottawa: Queen's Printer, March 1964.
Canada. Department of National Defence (Naval Service). *Naval Orders,* 1942-9.
–. *Report on Certain "Incidents" Which Occurred on Board HMC Ships ATHABASKAN, CRESCENT, and MAGNIFICENT and on Other Matters Concerning the Royal Canadian Navy.* Ottawa: Edmond Cloutier, King's Printer, 1949.
Canada. House of Commons. *Bill C-25: An Act to Amend the National Defence Act and to Make Consequential Amendments to Other Acts,* first reading, 4 December 1997.
–. *Equality for All: Report of the Parliamentary Committee on Equality Rights.* Ottawa: Queen's Printer, October 1985.
–. *Sessional Papers.* Ottawa: King's/Queen's Printer, 1867-1925.
–. *Special Committee on Bill No. 133, an Act Respecting National Defence: Minutes of Proceedings and Evidence.* Ottawa: King's Printer, 1950.
Canada. Maritime Command. *Guide to the Divisional System.* Winnipeg: Canadian Forces Training Material Production Centre, December 1985.
Canada. Militia, *Examination of Officers, Non-Permanent Active Militia, for Promotion: Papers Set in December, 1938 with Specimen Answers.* Ottawa: J.O. Patenaude, King's Printer, 1938.
–. *Examination of Officers, Non-Permanent Active Militia for Promotion: Papers Set in August 1940 with Notes to Solutions.* Ottawa: Edmond Cloutier, King's Printer, 1940.
–. *General Orders,* 1899-1946.
–. *Militia Orders,* 1899-1946.
Canada. Ministry of Overseas Military Forces of Canada. *A Report of the Ministry of Overseas Military Forces of Canada, 1918.* London: Ministry, Overseas Military Forces of Canada, 1918.
Canada. Mobile Command. *Reserve Commanders' Conference, 26 February 1972,* FMC 1180-22, 10 March 1972.
Canada. Office of the JAG. *Digest of Opinions and Rulings Compiled from the Records of the Office of the JAG at National Defence Headquarters.* Ottawa: Office of the JAG, 1942.
–. *Digest of Opinions and Rulings Compiled from the Records of the Office of the JAG,* Ottawa: Office of the JAG, 1944.

–. *You and the Law of War.* Ottawa: Office of the JAG, 1981.

Canada. Royal Canadian Air Force. *Extracts from the Manual of Air Force Law: Canadian Consolidation for Use of the Royal Canadian Air Force.* Ottawa: Edmond Cloutier, King's Printer, 1944.

–. *Financial Regulations and Instructions for the Royal Canadian Air Force on Active Service 1939.* Ottawa: Edmond Cloutier, King's Printer, 1940.

–. *Financial Regulations and Instructions for the Royal Canadian Air Force on Active Service 1939.* Ottawa: Edmond Cloutier, King's Printer, 1941.

–. *Financial Regulations and Instructions for the Royal Canadian Air Force on Active Service 1939.* Ottawa: Edmond Cloutier, King's Printer, 1943.

–. *Financial Regulations and Instructions for the Royal Canadian Air Force on Active Service 1945.* Ottawa: Edmond Cloutier, King's Printer, 1945.

–. *The King's Regulations and Orders for the Royal Canadian Air Force 1924.* Ottawa: King's Printer, 1924.

–. *King's Regulations for the Royal Canadian Air Force 1943.* Ottawa: Edmond Cloutier, King's Printer, 1943.

–. *The King's Regulations and Orders for the Royal Canadian Air Force,* 3 vols. Ottawa: Edmond Cloutier, King's Printer, 1951.

–. *Notes for the Guidance of Officers,* RCAF Pamphlet 4 (January 1964).

–. *Pay and Allowance Regulations for the Royal Canadian Air Force Permanent and Auxiliary 1924.* Ottawa: J.O. Patenaude, King's Printer, 1939.

–. *Pay and Allowance Regulations for the Royal Canadian Air Force 1946.* Ottawa: Edmond Cloutier, King's Printer, 1946.

–. *The Queen's Regulations and Orders for the Royal Canadian Air Force,* 3 vols. Ottawa: Edmond Cloutier, Queen's Printer, 1952.

Canada. Royal Canadian Navy. *Administrative and Secretariat Orders Naval Headquarters,* BRCN 126.

–. *General Orders Part 1: Administration, Personnel, and Financial,* 4 vols., 2 October 1964.

–. *The King's Regulations and Admiralty Instructions for the Government of His Majesty's Naval Service: reprinted for use H.M. Canadian Naval Forces,* 2 vols. and index. Ottawa: King's Printer, 1942.

–. *King's Regulations and Orders for the Royal Canadian Navy,* 3 vols. Ottawa: Edmond Cloutier, King's Printer, 1951.

–. *The King's Regulations for the Government of His Majesty's Canadian Naval Service 1945,* 2 vols. Ottawa: Edmond Cloutier, King's Printer, 1945.

–. *Manual of Advancement and Promotion,* 2 vols. Ottawa: Edmond Cloutier, Queen's Printer, 1954.

–. *The Queen's Regulations and Orders for the Royal Canadian Navy,* 3 vols. Ottawa: Edmond Cloutier, Queen's Printer, 1952.

–. *Regulations and Instructions for the Royal Canadian Navy 1937.* Ottawa: J.O. Patenaude, King's Printer, 1937.

–. *Regulations and Instructions for the Royal Canadian Navy 1940.* Ottawa: J.O. Patenaude, King's Printer, 1940.

–. *Regulations for Royal Canadian Naval Volunteer Reserve 1938.* Ottawa: J.O. Patenaude, King's Printer, 1938.

Canada. Senate. *Journals of the Senate of Canada.*

–. *Report of the Special Committee of the Senate on National Defence: Canada's Land Forces.* Ottawa: Supply and Services Canada, 1989.

–. *Report of the Sub-Committee on National Defence of the Standing Senate Committee on Foreign Affairs: Canada's Maritime Defence.* Ottawa: Supply and Services Canada, May 1983.

Carter, A.T. *The Admiralty Statutes,* 2 vols. London, UK: Eyre and Spottiswoode, King's Printer, 1905.

Claxton, Brooke. *Notes on Military Law and Discipline for Canadian Soldiers.* Montreal: McGill University Contingent, Canadian Officers Training Corps, 1939.

Clode, Charles Matthew. *The Administration of Justice under Military and Martial Law.* London, UK: John Murray, 1872.

–. *The Military Forces of the Crown: Their Administration and Government,* 2 vols. London, UK: John Murray, 1869.
–. *The Statute Law Relating to the Army.* London, UK: H.M. Stationery Office, 1877.
Cochran, Francis. *A Handy Text-Book on Military Law, arranged according to the Syllabus, Queen's Regulations, etc.* Edinburgh and London, UK: W. Blackwood and Sons, 1884.
Coddington, Fitzherbert John Osbourne. *The Young Officer's Guide to Military Law,* 19th ed. Aldershot, UK: Gale and Polden, 1943.
Collenette, David. *Budget Impact: National Defence.* Ottawa: Department of Finance, 1994.
Collins, G.R.N. *Pocket Manual of Military Law and Procedure,* London, UK: Hugh Rees, 1916.
Cox, George. *The Practice and Procedure of Courts-Martial and Disposal of Offences by Commanding Officers.* London, UK: Harrison and Sons, 1887,
D'Aguilar, George Charles. *Observations on the Practice and Forms of District, Regimental, and Detachment Courts Martial.* Dublin: M.H. Gill, 1866.
De Mulinen, Frederic. *Handbook on the Law of War for Armed Forces.* Geneva: International Committee of the Red Cross, 1987.
Dennistoun, Robert Maxwell. *Notes on District Courts Martial,* 2nd ed. London, UK: Hugh Rees, 1917.
–. *Notes on Military Law.* Winnipeg: Ladies' Home Workers Association of the 53rd Overseas Battalion, 1916.
Deschênes, Jules. *Commission of Inquiry on War Criminals Report Part 1: Public.* Ottawa: Supply and Services Canada, 1986.
Digan, G.C. *Synopsis of Military Law.* London, UK: W. Clowes and Sons, 1887.
Duckworth, Arthur Dyce. *An Introduction to Naval Court Martial Procedure,* 4th ed. Devonport, UK: Hiorns and Miller, 1948.
Edmonds, J.E., and L. Oppenheim. *Land Warfare: An Exposition of the Laws and Usages of War on Land, for the Guidance of Officers of His Majesty's Army.* London, UK: H.M. Stationery Office, Harrison and Sons, 1912.
Edwards, T.J. *The Non-Commissioned Officers' Guide to Promotion in the Infantry,* 2 vols. Aldershot, UK: Gale and Polden, 1927.
Fletcher, Henry Charles. *Report on the Military Academy at West Point, U.S.,* 1874.
Flower, Stephen. *Guide to Promotion: or Lectures on Fortification, Military Law, Tactics, etc.* London, UK: Clowes and Sons, 1883.
Ford, Arthur. *A Concise Text Book on Military Law,* 2nd ed. London, UK: Mitchell and Co.; Woolwich, UK: Boddy and Co., 1875.
Foster, Hubert. *Organization: How Armies are Formed for War.* London, UK: Hugh Rees, 1913.
Franklyn, Henry Bowles. *Outlines of Military Law and the Laws of Evidence.* London, UK: N.p., 1874.
Frost, O.M.T. *Vade-Mecum for Field-General Courts Martial,* 4th ed. Aldershot, UK: Gale and Polden, 1942.
Furse, A.P. *A Tabular Précis of Military Law, with explanatory notes based on the official textbooks for use of candidates for the military law examination.* London, UK: Macmillan and Co., 1896.
Gagnon, Charles. *Discipline, loi et devoirs militaires: précis elementaire.* Levis, QC: Quotidien, 1941.
Gall, Herbert Reay. *Questions and Answers on the Royal Military College Text Book of Military Law.* London, UK: Hugh Rees, 1904.
Gorham, Charles Alfred. *A Text Book of Military Law as Applicable to Persons Subject to the Army Discipline Act to Which Is Added Military Law as Applicable to Persons Subject to the Indian Articles of War,* 3rd ed. Calcutta: Brown and Co., 1880.
Great Britain. *An Act for Punishing Mutiny and Desertion, and for the Better Payment of the Army and Their Quarters (Passed 23d March 1866) ... Together with Rules and Articles of War.* London, UK: G. Eyre and W. Spottiswoode, 1866.
–. *Parliamentary Papers,* 1835-1953.
–. *Report from the Select Committee on the Naval Discipline Act, Together with the Proceedings of the Committee, Minutes of Evidence and Appendices.* London, UK: H.M. Stationery Office. 1956.

–. *Report of the Interdepartmental Committee on Proposed Disciplinary Amendments of the Army and Air Force Acts.* London, UK: H.M. Stationery Office, 1925.
Great Britain. Admiralty. *The King's Regulations and Admiralty Instructions for the Government of His Majesty's Naval Service 1906.* London, UK: H.M. Stationery Office, 1906.
–. *The King's Regulations and Admiralty Instructions for the Government of His Majesty's Naval Service,* 2 vols., London, UK: H.M. Stationery Office, 1937.
–. *The King's Regulations and Admiralty Instructions for the Government of His Majesty's Naval Service,* 2 vols. London, UK: H.M. Stationery Office, 1944.
–. *The Orders in Council for the Regulation of the Naval Service,* 4 vols. London, UK: H.M. Stationery Office, 1883-98.
Great Britain. Air Ministry. *The King's Regulations and Air Council Instructions for the Royal Air Force 1928.* London, UK: H.M. Stationery Office, 1934.
–. *The King's Regulations and Air Council Instructions for the Royal Air Force 1940.* London, UK: H.M. Stationery Office, 1940.
–. *The King's Regulations and Air Council Instructions for the Royal Air Force 1941.* London, UK: H.M. Stationery Office, 1941.
–. *Manual of Air Force Law 1921,* 1st ed. London, UK: H.M. Stationery Office, 1921.
–. *Manual of Air Force Law 1939,* 2nd ed. London, UK: H.M. Stationery Office, 1939.
–. *Royal Air Force War Manual,* Part I: Operations, February 1940.
Great Britain. 18th Corps. *Hints on Training.* France: Army Printing and Stationery Services, August 1918.
Great Britain. Horse Guards. Adjutant General's Office. *The King's Regulations and Orders for the Army.* London, UK: W. Clowes and Sons, 1837.
–. *The Queen's Regulations and Orders for the Army.* London, UK: H.M. Stationery Office, 1868.
Great Britain. War Office. *The Army Act, 1881, and certain other statutes relating to the Army, together with Rules of Procedure, 1881, and Rules for Summary Punishment,* 2nd ed. London: H.M. Stationery Office, 1882.
–. *Circular Memorandum on Courts-Martial for the Use of Convening and Staff Officers, and of Officers Giving Instruction on This Subject.* London, UK: Adjutant General's Branch, Stationery Services Press, 1916.
–. *Circular Memorandum on Courts Martial for Use on Active Service.* London, UK: Adjutant General's Branch, 1918.
–. *Circular Memorandum on Field General Courts-Martial on Active Service for Use in the United Kingdom: "The Green Book."* London, UK: Adjutant General, 1940.
–. *Discipline.* London, UK: H.M. Stationery Office, 1950.
–. *Examination of Officers for Promotion: Regular Army, Royal Marines, Indian Army, Supplementary Reserve and Territorial Army – (Voluntary Subjects), Papers Set in October, 1926 with Remarks by Examiners.* London, UK: H.M. Stationery Office, 1926.
–. *Field Service Pocket Book, 1911.* London, UK: H.M. Stationery Office, 1911.
–. *Field Service Pocket Book, 1913.* London, UK: H.M. Stationery Office, 1913.
–. *Field Service Pocket Book, 1914.* Reprint, with amendments, London, UK: H.M. Stationery Office, 1916.
–. *Field Service Pocket Book, 1932.* London, UK: H.M. Stationery Office, 1932.
–. *Field Service Pocket Book, 1939.* London, UK: William Clowes and Sons, H.M. Stationery, 1939.
–. *Field Service Regulations,* vol. 2. London, UK: H.M. Stationery Office, 1923.
–. *The King's Regulations and Orders for the Army 1912.* London, UK: H.M. Stationery Office, 1912.
–. *The King's Regulations for the Army and the Army Reserve 1923.* London, UK: H.M. Stationery Office, 1923.
–. *The King's Regulations for the Army and the Army Reserve 1935.* London, UK: H.M. Stationery Office, 1935.
–. *The King's Regulations for the Army and the Royal Army Reserve 1940.* London, UK: H.M. Stationery Office, 1941.
–. *The Law of War on Land Being Part III of the Manual of Military Law.* London, UK: H.M. Stationery Office, 1958.

–. *Manual of Military Law, 1884,* 1st ed. London, UK: H.M. Stationery Office, 1884.
–. *Manual of Military Law, 1887,* 2nd ed. London, UK: H.M. Stationery Office, 1887.
–. *Manual of Military Law, 1894,* 3rd ed. London, UK: H.M. Stationery Office, 1894.
–. *Manual of Military Law, 1899,* 4th ed. London, UK: H.M. Stationery Office, 1899.
–. *Manual of Military Law, 1907,* 5th ed. London, UK: H.M. Stationery Office, 1907.
–. *Manual of Military Law, 1914,* 6th ed. London, UK: H.M. Stationery Office, 1914.
–. *Manual of Military Law, 1929,* 7th ed. London, UK: H.M. Stationery Office, 1929.
–. *Manual of Military Law, 1951,* 8th ed. London, UK: H.M. Stationery Office, 1951.
–. *Manual of Military Law, 1956,* 9th ed. 2 Parts, London, UK: H.M. Stationery Office, 1956.
–. *Notes for Instructors on the Principles of Instruction 1943.* London, UK: H.M. Stationery Office, 1943.
–. *Notes for the Guidance of Staff and Other Officers Concerned in the Preparation of a Case for Trial by Court Martial, the Convening of the Court, the Trial, and the Confirmation of the Proceedings.* London, UK: Harrison and Sons, H.M. Stationery Office, 1929.
–. *Notes for Instructors on the Principles of Instruction 1939.* Ottawa: Edmond Cloutier, King's Printer, 1942.
–. *Notes on Procedure, etc. in Connection with Trials by Court Martial.* London, UK: H.M. Stationery Office, 1936.
–. *The Principles and Practice of Good Instruction, Part 1, for Officer and NCO Instructors 1947.* Ottawa: Edmond Cloutier, King's Printer, 1947.
–. *The Principles and Practice of Good Instruction, Part 2, for Officers Concerned with Organization of Training 1947.* Ottawa: Edmond Cloutier, King's Printer, 1947.
–. *The Principles of Training.* Ottawa: Edmond Cloutier, King's Printer, 1946.
–. *The Rights of a Soldier When in Arrest Charged with an Offence under the Army Act.* Ottawa: J.O. Patenaude, King's Printer, 1940.
–. *Rules of Procedure for Courts Martial and Other Matters.* London, UK: H.M. Stationery Office, 1947.
–. *Staff Manual: War (Provisional) 1912.* London, UK: General Staff, War Office, 28 October 1912.
Grierson, Francis D. *The A.B.C. of Military Law: A Concise Guide for the Use of Officers, N.C.O.'s and Men.* London, UK: T. Fisher Unwin, 1916.
Group Captain. *The Air Force Guide.* Toronto: Copp Clark, 1940.
Gunter, Edward. *Outlines of Military Law and Customs of War.* London, UK: W. Clowes and Sons, 1897.
Hansford, C.C. *Brief Notes on Discipline: A Handbook of Courts Martial Duties Discipline, etc. for Young Officers.* Toronto: McLeod, 1918.
Harcourt, Francis Vernon. *Hints to Young Officers on the Principles of Military Law and on the Practice of Courts Martial.* London, UK: W. Houghton, 1833.
Harry, Ernest. *From Crime to Court-Martial: A Simplified Rendering and Index of Those Parts of the "Manual of Military Law" and "King's Regulations" Which Deal with a Soldier's Offences and Punishments.* London, UK: Gale and Polden, 1918.
Hayman, Percival Mills Cobham. *Some Elementary Notes on Military Law and Procedure.* 4th ed. London, UK: Forster Groom and Co., 1943.
Hellyer, Paul. *Address on the Canadian Forces Reorganization Act, on moving second reading of Bill C-243 in the House of Commons,* 7 December 1966.
Hickman, William. *A Treatise on the Law and Practice of Naval Courts Martial.* London, UK: John Murray, 1851.
Holland, Thomas Erskine. *The Laws and Customs of War on Land, as Defined by the Hague Convention of 1899.* London, UK: Harrison and Sons, 1904.
–. *The Laws of War, Written and Unwritten.* Oxford, UK: Clarendon Press, 1908.
James, Walter Haweis. *1,260 Questions in Topography, Tactics, Military Law, Fortification, Military Administration, and Drill: Chiefly Those Set at the Various Examinations Held during the Past Seven Years at the Royal Military College, Sandhurst, and for the Admission of Militia Officers to the Army.* London, UK: Queen's Printer, Harrison, 1881.
Jones, Douglas. *Notes on Military Law for the Use of the Cadets of the Royal Military College of Canada.* Ottawa: Maclean, Roger, 1880.

–. *Textbook of Military Law: For Use of the Gentlemen Cadets of the Royal Military College of Canada.* Kingston, ON: Daily News Steam Print House, 1882.

Keefler, J.K. *Junior Officer's Guide.* Pamphlet. Toronto: Canadian Military Journal, 1952.

Kellock, R.L. *Report on the Halifax Disorders, May 7th-8th, 1945.* Ottawa: Edmond Cloutier, King's Printer, 1945.

Lamerson, C.D. "Combat Related Employment of Women (CREW) in the Army: Trial Research Plan." Working Paper 89-2. Canadian Forces Personnel Applied Research Unit, Willowdale, ON, July 1989.

–. "Combat Related Employment of Women: The Behavioural Science Approach." Canadian Forces Personnel Applied Research Unit, Willowdale, ON, June 1989.

–. "The Evolution of a Mixed Gender Canadian Forces." Canadian Forces Personnel Applied Research Unit, Willowdale, ON, 26 October 1989.

Langford, R.J.S. *Corporal to Field Officer* Toronto: Copp Clark Co., 1939. This book appeared in eight editions between 1939 and 1944.

Le Bill de la Marine. Pamphlet. N.p.: n.p., 1910.

Lower Canada. Militia. Office of the Adjutant General. *Rules and Regulations for the Formations, Field-Exercises, and Movements of the Militia of Lower Canada.* Quebec: J. Neilson, 1804.

Macpherson, James Pennington. *A Catechism on Military Law as Applicable to the Militia of Canada: Consisting of Questions and Answers on the Militia Act, 1883.* Montreal: J. Lovell and Son, 1886.

McArthur, John. *Principles and Practice of Naval and Military Courts Martial, with an Appendix Illustrative of the Subject.* 2 vols. London, UK: A. Strahan, 1813.

Metropolitan College, St. Albans. *Military Law,* Course 317A. Watford, UK: William Brendon and Son, 1942.

Morgan, Hill Faulconer. *A Summary of Military Law, etc.* London, UK: Marcus Ward and Co., 1883.

Morrison, Colquhon Grant. *Notes on Military Law, Organisation, and Interior Economy for Use at the Royal Military College.* London, UK: H.M. Stationery Office, 1895.

Napier, Charles J. *Remarks on Military Law and the Punishment of Flogging.* London, UK: J. and W. Boone, 1837.

Newman, John Cartwright Harding. *Notes on Military Law.* London, UK: Hugh Rees, 1906.

The Non-Commissioned Officers' Guide to Promotion in the Infantry. London, UK: Gale and Polden, 1915.

Nordon, Charles Louis. *The First Principles of Military Law for the Guidance of Officers and Candidates for Commissions.* Berkhamsted, UK: Loosley and Sons, 1918.

O'Dowd, James C. *Practical Hints to Courts Martial, upon many matters usually coming under their notice.* London, UK: W. Clowes and Sons, 1882.

Otter, William D. *The Guide: A Manual for the Canadian Militia (Infantry), Embracing the Interior Economy, Duties, Discipline, Dress, Books and Correspondence of a Regiment in Barracks, Camp, or Headquarters,* 2nd ed. Toronto: Copp Clark, 1885. This book appeared in nine editions between 1880 and 1914.

Park, R.E. "Overview of the Social/Behavioural Science Evaluation of the 1979-1985 Canadian Forces Trial Employment of Service Women in Non-Traditional Environments and Roles." Research Report 86-2. Canadian Forces Personnel Applied Research Unit, Willowdale, ON, May 1986.

Pendlebury, William Johann von Monté. *A Précis of the King's Regulations and the Manual of Military Law for Officers.* Shrewsbury, UK: Wilding and Son, 1943.

Pope, E.W. *The Canadian Officer's Guide to the Study of Military Law.* London, UK: Methuen and Co., 1916.

Pratt, Sisson Cooper. *Guide to Promotion. An Aid to Officers ... in Preparing for Examination in Regimental Duties.* London, UK: E. Stanford, 1892. 2nd ed., 1896.

–. *Military Law: Its Procedure and Practice.* London, UK: Kegan Paul and Co., 1883. This book appeared in nineteen editions between 1883 and 1915.

–. *The Military Law Examiner ... Being the Answers to Questions Set at Public Examinations in Military Law 1890 to 1895.* London and Aldershot, UK: Gale and Polden, 1895. This book appeared in eight editions between 1895 and 1911.

–. *Notes on Tactics and Military Administration.* Woolwich, UK: F.J. Caltermole, 1889.

Pullar, Laurence James Leslie. *A Guide to Courts Martial Procedure.* London, UK: Sifton, Praed and Co., 1943.

Questions on Military Law, etc. Yorktown, Surrey, UK: W. Webb, 1882.

Scoble, Thomas C. *The Canadian Volunteer's Hand Book for Field Service.* Toronto: Henry Rowsell, 1868.

Shurlock, Harold Harry Matthew. *Army District Court-Martial Procedure and Notes on Field General Court Martial Procedure.* Aldershot, UK: Gale and Polden, 1941.

–. *Royal Air Force Court-Martial Procedure, and Notes on Field General Court-Martial Procedure.* Aldershot, UK: Gale and Polden, 1941.

–. *600 Questions and Answers on Air Force Law.* Aldershot, UK: Gale and Polden, 1939. This book appeared in ten editions between 1939 and 1954.

–. *600 Questions and Answers on Military Law.* Aldershot, UK: Gale and Polden, 1939. This book appeared in seven editions between 1939 and 1955.

Siddons, J.H. *The Canadian Volunteers' Hand-Book: A Compendium of Military Facts and Suggestions Adapted to Field Service.* Toronto: Rollo and Adam, 1863.

Simmons, Thomas Frederick. *Remarks on the Constitution and Practice of Courts Martial; with a Summary of the Law of Evidence as Connected Therewith, and Some Notice of the Criminal Law of England with Reference to the Trial of Civil Offences.* London, UK: T. Egerton, 1830. This book appeared in seven editions between 1830 and 1875. F. Pinkney published editions 2 through 5. John Murray published editions 6 and 7.

Singer, Burrell M., and R.J.S. Langford. *Handbook of Canadian Military Law.* Toronto: Copp Clark, 1941.

Smith, Brian A. *What's Fair: The Geneva Conventions: Relief and Protection of the Wounded.* Ottawa: Canadian Red Cross Society, 1985.

Speeches of the Hon. G.E. Cartier on Submitting the Militia Bill and the Resolutions Concerning the Fortifications. Ottawa: G.E. Desbarats, 1868.

Story, Philip. *Summary of Military Law and Procedure for the Use of Officers of the Regular Forces and Militia.* London, UK: Rivingtons, 1886.

Suzor, Louis Timothée, ed. *Code militaire.* Quebec: G. and G.E. Desbarats, 1864.

Taschereau, Joseph Ernest de Montarville. *Petit Code Militaire: à l'usage des officiers, sous-officers et soldats Canadiens-français de la milice active du Canada.* Quebec: A. Coté, 1884.

Thompson, Joshua. *Militia List for Canada West: And, an Abridged System of Infantry Drill, Blank Forms of Annual, Company and Recommendation Returns: Also, Blank Forms Required in Ordinary Courts Martial.* Toronto: S. Derbishire and G. Desbarats, Queen's Printer, 1851.

Thring, Theodore. *Manual of Naval Law and Court Martial Procedure, in Which is Embodied Thring's Criminal Law of the Navy; Together with the Naval Discipline Act and an Appendix of Practical Forms.* London, UK: Stevens and Sons, 1901.

Townshend-Stephens, R. *A Practical Digest of Military Law.* London, UK: Sifton Praed and Co., 1933.

Tulloch, Alexander Bruce. *Elementary Lectures on Military Law.* London, UK: W. Mitchell and Co., 1872.

21st Army Group. Canadian Section. General headquarters 1st echelon. *Commanding Officers' Guide to Discipline (Canadian),* 1944.

United States. Department of Defence. *Manual for Courts-Martial 1951.* Washington, DC: Government Printing Office, 1951.

United States Army. *Fundamentals of Military Law,* ROTCM 145-85. Washington, DC: Headquarters, Department of the Army, September 1976.

–. *A Manual for Courts-Martial 1928.* Washington, DC: Government Printing Office, 1927.

University of Manitoba Contingent Canadian Officers Training Corps. *Notes and Excerpts from Official Publications for the Qualification of Officers and Non-Commissioned Officers of the Canadian Army (Reserve),* 2 vols. October 1942.

University of Toronto Contingent Canadian Officers Training Corps. *Lecture Notes for Officer Training Canadian Army (Reserve).* Toronto: University of Toronto Press, 1943.

Wilkins, Robert James, and Walter Sydney Chaney. *Handbook of Military Law.* London, UK: William Clowes and Sons, 1930.
Wolseley, Garnet Joseph. *The Soldier's Pocket-Book for Field Service,* 2nd ed. London, UK, and New York: Macmillan and Co., 1871. This book appeared in four editions between 1869 and 1882. Detailed coverage of military law began in the 2nd edition.
Wood, W.B. *The Complete Guide to Military Lectures (for Candidates for Lieutenants', Captains', and Field Officers' Certificates).* Winnipeg: Military News Agency, 1916.
Woodhouselee, Alexander Fraser Tytler. *An Essay on Military Law and the Practice of Courts-Martial.* London, UK: T. Egerton, 1814.
Woosnam, C.E. *Synopsis of Military Law and Discipline,* 2nd ed. Aldershot, UK: A.S.C. Printing Works, 1918.
Young, Clarence Richard. *Notes on Elementary Military Law for Canadian Officers.* Toronto: University of Toronto Press, 1939.
Younghusband, G.J. *The Queen's Commission.* London, UK: John Murray, 1891.

Newspapers and Periodicals
Alberta Military Institute Annual Journal
Canadian Army Journal
Canadian Defence Quarterly
Canadian Infantry Association Annual Reports
Canadian Military Gazette
Canadian Military Review
Canadian Militiaman
Command and Staff Review (Canadian Forces Command and Staff College)
Crowsnest
Maclean's
Military Topics
Naval Institute Proceedings
Roundel
Saturday Night
Selected Papers from the Transactions of the Canadian Military Institute
Sentinel
Supreme Court Reports
Toronto Star
Vancouver Sun
Volunteer and Military and Naval Gazette

Secondary Sources
Allard, Jean V. (with Serge Bernier). *The Memoirs of General Jean V. Allard.* Vancouver: UBC Press, 1988.
Archambault, Peter. "The Canadian Naval Mutinies of the 1940s and the Imperial Naval Tradition." M.A. thesis, University of New Brunswick, 1993.
Arnold, Fredrik von. "British Military Law and the Supervision of Its Application." *Military Law and Law of War Review* 27 (1988): 471-507.
Art, Robert J., Vincent Davis, and Samuel P. Huntington, eds. *Reorganizing America's Defense: Leadership in War and Peace.* Washington, DC: Pergamon-Brassey's, 1985.
Atkins, G.M. "An Ombudsman for the Canadian Forces: Re-establishing an Ethical Framework." Extended essay, Canadian Forces Command and Staff College, 1993.
Avins, Alfred. "Historical Origins of Desertion through Dual Enlistment." *Law Quarterly Review* 77 (1961): 501-25.
–. "The Testing of the Prolonged Absence Rule in Military Desertion by Questionnaire." *Criminal Law Quarterly* 6 (1963-4): 116-44.
Babington, Anthony. *For the Sake of Example: Capital Courts-Martial 1914-1920.* New York: St. Martin's Press, 1983.
Barnes, Rudolph C., Jr. *Military Legitimacy: Might and Right in the New Millennium.* London, UK: Frank Cass, 1996.

Beckett, I.F.W. "The Problem of Military Discipline in the Volunteer Forces, 1859-1899." *Journal of the Society for Army Historical Research* 56 (1978): 66-78.

Bellen, Edward J. "The Revolution in Military Law." *American Bar Association Journal* 54 (1968): 1194-8.

Bercuson, David Jay. *Significant Incident: Canada's Army, the Airborne, and the Murder in Somalia.* Toronto: McClelland and Stewart, 1996.

–. *True Patriot: The Life of Brooke Claxton 1898-1960.* Toronto: University of Toronto Press, 1994.

Bishop, J.H. "British Military Justice: Past Developments, Present Dangers, and Future Possibilities." LLM thesis, King's College, University of London, 1972.

Bishop, Joseph W., Jr. *Justice under Fire: A Study of Military Law.* New York: Charterhouse, 1974.

Blair, C.F. "Military Efficiency and Military Justice: A Peaceful Co-existence?" *University of New Brunswick Law Journal* 42 (1993): 237-41.

Blanco, Richard L. "Attempts to Abolish Branding and Flogging in the Army of Victorian England before 1881." *Journal of the Society for Army Historical Research* 45 (autumn 1968): 137-45.

Bland, Douglas. *The Administration of Defence Policy in Canada 1947-1985.* Winnipeg: Ronald P. Frye, 1987.

–. *Chiefs of Defence: Government and the Unified Command of the Canadian Armed Forces.* Toronto: Canadian Institute of Strategic Studies, 1995.

–. *National Defence Headquarters: Centre for Decision.* Ottawa: Commission of Inquiry into the Deployment of Canadian Forces to Somalia, 1997.

Borek, Ted B. "Legal Services during War." *Military Law Review* 120 (1988): 19-58.

Bothe, Michael, ed. *National Implementation of International Humanitarian Law: Proceedings of an International Colloquium Held at Bad Hamburg, June 17-19, 1988.* Dordrecht, Boston and London, UK: Martinus Nijhoff, 1990.

Boutilier, James A., ed. *The RCN in Retrospect, 1910-1968.* Vancouver: University of British Columbia Press, 1982.

Bridges, Barry. "Lord Kitchener and the Morant-Handcock Executions." *Journal of the Royal Australian Historical Society* 73 (1987): 24-40.

Brode, Patrick. "Bruce Macdonald and the Drafting of Canada's War Crimes Regulations, 1945." *Law Society of Upper Canada Gazette* 24 (December 1995): 274-82.

–. *Casual Slaughters and Accidental Judgments: Canadian War Crimes and Prosecutions, 1944-1948.* Toronto: University of Toronto Press, Osgoode Society, 1997.

Brown, James, and Michael J. Collins, eds. *Military Ethics and Professionalism: A Collection of Essays.* Washington, DC: National Defense University Press, 1981.

Burroughs, Peter. "Crime and Punishment in the British Army, 1815-1870." *English Historical Review* 100 (1985): 545-71.

–. "Tackling Army Desertion in British North America." *Canadian Historical Review* 61 (March 1980): 28-68.

Byers, R.B. "The Canadian Military and the Use of Force: End of an Era?" *International Journal* 30 (1975): 284-98.

–. "Perceptions of Parliamentary Surveillance of the Executive: The Case of Canadian Defence Policy." *Canadian Journal of Political Science* 5 (1972): 234-50.

–. "Structural Change and the Policy Process in the Department of National Defence: Military Perceptions." *Canadian Public Administration* 16 (1973): 220-42.

Byers, R.B., and Colin S. Gray, eds. *Canadian Military Professionalism: The Search for Identity.* Toronto: Canadian Institute for International Affairs, 1973.

Cameron, James M. *Murray: The Martyred Admiral.* Hantsport, NS: Lancelot Press, 1980.

Campbell, Ian J., and Robert L. Bennett. *Abbaye D'Ardenne June 1944: Twenty Canadian Prisoners of War.* Buron, Calvados, France: L'Association des Amis du Canada, 1984.

Canada Commissioners. "Courts Martial: Use of Self-criminating Evidence. Report." *Proceedings Uniform Law Conference of Canada* 56 (1974): 136-44.

"Canadian Law Concerning Trials of War Criminals by Military Courts." *Law Reports of Trials of War Criminals* 4 (1948): 125-30.

Carter, Kim. "Proof beyond a Reasonable Doubt? Collecting Evidence for the International Criminal Tribunal for the Former Yugoslavia." *Canadian Yearbook of International Law* (1993): 235-63.

Chambers, Ernest J. *The Canadian Militia: A History of the Origin and Development of the Force.* Ottawa and Montreal: Mortimer Press, 1907.

Claver, Scott. *Under the Lash: A History of Corporal Punishment in the British Armed Forces.* London, UK: Torchstream Books, 1954.

Cohen, Eliot A. *Citizens and Soldiers.* Ithaca, NY: Cornell University Press, 1985.

Cohen, Marshall, Thomas Nagel, and Thomas Scanlon, eds. *War and Moral Responsibility.* Princeton, NJ: Princeton University Press, 1974.

Cooke, Owen Arnold. *The Canadian Military Experience 1867-1983: A Bibliography,* 2nd ed. Ottawa: Directorate of History, Department of National Defence, 1984.

–. "Organization and Training in the Central Canadian Militia 1866-1885." M.A. thesis, Queen's University, 1974.

Copp, Terry, and Bill McAndrew. *Battle Exhaustion: Soldiers and Psychiatrists in the Canadian Army, 1939-1945.* Montreal and Kingston: McGill-Queen's University Press, 1990.

Corry, David J. "Military Law under the Charter." *Osgoode Hall Law Journal* 24 (1986): 67-120.

Cotton, Charles A. "The Divided Army: Role Orientations among Canada's Peacetime Soldiers." Ph.D. diss., Carleton University, 1980.

Cotton, Charles A., Rodney K. Crook, and Frank C. Pinch. "Canada's Professional Military: The Limits of Civilianization." *Armed Forces and Society* 4 (1978): 365-90.

Creighton, Geoffrey. "Superior Orders and Command Responsibility in Canadian Criminal Law." *University of Toronto Faculty of Law Review* 38 (1980): 1-32.

Creveld, Martin van. *The Training of Officers: From Military Professionalism to Irrelevance.* New York: Free Press, 1990.

Critchley, W. Harriet. "Civilianization and the Canadian Military." *Armed Forces and Society* 16 (1989): 117-36.

Cross, Michael, and Robert Bothwell, eds. *Policy by Other Means: Essays in Honour of C.P. Stacey.* Toronto: Clarke, Irwin and Co., 1972.

Crowe, Alfred J. "Droit militaire canadien," *Thémis* (1958-9): 81-8.

Denison, George T. *Soldiering in Canada: Recollections and Experiences.* Toronto: Macmillan, 1900.

Dennistoun, Robert. "Canadian Military Law Overseas." *Canada Law Journal* 56 (1920): 41-50, 121-4.

Denton, Edgar, III, ed. *Limits of Loyalty.* Waterloo, ON: Wilfrid Laurier University Press, 1980.

Desbarats, Peter. *Somalia Cover-Up: A Commissioner's Journal.* Toronto: McClelland and Stewart, 1997.

"Desertion: from Military Unit. Annotated to *Rex* v. *Poulin* (1916)." *Dominion Law Reports* 31 (1917): 14-8.

"The Diary of Lieut. J.A.V. Preston, 1885." *Saskatchewan History* 8 (1955): 95-107.

Dinwiddy, J.R. "The Early Nineteenth Century Campaign against Flogging in the Army." *English Historical Review* 97 (1982): 308-31.

Doi, Michael. "The Judicial Independence of Canadian Forces General Courts Martial: An Analysis of the Supreme Court of Canada Judgment in R. v. Généreux." *Dalhousie Law Journal* 16 (1993): 234-69.

Donagan, Barbara. "Codes and Conduct during the English Civil War." *Past and Present* 116 (1988): 65-95.

Donaghy, Greg. "The Rise and Fall of Canadian Military Assistance in the Developing World, 1952-1971." *Canadian Military History* 4 (1995): 75-84.

Douglas, W.A.B. "Why Does Canada Have Armed Forces?" *International Journal* 30 (1975): 259-83.

Douglass, John Jay. "Military Law: Stepchild of Legal Education." *Journal of Legal Education* 26 (1974): 467-94.

Draper, G.I.A.D. "The Exercise of Criminal Jurisdiction under the NATO Status of Forces Agreement, 1951." *Transactions of the Grotius Society* 44 (1958): 9-28.

Eagan, R.J. "Impact of the Canadian Forces Personnel System on the Canadian Military Ethos." Extended essay, Canadian Forces Command and Staff College, 1987.

Eggenberger, J.C. "Toward a General Model of Military Leadership for the Canadian Armed Forces." Departmental manuscript 79-1. Kingston: Department of Military Leadership and Management, Royal Military College of Canada, May 1979.

Elliot, Stuart Robert. *Scarlet to Green: A History of Intelligence in the Canadian Army, 1903-1963.* Toronto: Canadian Intelligence and Security Association, 1981.

Ewart, J.S. "Canada and War." *Canadian Bar Review* 10 (1932): 495-506.

Facey-Crowther, David R. "Militiamen and Volunteers: The New Brunswick Militia 1787-1871." *Acadiensis* 20 (1990): 148-73.

Fay, James B. "Canadian Criminal Law: An Examination of Military Justice." LLM thesis, Dalhousie University, 1974.

–. "Canadian Military Criminal Law: An Examination of Military Justice." *Chitty's Law Journal,* Part I, 23 (1975): 120-38; Part II, 23 (1975): 156-75; Part III, 23 (1975): 195-216; Part IV, 23 (1975): 228-52.

Fenrick, William John. "The Exclusion Zone Device in the Law of Naval Warfare." *Canadian Yearbook of International Law* 24 (1986): 91-126.

–. "In the Field with UNCOE: Investigating Atrocities in the Territory of Former Yugoslavia." *Military Law and Law of War Review* 34 (1995): 35-64.

–. "International Legal Aspects of Canadian Forces Experience in the Recent Gulf Conflict." *Canadian Council on International Law* (1991): 11-7.

–. "The Law of War at Sea Today: A Perspective from Canada." *Canadian Forces JAG Journal* 3 (1989): 17-25.

–. "Legal Aspects of Targeting in the Law of Naval Warfare." *Canadian Yearbook of International Law* 29 (1991): 238-82.

–. "Legal Limits on the Use of Force by Canadian Warships Engaged in Law Enforcement." *Canadian Yearbook of International Law* 18 (1980): 113-45.

–. "New Developments in the Law Concerning the Use of Conventional Weapons in Armed Conflict." *Canadian Yearbook of International Law* 19 (1981): 229-56.

–. "The Prosecution of War Criminals in Canada." *Dalhousie Law Journal* 12 (1989): 256-97.

–. "The Rule of Proportionality and Protocol I in Conventional Warfare." *Military Law Review* 98 (fall 1982): 91-127.

Ferretti, Aleardo, ed. *International Rules of Warfare and Command Responsibility: ICRC East Asia Regional Seminar on the Instruction of the Law of War.* Bangkok: ICRC Regional Delegation for East Asia, 1998.

Fidell, Eugene R. "The Culture of Change in Military Law." *Military Law Review* 126 (1989): 125-32.

Flemming, S.B. *Civilianization and Contemporary Social Theory: Alternative Approaches to Armed Forces and Society.* ORAE Report No. 439. Ottawa: Department of National Defence, Operational Research and Analysis Establishment, January 1988.

–. "Civilianization Theory and Martial Discipline in the Canadian Forces in the Post-Korean War Period." Staff Note 2/89. Ottawa: Operational Research and Analysis Establishment. Directorate of Social and Economic Analysis, 1989.

–. *The Hearts and Minds of Soldiers in Canada: The Military Ethos Scale (MES) in Retrospect.* Ottawa: Operational Research and Analysis Establishment, Directorate of Social and Economic Analysis, 1989.

Fletcher, Henry Charles. "A Volunteer Force, British and Colonial, in the Event of War." *Royal United Services Institute Journal* 21 (1877): 631-58.

Foster, Tony. *Meeting of Generals.* Toronto: Methuen, 1986.

Fotion, N., and G. Elfstrom. *Military Ethics: Guidelines for Peace and War.* Boston: Routledge and Kegan Paul, 1986.

Frey, Sylvia F. "Courts and Cats: British Military Justice in the Eighteenth Century." *Military Affairs* 43 (1979): 5-11.

Friedland, Martin L. *Controlling Misconduct in the Military.* Ottawa: Commission of Inquiry into the Deployment of Canadian Forces to Somalia, 1997.

Frost, Charles Sydney. *Once a Patricia: Memoirs of a Junior Infantry Officer in World War II.* St. Catharines, ON: Vanwell, 1988.

Gabriel, Richard A. *To Serve with Honor: A Treatise on Military Ethics and the Way of the Soldier.* Westport, CT: Greenwood, 1982.

Gagnon, Jean-Pierre. *Le 22e bataillon (canadien-français) 1914-1919: Étude socio-militaire.* Ottawa and Quebec City: Les Presses de l'Université Laval, 1986.

Gans, Arthur E. "Ethics and International Humanitarian Law: A New Direction for Officer Instruction in the Canadian Army." Extended essay, Department of Theology, University of Toronto, 1991.

–. "Vocation or Job: A Warrior's Place in a Rights-Driven Society." *Canadian Defence Quarterly* 24 (December 1994): 10-3.

Gardam, David. "Canadian Military Professionalism: Are We Losing It?" Extended essay, Canadian Forces Command and Staff College, 1995.

Gardner, Ray. *Wanted for Murder ... SS Brigadeführer Kurt Meyer.* Pamphlet. Vancouver, 1951.

Gates, John M. "The 'New' Military Professionalism." *Armed Forces and Society* 11 (1985): 427-36.

Generous, William T., Jr. *Swords and Scales: The Development of the Uniform Code of Military Justice.* Port Washington, NY: Kennikat, 1973.

Ginsburgh, Robert N. "Military Ethics in a Changing World." *Air University Review* 27 (1976): 2-10.

Glenesk, Larry. "Canadian Forces Code of Military Ethics." Extended essay, Canadian Forces Command and Staff College, 1989.

Goetze, Bernd A. *Military Professionalism: The Canadian Officer Corps.* National Security Series No. 3/76. Kingston, ON: Centre for International Relations, Queen's University, 1976.

Gold, Marc. "Canadian Bill of Rights – Fair Hearing – Equality before the Law – National Defence Act – Court Martial Jurisdiction." *Canadian Bar Review* 60 (1982): 137-51.

Goldstein, Elliott. "Videotape Evidence in Canadian Military Courts." *Canadian Forces JAG Journal* 2 (1987): 59-74.

Gordon, Donald C. *The Dominion Partnership in Imperial Defense. 1870-1914.* Baltimore: Johns Hopkins University Press, 1965.

Green, Leslie C. "Canada's Role in the Development of the Law of Armed Conflict." *Canadian Yearbook of International Law* 18 (1980): 91-112.

–. "Canadian Law and the Punishment of War Crimes." *Chitty's Law Journal* 28 (1980): 249-54.

–. "Canadian Law, War Crimes and Crimes against Humanity." *British Yearbook of International Law* 59 (1988): 217-35.

–. "The Defence of Superior Orders in the Modern Law of Armed Conflict." *Alberta Law Review* 31 (1993): 320-33.

–. "The Environment and the Law of Conventional Warfare." *Canadian Yearbook of International Law* 29 (1991): 222-37.

–. *Essays on the Modern Law of War.* Dobbs Ferry, NY: Transnational Publishers, 1985.

–. "The Geneva Humanitarian Law Conference 1975." *Canadian Yearbook of International Law* 13 (1975): 295-305.

–. "The German Federal Republic and the Exercise of Criminal Jurisdiction." *University of Toronto Law Journal* 43 (1993): 207-15.

–. "Humanitarian Law and the Man in the Field." *Canadian Yearbook of International Law* 14 (1976): 96-115.

–. *International Law: A Canadian Perspective.* Toronto: Carswell, 1984.

–. "The Law of Armed Conflict and the Enforcement of International Law." *Canadian Yearbook of International Law* 22 (1984): 3-25.

–. "The Man in the Field and the Maxim *Ignorantia Juris Non Excusat.*" *Revue de droit de l'Université de Sherbrooke* 10 (1979): 135-56.

–. "The New Law of Armed Conflict." *Canadian Yearbook of International Law* 15 (1977): 3-41.

–. "Rewriting the Laws of War: The Geneva Protocols of 1977." *International Perspectives* (November/December 1977): 36-43.

–. "The Role of Legal Advisors in the Armed Forces." *Chitty's Law Journal* 26 (1978): 18-24.

–. "Superior Orders and Command Responsibility." *Canadian Yearbook of International Law* 27 (1989): 167-202.

–. "Superior Orders and the Reasonable Man." *Canadian Yearbook of International Law* 8 (1970): 61-103.

–. *Superior Orders in National and International Law.* Leyden, Netherlands: A.W. Sijthoff, 1976.

–. "A Wartime Lawyer Reminisces." *Canadian JAG Journal* 3 (1989): 1-16.

Groll-Ya'ari, Yedidiah. "Toward a Normative Code for the Military." *Armed Forces and Society* 20 (1994): 457-72.

Guggisberg, Frederick Gordon. *"The Shop": The Story of the Royal Military Academy.* London, UK: Cassell and Co. 1900.

Hackett, John Winthrop. *The Profession of Arms.* London, UK: Times Publishing Co. 1964.

Hanson, Jim, and Susan McNish, eds. *The Military in Modern Democratic Society.* Toronto: Canadian Institute of Strategic Studies, 1996.

Harries-Jenkins, Gwyn. "The Development of Professionalism in the Victorian Army." *Armed Forces and Society* 1 (1975): 472-89.

Harris, Stephen John. *Canadian Brass: The Making of a Professional Army 1860-1939.* Toronto: University of Toronto Press, 1988.

Hartle, Anthony E. *Moral Issues in Military Decision Making.* Lawrence, KS: University Press of Kansas, 1989.

Harwood, J.R. "Strengthening Ethical Vision in the Canadian Forces." Extended essay, Canadian Forces Command and Staff College, 1994.

Haycock, Ronald. *Sam Hughes: The Public Career of a Controversial Canadian.* Waterloo, ON: Wilfrid Laurier University Press, 1986.

Heard, Andrew D. "Military Law and the Charter of Rights." *Dalhousie Law Journal* 11 (1987-8): 514-45.

Hellyer, Paul. *Damn the Torpedoes: My Fight to Unify Canada's Armed Forces.* Toronto: McClelland and Stewart, 1990.

Herfst, G. "Meeting the Needs of Military Justice: An Examination of the Military Rules of Evidence." LLM thesis, Dalhousie University, 1995.

–. "Survey of Canadian Military Law." Advanced Criminal Law assignment. University of Calgary, 4 December 1981.

Higginbotham, Robert. "Case Studies in the Law of Land Warfare." *Military Review* 63 (January 1983): 58-66.

Hildebrandt, Walter. "Ending the Resistance: The Northwest Campaign of 1885 and the Fall of Batoche." *Journal of the West* 32 (1993): 38-46.

Hines, A.G. "Military Ethics: A Code for the Canadian Forces." Extended essay, Canadian Forces Command and Staff College, 1992.

Hingorani, R.C. *Prisoners of War.* 2nd ed. New Delhi: Oxford and IBH Publishing, 1982.

Hiscox, Diane, ed. *International Peace and Security: Proceedings of the 1994 Conference of the Canadian Council on International Law.* Ottawa: Canadian Council on International Law, 1995.

Ho, Rubsun. "A World That Has Walls: A *Charter* Analysis of Military Tribunals." *University of Toronto Faculty of Law Review* 54 (winter 1996): 149-85.

Hodgins, W.E. "Law Applicable to the Militia of Canada." *Canadian Law Times* 21 (1901): 169-88.

–. "Military Law." *Canadian Law Times* 30 (1910): 485-96.

Hollies, Jack H. "Canadian Military Law." *Military Law Review* 13 (1961): 69-87.

–. "Courts Martial in the Canadian Forces." *Criminal Law Quarterly* 2 (1959-60): 67-76.

–. "Hearsay as the Basis of Opinion Evidence." *Criminal Law Quarterly* 10 (1967-8): 288-304.

–. "Review of Alfred Avins' *The Law of AWOL.*" *Canadian Bar Review* 35 (1957): 999-1003.

Hough, Lynne. "No Life Like It," *Canadian Lawyer* 6 (October 1982): 12-5.

Hughes-Morgan, David. "Disobedience to a Lawful Military Command." *Journal of the Royal United Services Institute for Defence Studies* 122 (1977): 9-16.

Huntington, Samuel P. *The Soldier and the State*. New York: Vintage Books, 1957.

Ignatieff, Michael. *The Warrior's Honor*. Toronto: Viking, 1997.

Jackson, B.R. "Ethics, Leadership, and the Canadian Forces." Extended essay, Canadian Forces Command and Staff College, 1989.

Jacobs, James B. "Legal Change within the United States Armed Forces since World War II." *Armed Forces and Society* 4 (1978): 391-421.

James, Lawrence. *Mutiny: In the British and Commonwealth Forces, 1797-1956*. London, UK: Buchan and Enright, 1987.

Janowitz, Morris. *The Professional Soldier*. New York: Free Press, 1971.

Jones, David R., Fred Crickard, and Todd R. Yates. *Ethics and Canadian Defence Policy: Conference Proceedings*. Halifax: Centre for Foreign Policy Studies, Dalhousie University, 1992.

Jones, Robert W. "Truth, Duty, Valour (and Don't Get Caught): The Need for a Code of Ethics for the Canadian Forces." Extended essay, Canadian Forces Command and Staff College, 1995.

Joseph, Robert E. "The Need for Including a Course on Military Justice in the Law School Curriculum." *Journal of Legal Education* 7 (1954): 79-83.

Juliani, Tony Joseph, and Charles Kenneth Talbot. *Military Justice: A Selected Annotated Bibliography*. Ottawa: CRIMCARE, 1981.

Karsten, Peter. *Law, Soldiers and Combat*. Westport, CT: Greenwood Press, 1978.

Kasurak, Peter C. "Civilianization and the Military Ethos: Civil-Military Relations in Canada." *Canadian Public Administration* 25 (1982): 108-29.

Kronenberg, Vernon J. *All Together Now: The Organization of the Department of National Defence in Canada 1964-1972*. Toronto: Canadian Institute of International Affairs, 1973.

Lang, D., ed. *Leadership for the 1990s: Report of a Leadership Symposium Held at Royal Roads Military College 15, 16, 17 June, 1981*. Victoria: Department of Military Leadership and Management, Royal Roads Military College, June 1981.

Laplante, Laurent. "Why a Specific Justice System for the Military?" *Justice Report* 10 (1994): 6-8.

Lawson, William J. "Canadian Military Law." *Canadian Bar Review* 29 (1951): 241-55.

Lazar, Harvey. "Parliamentary Control of Defence in Canada, 1945-1962." M.A. thesis, University of British Columbia, 1963.

Leger, Francis A. "Military Criminality in Canada." *Military Law and Law of War Review* 9 (1970): 297-8.

Lewis, Ira. "Public Service 2000 and Cultural Change in the Department of National Defence." *Canadian Public Administration* 37 (1994): 249-66.

Lockyer, James E. "Charter Implications for Military Justice: A Commentary on Zillman and Blair." *University of New Brunswick Law Journal* 42 (1993): 243-55.

Lunau, Ronald D. "Military Tribunals under the Charter." *National Journal of Constitutional Law* 2 (1992): 197-216.

Macdonald, Bruce J.S. *The Trial of Kurt Meyer*. Toronto: Clarke, Irwin, and Co., 1954.

Macdonald, R. St. J., ed. *Canadian Perspectives on International Law and Organization*. Toronto: University of Toronto Press, 1974.

MacLaren, Roy. *Canadians on the Nile 1882-1898*. Vancouver: University of British Columbia Press, 1978.

Macquarrie, J.C. "Canada Expects ... : A Case for Formal Ethics Education in the Canadian Forces." Extended essay, Canadian Forces Command and Staff College, 1989.

Madsen, A.J. *Training Perspective of CF Ethos and Values*. Astra, ON: Canadian Forces Training System Headquarters, 1988.

Madsen, Chris. "Victims of Circumstance: The Execution of German Deserters by Surrendered German Troops under Canadian Control in Amsterdam, May 1945." *Canadian Military History* 2 (1993): 93-113.

Mahon, Gerard. "Military Ethics: A Culture Change." Extended essay, Canadian Forces Command and Staff College, 1991.

Maloney, Sean M. "'Missed Opportunity': Operation Broadsword, 4 Brigade and the Gulf War, 1990-1991." *Canadian Military History* 4 (1995): 36-46.

Margolian, Howard. *Conduct Unbecoming: The Story of the Murder of Canadian Prisoners of War in Normandy.* Toronto: University of Toronto Press, 1998.

Martins, Mark S. "Rules of Engagement for Land Forces: A Matter of Training, Not Lawyering." *Military Law Review* 143 (1994): 1-160.

Mason, J.A.R. "Military Tribunals – Restraint of by Civil Courts – Habeas Corpus and Prohibition." *Canadian Bar Review* 24 (1946): 210-7.

Mason, John W. "Basic Freedoms in the Canadian Armed Forces." M.A. thesis, Carleton University, 1972.

Matthews, Lloyd J., and Dale E. Brown, eds. *The Parameters of Military Ethics.* London, UK: Pergamon-Brassey's International Defence Publishers, 1989.

Mayo, Margo J. "Computer Assisted Learning in the Canadian Forces: Training the Trainers." M.Sc. thesis, University of Calgary, 1990.

McDonald, Ronald Arthur. "Equality Issues in the Canadian Forces under the Canadian Charter of Rights and Freedoms: A Study of the Effect of the Canadian Charter of Rights and Freedoms on Certain Policies of the Canadian Forces." LLM thesis, Queen's University, 1986.

–. "The Legal Branch Law Firm of the Canadian Forces." *Canadian Forces JAG Journal* 2 (1987): 1-4.

–. "The Trail of Discipline: The Historical Roots of Canadian Military Law." *Canadian Forces JAG Journal* 1 (1985): 1-28.

McDougall, Bruce. "Be All You Can Be." *Canadian Lawyer* 15 (May 1991): 26-8.

McGowan, James J., Jr. "Training in the Geneva and Hague Conventions: A Dead Issue?" *Military Law and Law of War Review* 14 (1975): 51-68.

McLin, J.B. *Canada's Changing Defence Policy, 1957-1963.* Baltimore: Johns Hopkins University Press, 1967.

McNeil, D.G. "Ethics and the Canadian Professional Officer." Extended essay, Canadian Forces Command and Staff College, 1984.

Meron, Theodor. "Civil Jurisdiction of Canadian Courts over United States Military Personnel in Canada." *University of Toronto Law Journal* 12 (1957-8): 67-78.

Meyer, Kurt. *Grenadiers.* Winnipeg: J.J. Fedorowicz, 1994.

Miller, Carman. "Chums in Arms: Comradeship among Canada's South Africa War Soldiers." *Social History* 18 (1985): 359-73.

–. *Painting the Map Red: Canada and the South African War, 1899-1902.* Montreal and Kingston: McGill-Queen's University Press, 1993.

–. "Sir Frederick William Borden and Military Reform, 1896-1911." *Canadian Historical Review* 50 (1969): 265-84.

Miller, D.M. "Next Stage in Humanitarian Law." *International Perspectives* (November/December 1972): 51-7.

Moore, William. *The Thin Yellow Line.* London, UK: Leo Cooper, 1974.

Morgan, Edmund. "The Background of the Uniform Code of Military Justice." *Vanderbilt Law Review* 6 (1953): 169-85.

Morgan-Owen, J.G. "The Attitude of the Public in the United Kingdom to the Administration of Justice in the Armed Forces." *Military Law and Law of War Review* 19 (1980): 356-60.

Morrison, Alex, ed. *Peacekeeping, Peacemaking or War: International Security Enforcement.* Toronto: Canadian Institute of Strategic Studies, 1994.

Morton, Desmond, "Aid to the Civil Power: The Canadian Militia in Support of Social Order, 1867-1914." *Canadian Historical Review* 51 (1970): 407-25.

–. *Canada and War.* Toronto: Butterworths, 1981.

–. *The Canadian General Sir William Otter.* Toronto: Hakkert, 1974.

–. "Kicking and Complaining: Postwar Demobilization Riots in the Canadian Expeditionary Force 1918-1919." *Canadian Historical Review* 61 (1980): 334-60.

–. *The Last War Drum: The North West Campaign of 1885.* Toronto: Hakkert, 1972.

–. *A Military History of Canada.* Edmonton: Hurtig Publishers, 1985.

–. *Ministers and Generals: Politics and the Canadian Militia 1868-1904*. Toronto: University of Toronto Press, 1970.

–. *A Peculiar Kind of Politics: Canada's Overseas Ministry in the First World War*. Toronto: University of Toronto Press, 1982.

–. "The Supreme Penalty: Canadian Deaths by Firing Squad in the First World War." *Queen's Quarterly* 79 (autumn 1972): 345-52.

Morton, Desmond, and Glenn Wright. *Winning the Second Battle: Canadian Veterans and the Return to Civilian Life, 1915-1930*. Toronto: University of Toronto Press, 1987.

Mowat, H.M. "The Law and the Soldier." *Canadian Law Times* 18 (1898): 97-107.

Mowbray, J.A. "Militiaman: A Comparative Study of the Evolution of Organisation in the Canadian and British Voluntary Citizen Military Forces, 1896-1939." Ph.D. diss., Duke University, 1975.

Oliver, R.G. "Canadian Military Law." *Chitty's Law Journal* 23 (1975): 109-19.

Orde, Reginald John. "Canadian Military Law." *Federal Bar Association Journal* 5 (1943): 29-39, 61-2.

–. "Some Aspects of Canadian Service Law and of the Office of the JAG in Canada." *The Judge Advocate Journal* 1 (December 1944): 8-11, 18.

–. "The Statute of Westminster: Notes on the Application of the Statute and Complementary Legislation to the Armed Forces of Canada." *Canadian Defence Quarterly* 11 (1933-4): 213-23.

O'Reilly, James, and Healy, Patrick. *Independence in the Prosecution of Offences in the Canadian Forces: Military Policing and Prosecutorial Discretion*. Ottawa: Commission of Inquiry into the Deployment of Canadian Forces to Somalia, 1997.

O'Roark, Dulaney L., Jr. "Transformational Leadership: Teaching the JAG Elephant to Dance." *Military Law Review* 146 (1994): 224-33.

O'Sullivan, P. *Military Law and the Supremacy of the Civil Courts*. London, UK: Stevens and Sons, 1921.

Owen, J.F. "The Military Defence Forces of the Colonies." *Proceedings of the Royal Colonial Institute* 21 (1890): 277-326.

Parizeau, Jean. "Force armeé et maintien de l'ordre au Canada, 1867: Un siècle d'aide au pouvoir civil." Ph.D. diss., Université Paul Vléry III Montpellier Centre d'histoire militaire et d'études de défense nationale, 1981.

Penlington, Norman. *Canada and Imperialism, 1896-1899*. Toronto: University of Toronto Press, 1965.

–. "General Hutton and the Problem of Military Imperialism in Canada, 1898-1900." *Canadian Historical Review* 24 (1943): 156-76.

Perry, Warren. "Military Reforms of General Sir Edward Hutton in New South Wales: 1893-96." *Australian Quarterly* 28 (1956): 65-75.

Pineau, Michele A. "Civilians under Military Justice: A Canadian Study." *McGill Law Journal* 25 (1979): 3-31.

Ponton, William N. "A Legal Clearing House." *Canadian Law Times* 25 (1905): 10-8.

Porter, Gerald. *In Retreat: The Canadian Forces in the Trudeau Years*. Vancouver: Deneau and Greenberg, 1979.

Preston, Richard Arthur. *Canada's RMC: A History of the Royal Military College of Canada*. Toronto: University of Toronto Press, 1969.

–. *Canada and "Imperial Defense": A Study of the Origins of the British Commonwealth's Defense Organization, 1867-1919*. Toronto: University of Toronto Press, 1967.

–. "Military Education, Professionalism, and Doctrine." *Revue internationale d'histoire militaire* 54 (1982): 273-301.

–. "The Military Structure of the Old Commonwealth." *International Journal* 17 (1961-2): 98-121.

–. "Perspectives in the History of Military Education and Professionalism." *Harmon Memorial Lectures in Military History* 22 (1980): 1-37.

–. "The Profession of Arms in Post-War Canada, 1945-1970." *World Politics* 23 (1971): 189-214.

–. *To Serve Canada: A History of the Royal Military College since the Second World War*. Ottawa: University of Ottawa Press, 1991.

Preston, Richard A., and Ian Wards. "Military and Defense Development in Canada, Australia and New Zealand: A Three-Way Comparison." *War and Society* 5 (1987): 1-21.

Prichard, M.J. "The Army Act and Murder Abroad." *Cambridge Law Journal* 12 (1954): 232-41.

Putkowski, Julian. *The Kinmel Park Camp Riots 1919.* Clwyd, Wales: Flintshire Historical Society, 1989.

Putkowski, Julian, and Julian Sykes. *Shot at Dawn.* Barnsley, South Yorkshire, UK: Wharncliffe Publishing, 1989.

Rasor, Eugene L. *Reform in the Royal Navy: A Social History of the Lower Deck 1850-1880.* New York: Archon Books, 1976.

Raushenbush, Walter B. "Military Law Courses Can Serve Scholarly Objectives." *Journal of Legal Education* 16 (1963): 191-7.

Ray, Randy. "Law in the Trenches." *National* 4 (March 1995): 12-24.

Reynolds, Eric T. "Ethical Competence and the Profession of Arms: A Contemporary Challenge to Military Institutions." *Canadian Defence Quarterly* 23 (December 1993): 30-6.

Rigby, William Cattron. "Military Justice in the British Commonwealth." *Federal Bar Association Journal* 4 (1942): 291-4, 323-8.

Roberts, Leslie. *There Shall Be Wings: A History of the Royal Canadian Air Force.* Toronto: Clarke, Irwin and Co., 1959.

Rogers, A.P.V. *Law on the Battlefield.* Manchester and New York: Manchester University Press, 1996.

–. "War Crimes Trials under the Royal Warrant: British Practice 1945-1949." *International and Comparative Law Quarterly* 39 (1990): 780-800.

Rossignol, Michel. *International Conflicts: Parliament, the National Defence Act, and the Decision to Participate.* Background Paper BP-303E. Ottawa: Research Branch, Library of Parliament, 1992.

–. *National Defence Act: Reform of the Military Justice System.* 96-1E. Ottawa: Research Branch, Library of Parliament, 22 January 1997.

Rowe, Peter J. *Defence: The Legal Implications, Military Law, and the Laws of War.* London and Toronto: Brassey's Defence Publishers, 1987.

–. "Military Justice within the British Army." *Military Law Review* 94 (1981): 99-134.

–, ed. *The Gulf War 1990-91 in International and English Law.* London, UK: Routledge/Sweet and Maxwell, 1993.

Roy, Reginald H. *For Most Conspicuous Bravery: A Biography of Major-General George R. Pearkes, V.C., through Two World Wars.* Vancouver: University of British Columbia Press, 1977.

–. "With the Midland Battalion to Batoche." *Saskatchewan History* 32 (spring 1979): 41-60.

Rubin, Gerry R. "The Legal Education of British Army Officers, 1860-1923." *Journal of Legal History* 15 (1994): 223-51.

–. "Parliament, Prerogative, and Military Law: Who Had Legal Authority over the Army in the Later Nineteenth Century." *Journal of Legal History* 18 (April 1997): 45-84.

–. "The Status of the JAG of the Forces in the United Kingdom since the 1930's." *Military Law and Law of War Review* 33 (1994): 243-71.

Saskatchewan and Canada Commissioners. "Use of Self-criminating Evidence Given before Military Boards of Inquiry. Reports." *Proceedings Uniform Law Conference of Canada* 57 (1975): 211-5.

Schafer, Arthur. *The Buck Stops Here: Reflections on Moral Responsibility, Democratic Accountability and Military Values.* Ottawa: Commission of Inquiry into the Deployment of Canadian Forces to Somalia, 1997.

Schlueter, David A. "The Court-Martial: A Historical Survey." *Military Law Review* 87 (1981): 129-66.

–. "Military Justice for the 1990's: A Legal System Looking for Respect." *Military Law Review* 133 (1991): 1-29.

Sears, Jason. "Discipline in the Royal Navy, 1913-1946." *War and Society* 9 (1991): 39-60.

Sellar, Watson. "Canadian Non-Permanent Militia Units." *Canadian Bar Review* 24 (1946): 98-106.

Sellen, Keith L. "The United States Military Academy Law Department – Yesterday and Today: Purpose – Challenge – Reward." *Federal Bar News and Journal* 37 (1990): 231-9.

Sharma, O.P. *Military Law in India,* 2nd ed. Bombay: N.M. Tripathi Private, 1990.

Shaw, Henry L. "Running the Gauntlet." *Journal of the Society for Army Historical Research* 41 (1963): 219-20.

Shipp, John. *Flogging and Its Substitute: Advice from the Ranks; or, a Letter to Sir Francis Burdett, on the Barbarous and Degrading System of Flogging Soldiers and Sailors.* London, UK: Whittaker, Treacher, 1831.

Simpson, James M. "The Defence of Superior Orders in Canada: A Review of *Superior Orders in National and International Law.*" *Canadian Yearbook of International Law* 15 (1977): 306-14.

–. *Law Applicable to Canadian Forces in Somalia 1992/93.* Ottawa: Commission of Inquiry into the Deployment of Canadian Forces to Somalia, 1997.

Smith, Bruce T. "Uncle Sam's Newest Recruits: A Look at Three JAG Schools, Their Curricula, and Continuing Education Programs." *Federal Lawyer* 42 (September 1995): 22-6.

Smith, E.A. "Educating the Soldier in the Nineteenth Century." *Journal of the Society for Army Historical Research* 65 (1987): 35-45.

Smith, S.E. "Constitutional Law – Provincial Act Requiring Motor Car Drivers to Be Licensed – Applicability to Military Officer." *Canadian Bar Review* 8 (1930): 747-9.

Sokolsky, Joel J. "Domestic Disturbances and the Military: The Canadian Experience." *Parameters* 23 (1993): 93-101.

Stacey, Charles Perry. *Arms, Men and Governments: The War Policies of Canada 1939-1945.* Ottawa: Queen's Printer, 1970.

–. *Canada and the British Army 1846-1871.* Toronto: University of Toronto Press, 1963.

Stacey, Charles Perry, and Barbara Wilson. *The Half-Million: The Canadians in Britain, 1939-1946.* Toronto: University of Toronto Press, 1987.

Stanley, George F.G. *Canada's Soldiers: The Military History of an Unmilitary People.* Toronto: Macmillan, 1960.

–. "Gabriel Dumont's Account of the North West Rebellion 1885." *Canadian Historical Review* 30 (1949): 249-69.

Starkman, Bernard. "Canadian Military Law: The Citizen as Soldier." *Canadian Bar Review* 43 (1965): 414-52.

Steiner, E.E. "Separating the Soldier from the Citizen: Ideology and Criticism of Corporal Punishment in the British Armies, 1790-1815." *Social History* 8 (1983): 19-35.

Steppler, G.A. "British Military Law, Discipline, and the Conduct of Regimental Courts Martial in the later Eighteenth Century." *English Historical Review* 102 (1987): 859-81.

Stirling, John. *The Colonials in South Africa 1899-1902: Their Record Based on the Despatches.* Edinburgh: Blackwood, 1907.

Stone, Jay Charles. "The Boer War and Its Effects on British Military Reform." Ph.D. diss., City University of New York, 1985.

Strange, Thomas Bland. *Gunner Jingo's Jubilee.* 1896. Reprint, Edmonton: University of Alberta Press, 1988.

Street, Harry. "Crown: Action for Loss of Services of a Soldier. Comment on R. v. Richardson and Adams (1948). 2 D.L.R. 305." *Canadian Bar Review* 26 (1948): 994-8.

Stuart-Smith, James. "Military Law: Its History, Administration, and Practice." *Law Quarterly Review* 85 (1969): 478-504.

–. "Without Partiality, Favour or Affection: An Account of the History and Present Functions of the Judge Advocate at a British Court Martial." *Military Law and Law of War Review* 2 (1963): 223-46.

Suard, Vincent. "La justice militaire française et la peine de mort au début de la première guerre mondiale." *Revue d'histoire moderne et contemporaine* 41 (1994): 136-53.

Swainson, Arthur K. "The Rules of Evidence at Courts Martial: A Study of the Military Rules of Evidence." *Chitty's Law Journal* Part, I, 25 (1977): 272-83; Part II, 25 (1977): 312-20; Part III, 25 (1977): 339-45; Part IV, 26 (1978): 25-31; Part V, 26 (1978): 52-62; Part VI, 26 (1978): 160-6; Part VII, 26 (1978): 212-16; Part VIII, 26 (1978): 227-44.

Symons, Ellen. "Under Fire: Canadian Women in Combat." *Canadian Journal of Women and Law* 4 (1991): 477-511.

Syvertsen-Bitten, Elizabeth A. "Distributed Training in the Canadian Forces: A Decision Model." M.A. thesis, University of Calgary, 1994.

Taylor, Zak. "The Military Justice Debate." *Armed Forces and Society* 2 (1976): 468-71.

Thuen, Eldren B. "The Need for a Creed: Why the CF Needs a Written Code of Ethics." Extended essay, Canadian Forces Command and Staff College, 1995.

Tooley, Robert. "Appearance or Reality? Variations in Infantry Courts Martial, 1st Canadian Division: 1940-1945." *Canadian Defence Quarterly,* Part I, 22 (October 1992): 33-9; Part II, 22 (December 1992): 40-7.

Torrance, Judy M. *Public Violence in Canada, 1867-1972.* Kingston and Montreal: McGill-Queen's University Press, 1986.

Tremeear, W.J. "Military Law – Powers of Arrest: Annotated Re Harris (1909)." *Canadian Criminal Cases* 15 (1910): 375-9.

Tucker, Gilbert Norman. *The Naval Service of Canada.* 2 vols. Ottawa: King's Printer, 1952.

United States Army. *The Army Lawyer: A History of the JAG's Corps, 1775-1975.* Washington, DC: Government Printing Office, 1976.

Vince, Donald M.A.R. "Development in the Legal Status of the Canadian Military Forces, 1914-1919, as Related to Dominion Status." *Canadian Journal of Economics and Political Science* 20 (1954): 357-70.

Vokes, Chris, and John P. Maclean. *Vokes: My Story.* Ottawa: Gallery Books, 1985.

Wakin, Malham M. *War, Morality and the Military Profession.* Boulder, CO: Frederick A. Praeger, 1986.

Walker, Janet. "A Farewell Salute to the Military Nexus Doctrine." *National Journal of Constitutional Law* 2 (1993): 366-78.

–. "Military Justice: From Oxymoron to Aspiration." *Osgoode Hall Law Journal* 32 (1994): 1-32.

"War – Foreign Forces in Canada – Desertion by Enlisted Foreign Nationals Resident in Canada – Arrest and Detention." *Canadian Bar Review* 20 (1942): 167-70.

Watkin, Kenneth W. "Canadian Military Justice: Summary Proceedings and the Charter." LLM thesis, Queen's University, 1990.

–. "Legal Aspects of Internal Security: A Soldier's Protections and Obligations." *Canadian Forces JAG Journal,* Part I, 1 (1985): 51-79; Part II, 2 (1987): 5-30.

Whalen, James M. "The Face of the Enemy: Kurt Meyer: Normandy to Dorchester." *The Beaver* 74 (April/May 1994): 20-3.

Wheeler, F.H. "Military Values: Should They Be Different from Civilian Society?" Extended essay, Canadian Forces Command and Staff College, 1988.

Whitburn, T.G. *The Re-establishment of an Ethical Environment in the Canadian Military.* Toronto: Canadian Forces Command and Staff College, 1991.

White, A.S. "Flogging in the Army." *Journal of the Society for Army Historical Research* 20 (1941): 114-5.

Whitfield, Carol M. "Desertion – That Disgraceful Crime: A Study of a Problem Affecting the British Army in North America, 1815-1865." Paper read at the Canadian Historical Association, Toronto, 1974, DHist 79/604.

–. *Tommy Atkins: The British Soldier in Canada, 1759-1870.* Ottawa: National Historic Parks and Sites Branch, Parks Canada, Environment Canada, 1981.

Wicksteed, R.J. *The Canadian Militia.* Ottawa: MacLean, Roger and Co., 1875.

Wiener, Frederick Bernays. *Civilians under Military Justice: The British Practice since 1689, Especially in North America.* Chicago and London: University of Chicago Press, 1967.

–. "The Teaching of Military Law in a University Law School." *Journal of Legal Education* 5 (1953): 475-99.

Wiktor, Christian L. *Canadian Bibliography of International Law.* Toronto: University of Toronto Press, 1984.

Willett, Terence C. *A Heritage at Risk: The Canadian Militia as a Social Institution.* Boulder, CO: Westview Press, 1987.

–. "The Reserve Forces of Canada." *Armed Forces and Society* 16 (1989): 59-76.

"Wills of Soldiers on Active Service." *Canadian Law Times* 34 (1914): 1166-72.

Wilson, H.J. "Jurisdiction over Foreign Armed Forces Which Enter Canada with Consent Express or Implied of the Government of Canada." *Canadian Bar Review* 21 (1943): 593-7, 665.

Wilson, James Brent. "Morale and Discipline in the BEF, 1914-1918." M.A. thesis, University of New Brunswick, 1978.

Winfield, Percy H. "Courts-Martial from the Lawyer's Point of View." *Law Quarterly Review* 34 (1918): 143-51.

Witton, George. *Scapegoats of Empire.* Melbourne: D.W. Paterson, 1907.

Wolfe, John P. "Changes in the Law of Armed Conflict." *Canadian Defence Quarterly* 8 (1978): 16-21, 48.

–. "Military Obedience in Canadian Internal Penal Law and in Law of War." *Military Law and Law of War Review* 10 (1971): 127-43.

Wood, Herbert Fairlie. *Strange Battleground: The Operations in Korea and Their Effects on the Defence Policy of Canada.* Ottawa: Roger Duhamel, Queen's Printer, 1966.

Worthington, Peter, and Kyle Brown. *Scapegoat: How the Army Betrayed Kyle Brown.* Toronto: Seal Books, 1997.

Wright, John De. "Armed Assistance to the Civil Power." *Law Society Gazette* 24 (1990): 302-14.

Zillman, Donald N. "What Military Criminal Law Can Teach Us: A United States Perspective." *University of New Brunswick Law Journal* 42 (1993): 229-35.

Index

Set in Stone by Brenda and Neil West, BN Typographics West
Printed and bound in Canada by Friesens
Copy editor: Robyn Packard
Proofreader: Darlene Money